Creatures of Change

Creatures of Change

An Album of Ohio Animals

by Carolyn V. Platt

photography by Gary Meszaros

The Kent State University Press

Kent, Ohio, & London

© 1998 by The Kent State University Press,
Kent, Ohio 44242
Library of Congress Catalog Card
Number 97-34531
ISBN 0-87338-585-3
Manufactured in Hong Kong

Title page photo: green salamander

*Library of Congress
Cataloging-in-Publication Data*
Platt, Carolyn V., 1943–
Creatures of change : an album of Ohio
animals / by Carolyn V. Platt,
photography by Gary Meszaros.
p.   cm.
Includes bibliographical references
(p.   ).
ISBN 0-87338-585-3 (cloth : alk. paper)
1. Zoology—Ohio. 2. Land settlement—
Environmental aspects—Ohio. I. Title.
QL 198.P58   1998
591.9771—dc21   97-34531

British Library Cataloging-in-Publication
data are available.

Contents

Acknowledgments

*T*hanks, first of all, go to my
parents, Grover C. and Virginia B. Platt of Bowling Green State
University, who, though they were historians, nurtured my love of
nature and the out-of-doors. Much of my interest in the interplay of
human and natural history comes from growing up with these two
remarkable people and with my sister Phyllis Platt. My husband Eric
Hoddersen has been my soul and inspiration and my companion on
walks, hikes, and canoe trips for a quarter of a century.

Without my collaborator Gary Meszaros, a fine photographer and
naturalist who always has a new photo series in hand, I would not
have produced half of what I've written. Editors Bill Baughman and
Aaron Leash of the Cleveland Museum of Natural History's *The
Explorer* gave me my start in writing, and the editorial staff at The
Ohio Historical Society's *Timeline* magazine—Chris Duckworth,
Jim Richards, David Simmons, William Keener, and Laurel Shan-
non—have afforded me scope, helpful criticism, and friendship.
Thanks, too, to the staff at the Kent State University Press, especially
Julia Morton, my editor for this book, designer Will Underwood,

and John Hubbell, Director of the Press. Friendly and competent Cleveland Museum of Natural History librarians Mary and Bill Baum and Wendy Wasman gave me access to many hard-to-locate materials. Lester Wyman, Debbie Rand, Bob McDonough, Betty Hoddersen, Bob Patrick, and Don Thompson have always listened.

Finally, but not lastly, are the many, many Ohio naturalists, both professional and amateur, who have shared their specialized knowledge gladly with a magpie generalist like me. Since I began writing in 1982, I have incurred debts to more people than I can remember, and I apologize to those I've omitted. Warm thanks for time, expertise, and encouragement to the following naturalists who helped me with these pieces: Carl Albrecht, Barbara Andreas, Bob Bartolotta, Jim Bissell, Richard Bradley, Denis Case, Sue Daly, Guy Denny, Bob Faber, Kim Flottum, Bob Glotzhober, Mike Hansen, Michael Hoggarth, Margaret Hodge, Steve Jordan, John MacGregor, Samuel Marshall, Tim Matson, Andrew McClure, Eric Metzler, Scott Moody, David Parshall, Richard Ramsey, Dan Rice, Martin Rosenberg, John Shuey, Bob Stoll, Edward Stroh, Chuck Strong, Sonja Tereguchi, Gildo Tori, Harvey Webster, and Jack Weeks.

Gary Meszaros extends special thanks to his wife Jane Meszaros and to his friends in the field: John MacGregor, Tim Matson, Andy McClure, Dan Rice, and Edward Stroh.

All of the written content of this book, except for the introductory materials and the chapter "Waterfowl Back from the Brink," as well as many of the photographs, originally appreared in The Ohio Historical Society's magazine *Timeline* in different design. Exact dates of magazine issues in which articles appeared are available at the end of this volume.

Introduction

A bald eagle flying over the
Ohio country in 1492 would have cocked its eye downward at a solid
expanse of venerable trees—here nature's fabric was woven in shades
of forest green, broken only seldom by the lighter greens and vivid
floral hues of prairie openings, the blue eyes of small glacial lakes, or
the waving emergent plants of the vast Lake Erie marshes. In these
primeval forests, grasslands, wetlands, and river systems lived a number and variety of animals difficult for us to imagine today.

Carolina parakeets chattered and wild turkeys gobbled in the
spring sunlight, and wolves' howls, owls' strange conversations,
cougars' screams, and the barking of foxes enlivened the winter
nights. An army of beavers dammed streams and created myriad
small wetlands and beaver meadows. The Erie marshes resounded
with voices of untold thousands of wild ducks and geese in autumn
and rang in spring with the mating songs of frogs and toads. Less
vocal species such as black bears, porcupines, wood bison, and
white-tailed deer haunted the woodland gloom or browsed the

GEOLOGIC MAP & CROSS SECTION OF OHIO

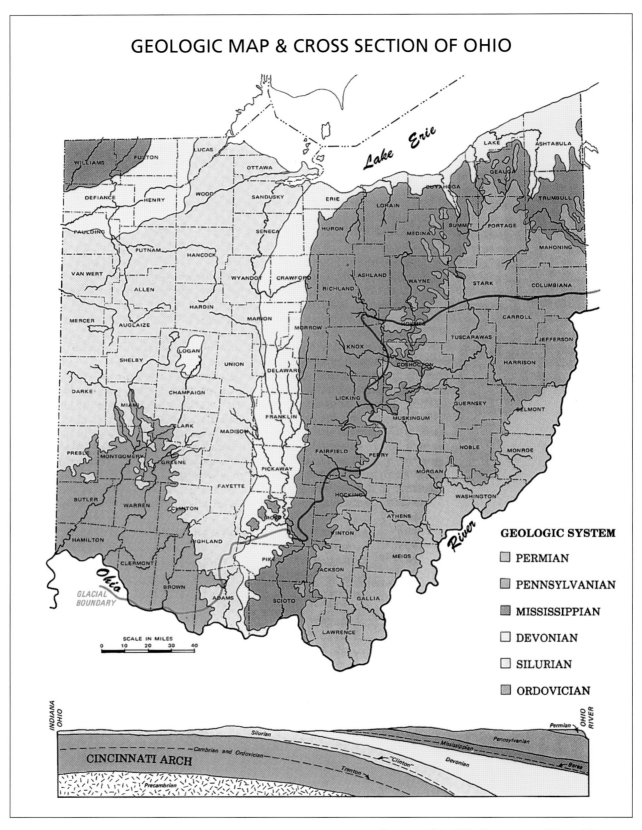

GEOLOGIC SYSTEM

- PERMIAN
- PENNSYLVANIAN
- MISSISSIPPIAN
- DEVONIAN
- SILURIAN
- ORDOVICIAN

SCALE IN MILES
0   10   20   30   40

Courtesy of the Ohio Department of Natural Resources

sunny edges where forest met prairie or beaver meadow. Vast flocks of passenger pigeons fed on abundant fruits and nuts of the forest, sometimes roosting in such numbers as to break large limbs from trees. Fishes thronged the pristine streams.

A great deal has changed since then, of course. Some creatures of the Ohio Country in 1492 are completely extinct or extirpated from the state today; others' numbers and kinds have dwindled; still others—once absent—have invaded from the south and west as forests disappeared under settlers' axes. Some earlier residents have returned to Ohio in this century with help from legislators, scientists, wildlife managers, and the public. Another group that includes raccoons, honey bees, and imported pests like Norway rats has benefited directly by exploiting the cities, suburbs, and farmlands of human beings.

These changes in animal populations were not solely the result of human interference: numbers always fluctuate, influenced by climate, food supplies, predator-prey relationships, and diseases and parasites, as well as other factors which we may not completely understand. The area's fauna was very different in 1492 than it had been twelve thousand years earlier at the end of the last ice age. Yet Ohio's animals are certainly entangled in the vast and sticky web that we, the preeminent creatures of change, have woven and that pessimistic souls believe may trap us too in the end. The history of animals in Ohio over the past two hundred years is one of constant change, a story that absorbs, disturbs, and sometimes even encourages.

To understand our area's fauna, readers should know something about the geology and soils that underpin its natural communities and which help to determine species' distribution. Ohio is the product of eons of gradual deposition in shallow inland seas, more eons of erosion once the seas withdrew, and a violent recent history when the continental glaciers rumbled out of the north, changing the look of much of the area and completely rearranging its drainage systems and plant communities. All of the state's visible bedrock was laid down between two and five hundred million years ago. The oldest rocks are exposed at the surface in the Cincinnati area, the youngest along the West Virginia border in the southeast. Limestones and dolomites, made of shelly materials deposited in clear, calm seas, underlie the western counties and cause that area's consistently hard water. These rocks erode easily in a moist climate, and so when the land rose and the seas withdrew, the elements began to wear them down to the relatively level surface that the glaciers and the forerunners of Lake Erie planed even smoother. Limestone is also the rock that forms Ohio's caverns and the giant cave systems of Pennsylvania, West Virginia, and Kentucky.

Sandstone, including the Hocking Hills' Black Hand, and various shales dominate the eastern counties. These layers, made up of water-sorted pebbles and rock particles, were deposited on top of the older limestones by runoff from mountains uplifted to the north and east. Though shale does not resist erosion well, sandstone is very resistant, so that where it was the major bedrock exposed or where it capped shale layers, the land remained rugged and dissected, slowing down the glaciers' invasion and leaving most of the state's eastern third unglaciated. Sandstone also collects rainwater and releases it in springs, which helps to explain why the greatest variety of salamanders inhabits Ohio's southeastern third. Whatever younger rocks were deposited above the limestones of western Ohio and the shales and sandstones of the eastern counties have disappeared, worn down by the rains, the rivers, and the ice of the past two hundred million years. Though Ohio boasts fine trilobite fossils, ancient fishes, and coal-age deposits, dinosaur fossils—if they were ever laid down in Ohio—have long since eroded away.

The reason for the differences in ages and types of bedrock in western and eastern Ohio is not really hard to understand. About two hundred million years ago, at the end of the Paleozoic Era, the Appalachian Mountains rose, and in related movements, rock layers tilted into a low arch whose axis ran from present-day Cincinnati northeastward to the Toledo–Port Clinton area. Rocks exposed on the back of this Cincinnati Arch eroded faster than those on its flanks. This means that in that part of Ohio, the older limestones and dolomites lie at the surface, with exposed layers getting younger and younger as one moves eastward or westward. Thus, eastern Ohio's outcrops are of younger sandstones and shales.

Understanding these regional bedrock differences and the extent of glaciation answers many questions about the look of the land, the varying plant communities on it, and the animals that inhabit them. Gardeners know that certain plants like limy soil, but that others are adapted to acid soil derived from sandstone and related rocks. Many other factors, including availability of water, climate and micro-climate, various adaptations, and competition with alien European plants that have invaded since settlement help define which plants grow where, but bedrocks and the soils they produce are vital determiners. Plant assemblages located on limestone- and dolomite-derived soils in western Ohio or in areas where limy glacial materials cover bedrock differ greatly from those growing on southeastern Ohio's acid soils.

Complicating these east-west bedrock differences are the effects of the Ice Age glaciers. For two hundred million years before the glaciers arrived, the area was drained by the Teays (rhymes with *days*) River and its tributaries. This ancient stream probably looped through ancestral Ohio from the southeast and exited west through what is now Indiana to join a northern embayment of the Gulf of Mexico. Botanists believe that a number of rare plants entered this area along the Teays' old course, which must have been a corridor for animal travel as well.

The glaciers bulldozed and dammed the Teays out of existence and fostered the upstart Ohio River. Today, water entering the Great and Little Miami, the Scioto, the Hocking, and the Muskingum Rivers drains into the Ohio, Mississippi, and Gulf of Mexico. North-flowing Ohio streams like the Maumee, Sandusky, Cuyahoga, and Grand deliver water to Lake Erie, the St. Lawrence, and the North Atlantic. A line snaking from northeastern Ohio southwest and south to the Ohio River marks the farthest extent of glaciation and segregates glaciated Allegheny plateau, lake plain, and till plain from the ruggedly dissected unglaciated plateau to the southeast. A look at a map of Ohio's original vegetation shows a division between beech-maple forests and mixed oak forests that roughly follows the line of the glaciers' farthest advance.

Naturally, since animals are more mobile than plants, their ranges correlate more loosely with bedrock, soil, and drainage boundaries than plants' do. Some creatures, like the coyote, thrive in all eighty-eight Ohio counties. Ranges of surprisingly many animals, however, correspond roughly with geological regions. For example, timber rattlesnakes and copperheads mainly lived in the southeastern unglaciated portion of the state, while massasaugas, or swamp rattlers, were adapted to wet prairies and swamps of the glaciated north and west. (The two rattlesnakes are extremely rare today, due to changes in land use and persecution by humans.) Black racers and closely related blue racers also divide the state roughly according to glacial margins: black racers inhabit southeastern Ohio and blue racers the glaciated counties, as do several other snakes that probably invaded western Ohio a few thousand years ago when drier weather caused the great tallgrass prairies to spread eastward. White-tailed deer have traditionally been more abundant in the rugged, wooded southeast, although they are now common even in the heavily

GLACIAL DEPOSITS OF OHIO

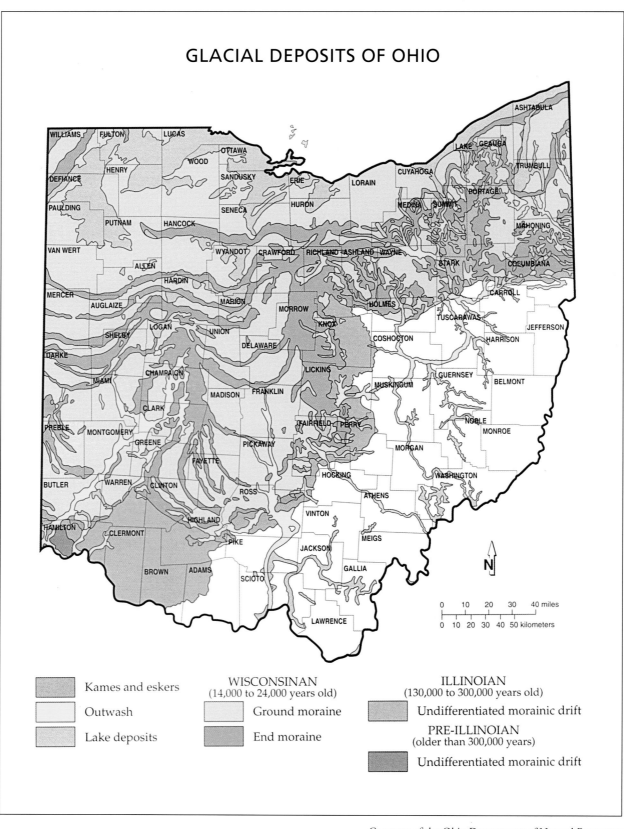

		WISCONSINAN (14,000 to 24,000 years old)		ILLINOIAN (130,000 to 300,000 years old)
	Kames and eskers			
	Outwash		Ground moraine	Undifferentiated morainic drift
	Lake deposits		End moraine	PRE-ILLINOIAN (older than 300,000 years) Undifferentiated morainic drift

Courtesy of the Ohio Department of Natural Resources

farmed northwestern corner of the state. Other animals discussed in this book show various and interesting relationships to Ohio's geology and botany.

The following pieces are gathered into four sections. These correspond roughly to how groups of animals have fared since the first Europeans appeared in this area and ended the long, stable relationship between Native Americans, the land, and the plants and animals on it. Section 1, "The Frontier Wars," discusses the struggles of settlers with large carnivores, such as timber wolves, and the devastating effects of the early fur trade on furbearers.

Section 2, "Decline and Recovery," deals with five species that once disappeared or nearly disappeared from Ohio but have returned more recently, sometimes with a vengeance: the beaver, wild turkey, white-tailed deer, wood duck, and Canada goose. The early fur trade extirpated Ohio beavers by the 1830s. Hunting did the same for the wild turkey and whitetail by about 1900, when wood ducks were also in serious decline. Concern for the future of Canada geese closed hunting seasons in 1946. All these animals have made dramatic recoveries in the past half century. These recoveries have been achieved firstly because farmers abandoned marginal land early in this century, and the state's forests have partially regrown, and secondly because hunting is now controlled, and wildlife management has become much more sophisticated.

Section 3, entitled "Mixed Effects," is the longest in this volume. It includes pieces on owls, snakes, salamanders and frogs, the little fish called darters and shiners, butterflies, and spiders. Rather than focusing on single species, as do the articles in Section 2, these pieces explore groups of animals. In these groupings, the effects of settlement and its aftermath have been uneven. Certain generalist or open-country species, such as great horned owls and barn owls, were favored over deep-wood types like the barred owl when the virgin woodlands fell to the ax; in the barn owl's case, decline set in later, when second-growth forest and intensive farming reduced its pasture and grassland hunting grounds. Among the fishes, species intolerant of siltation and pollution have suffered; among the butterflies, aggressive drainage has decimated specialists whose larvae feed on wetland plants. Often our knowledge of just what has happened to groups of so-called "lower animals" is sparse, since few cared to study them seriously or regarded their survival as important until recently.

Finally, Section 4 discusses "The Opportunists," including the coyote, the raccoon, and the honey bee. These and other species—

ORIGINAL VEGETATION OF OHIO

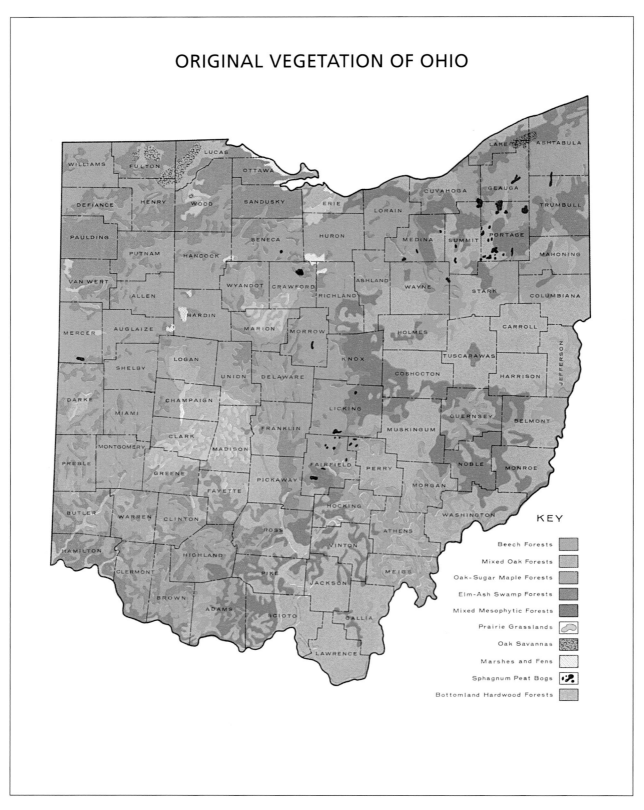

KEY

Beech Forests
Mixed Oak Forests
Oak-Sugar Maple Forests
Elm-Ash Swamp Forests
Mixed Mesophytic Forests
Prairie Grasslands
Oak Savannas
Marshes and Fens
Sphagnum Peat Bogs
Bottomland Hardwood Forests

Courtesy of the Ohio Department of Natural Resources

usually those that can exploit a variety of human-altered environments—have thrived under our influence, often whether we like it or not. Coyotes, which did not live in Ohio in any numbers two centuries ago, now inhabit all Ohio counties, and raccoon densities are higher in certain cities and suburbs than they are in the open countryside. Honey bees were introduced from Europe by early settlers and, until the last couple of years, included vast feral populations. Perhaps they should be removed from this "opportunists" section today, however. Until 1996 Ohio honey bees survived very nicely either in beekeeper's hives or in hollow trees and attic crawl spaces. Two parasitic mites introduced by honey bee importers and spread by large pollinating operations have suddenly wiped out 95 percent of "wild" bees and, as one expert says, have finally caused the domestication of *Apis mellifera,* which for the present can survive only in medicated hives. This is a graphic example of how fast and how devastating our influences can be on Ohio animals, whether native or introduced, and how quickly conditions for these creatures can change.

This book is not a field guide to Ohio wildlife—other books can fill that function more thoroughly. It is instead a collection of essays about representative animals and groups of animals loosely organized around the theme of changes since settlement. All but one of these pieces originally appeared in the Ohio Historical Society's magazine *Timeline* over a period of more than a decade. Although some material in the older articles has changed to a degree over time, I have updated information, especially statistics, in the short introductions to each of the book's sections. Photographer Gary Meszaros has illustrated the volume with color photos knowledgeably shot and carefully selected. He and I hope that our book will help readers to view Ohio's natural landscape and the animals that inhabit it with understanding and affectionate eyes; we also hope it will inspire Ohioans to work to foster these creatures and their changing natural communities rather than contributing to their decline.

The Frontier Wars

Settlers who began entering
the Ohio country in numbers after the Treaty of Greenville in 1795
were heirs to attitudes toward wilderness formed during more than a
thousand years of western European culture and based on even
older belief systems. In the Book of Genesis, God gave man "do-
minion over the fish of the sea, and over the fowl of the air, and over
the cattle, and over all the earth, and over every creeping thing that
creepeth upon the earth." Early immigrants, if they bothered to
think about it, considered themselves very much Adam's heirs. They
also inherited deep distrust of forest environments: Since before A.D.
800, when chronicles referred to the Anglo-Saxon farmer as the
"grey enemy of the wood," Europeans had viewed that continent's
wide forests as alien to humans—places of awe and horror and be-
wilderment. The early Christian church advocated clearing this
abode of the devil and of natural sin.

Ohio settlers set themselves to the task of clearing the abode of
the devil—whom they often saw in the guise of the Indians they
imagined lurking behind the great forest boles—with almost religious

fervor. By 1859 they had deforested an estimated 12.6 million acres in Ohio alone. By 1900, only about 15 percent of the state was wooded. They also declared war on large carnivores, the devil's minions, such as bears, cougars, and wolves. To be fair, bears and cougars could sometimes be dangerous, and wolves, though not threatening to human beings, had figured in so many lurid folk tales over the centuries that they were universally hated and feared. All of these creatures sometimes took sheep, cows, pigs, and other livestock, especially as settlers disrupted their forest environments and killed their natural prey. Other animals, such as wood bison and white-tailed deer, were put to use for food, hides, and trade. Authorities offered bounties for killing wolves and cougars and sometimes exacted penalties from those who did not account for their quota of dead gray squirrels, whose huge numbers made them a threat to crops.

Sometimes large-scale hunts were held, the most successful of these being the Great Hinckley Hunt of December 14, 1818. Meetings were held in the surrounding townships to organize a "war of extermination" upon bears and wolves. Six hundred men and boys carrying muskets, bayonets, butcher knives, and axes formed a cordon around the township's perimeter and drew the circle tight. Dogs then drove the animals caught inside it into the men's musket fire. At the end, hunters shot down into masses of panicked animals trapped in the bed of a frozen stream with steep, high banks. The body count was three hundred deer, twenty-one bears, seventeen wolves, and numbers of turkeys, foxes, raccoons, and other small game. The men celebrated that night with barbecued bear meat and large quantities of whiskey.

The "war of extermination" and the destruction of the forests spelled doom for the big meat eaters: in 1818, the same year as the Hinckley hunt, the wolf bounty was discontinued. In 1838 the pioneer naturalist Jared Kirtland observed that the cougar or "mountain tiger" had disappeared from the state. Wolves will probably never again howl or big cats scream in Ohio, but attitudes toward these large predators are now beginning to shift dramatically. Timber wolves have been reintroduced successfully to Yellowstone National Park and the northern Rockies since January 1995, culminating a decade-long struggle with local agricultural interests. Today serious consideration is being given to returning them to New York State's Adirondack Mountains.

By 1830 beavers were also only a memory in the young state of Ohio. The fur trade, of course, was their nemesis, fueled by the European love of beaver hats. Trappers had taken them and other furbearers in great numbers here for two hundred years. Black bears, wood bison, and elk were also rare by 1800, and lynx, bobcats, martens, and fishers essentially vanished by mid-century. Before 1976, when the Ohio Department of Natural Resources began reintroducing river otters into the state, no wild breeding population of those playful creatures survived in Ohio. Less desirable furbearers and ones that adapted well to living among humans fared better, of course, particularly skunks, raccoons, minks, and foxes. Opossums have entered Ohio from the south and are thriving here, and there is some evidence that small numbers of black bears may be returning to a few eastern counties.

Man's Best Enemy

The Wolf

*T*he gaunt gray shape of the wolf lopes through the folktales of a hundred cultures; its eerie howls reverberate in myths of the world's beginning and end. A Menomeni Indian story tells of the first man's birth as a wolf's twin. Norse myths, on the other hand, predict that the monstrous wolf Fenrir will break free on Doomsday to devour the earth and sun. Today, few people ever see these animals outside zoos, but their shadows still lurk in our collective dreams; the word "wolf" has come to symbolize much that is menacing both in nature and within the human heart. People try both to keep the wolf of famine from the door and to protect their daughters from wolf whistles and their sexual aftermath. Sadly, stereotyping of wolves and the mistaken attitudes of many stock raisers and hunters that rise out of such stereotyping are now serious threats to survival of the real wolf—an impressive and often beneficial predator which modern wildlife biologists have learned to respect.

On the face of it, people's reactions to wolves seem out of proportion to any influence—good or evil—that modern wolves exert

Page 14: Of all the large predators encountered by early settlers in Ohio, the gray wolf was the most reviled and feared. Although native American people were inclined to admire the wolves that hunted in packs as they themselves often did, stock-herding Europeans saw wolves as vicious competitors and as symbols of lurking evil. The real wolf, although a powerful carnivore, is a much different creature from the ravening beast of myth and legend.

Below: According to John James Audubon, "There is a strong feeling of hostility entertained by the settlers of the wild portions of the country, toward the Wolf, as his strength, agility, and cunning . . . tend to render him the most destructive enemy. . . . Therefore, in our country, he is not more mercifully dealt with than in any other part of the world."

on human lives. By mid-century these big, grizzled animals had disappeared from nearly 99 percent of their original American range. Although they still survive in Canada, Alaska, and as remnants in northern Minnesota, Michigan, the Gulf Coast, and Mexico, mankind could wipe them out in a few years with poison, traps, planes, and helicopters.

If *Canis lupus* no longer is a serious competitor with *Homo sapiens* for food, no longer a threat to life, why do emotions still run so high? Why the continual argument, especially in Minnesota, Canada, and Alaska, over whether to preserve wolves or exterminate them? Wolves no longer threaten livestock seriously. Ecologists also believe that their selective preying actually helps to keep deer, moose, and caribou populations healthy. Counter to visions of slavering packs nipping at the heels of lonely travelers, wolves do not endanger humans. No case has ever been proved of non-rabid wolf attack on anyone in North America, and rabies is rarely found in American wolves.

But feelings about wolves are rooted more deeply than thoughts of personal self-interest. They stem not simply from relations with the creatures themselves, but from human attitudes about nature and wilderness, from our hatred and fear of the wild, as well as our longing and love for it.

Whether wolves survive at all depends on to what degree humans change their traditional view of nature: Is the howling of a pack of wolves a sinister sound of the menacing unknown or the joyous song of unregimented nature? Do wolves have the right to share the earth with human beings or not? Opinions vary widely, and on the answers to these questions hangs the fate not only of wolves, but of many other predators as well.

Historically, the way people thought of wolves changed as their own cultures evolved. American Indians viewed wolves with awe, but seldom with Europeans' unreasoning fear and hate. They thought of wolves as brothers because wolves lived lives like theirs. Both stalked the large grazers that browsed in eastern woodlands and surged across the western grasslands, and both of their lives involved skill, endurance, and risk-taking. Hunting large, dangerous animals required cooperation and loyalty to the tribe or pack—neither brave nor wolf could normally kill a bison alone. Indians thought of wolves as a family parallel to the human one, as sharers of a generally harmonious natural order. The wolf-qualities of strength, endurance, and stealth were, to them, worthy of emulation and reverence. Many Indian stories told of wolves that sheltered men and women lost or driven out of their tribes, that taught them medicine ways, and that inspired warrior cults. Warriors emulated the strength and formidable fighting skills of the wild wolves of the woods and plains and imitated their soulful howls in songs and chants. Significantly, these same men viewed servile camp dogs with disdain and never made pets of them.

On the other side of the world, lifestyles and attitudes had changed a great deal. People there had learned to domesticate sheep, goats, cattle, and pigs, and had revolutionized their whole way of relating to the natural world. They had begun to change it, control it, to stand aside consciously from the rest of creation. Old world herders and farmers began to see themselves as subduers of nature and as rulers over it. Genesis provides the classic statement of this belief:

> Be fruitful and multiply, and replenish the earth, and subdue it:
> and have dominion over the fish of the sea, and over the fowl of
> the air, and over every living thing that moveth upon the earth.

As more cultures changed from hunting and gathering to herding and farming, attitudes toward wolves shifted from respect to mistrust, from light to dark. These powerful beasts with long white

In fairness to the early settlers, eastern timber wolves probably did cause important livestock losses. Steel traps and effective poisons were yet to be invented, and the small island farms lost in dark canine teeth that could rip and disembowel precious sheep or cattle could hardly be seen as brother creatures. The wolf harrying the fold became an enemy and competitor. It was a direct threat to survival: powerful, menacing, beyond human control.

The Bible and later Christian writings teem with fearful references to the wolf. Such an animal must come straight from the Devil, who

LOSSING-BARRITT

Lurid tales of attacks by wolves helped fuel popular hatred of these powerful predators. This image, in which Big Brother tries to protect his smaller siblings, appeared in 1881 in *Johnson's Natural History, Comprehensive, Scientific, and Popular, Illustrating and Describing the Animal Kingdom, with its Wonders and Curiosities, from Man Through all the Divisions, Classes, and Orders . . . .* by Hon. S. G. Goodrich.

oceans of forest often felt under siege. (If the Indians sometimes viewed wolves as their twins, the settlers often thought of the two as infernal siblings as well.) As early as 1630, Massachusetts authorities paid bounties for killing wolves; by the mid-eighteenth century, eastern wolves and other large predators were in retreat. Seventeen wolves met their end in the Great Hinckley, Ohio, Hunt of 1818. The great eastern forests fell before the axe, cover and prey were decimated; by 1900 wolves had disappeared completely from most eastern states.

The Great Plains wolf was not seriously threatened until the second half of the nineteenth century, when hunters wiped out the vast

bison herds, and ranchers formed livestock associations to deal with cattle rustling and wolf predation. Rangemen and professional "wolfers" used traps and strychnine wholesale, killing uncountable animals besides wolves with the poisoned meat: bears, ferrets, skunks, badgers, coyotes, weasels, eagles, ravens. Poison-contaminated grass even killed bison and other grazing animals. Wolves were caught in a scissors effect: hunters and stockmen eliminated their natural prey, encouraging them to develop a taste for livestock. Then they killed them mercilessly as stock-eating vermin. At the turn of the twentieth century, wolves survived only in mountain areas where more of their natural prey like elk and deer remained, and where they were more difficult to trap.

There the war against wolves should have ended, since the hounded beasts no longer posed a serious threat to sheep and cattle.

Goodrich also passed along uncritically this lurid chase tale from Russia: "We are told that a woman, in Russia, accompanied by three of her children, was one day in a sledge, when they were pursued by a number of wolves.... For the preservation of her own life, and that of the remaining children, the poor frantic creature cast one of them to her blood-thirsty pursuers." The woman ends up throwing all three of her children to the wolves and is executed by a peasant for unmaternal behavior. In another version of the tale, the victim is a young bride.

But this was far from the case. At a time when humans and wolves might have coexisted successfully in the animals' now restricted ranges, the war escalated even further. State legislators stepped up bounty programs, paying thousands upon thousands of dollars for wolf extermination. Montana alone paid $342,764 in bounties between 1883 and 1918.

The final campaign in the wolf wars began in 1915, when Congress appropriated money to control animals thought to harm agriculture. Between 1915 and 1940, federal hunters killed 24,132 northern gray wolves and southern red wolves. Today, gray wolves survive only in restricted areas in northern Minnesota and Michigan, with a few stragglers remaining in northwestern Montana and Idaho. The red wolf, a smaller species or subspecies (classifications vary), is near extinction in Texas and Louisiana, and only a few Mexican wolves still live in northern Mexico. In Alaska and in Canada alone do American wolves remain in any numbers, partly because the far North is so vast and so unsuitable for stock raising, partly because the government agencies did not control wolves intensively there until the 1950s. Bounty systems, however, were in place until well into the 1960s, both in the United States and Canada.

What seems most remarkable about the past hundred years is the virulence of feelings about wolves and how slowly general attitudes toward them have changed. Wolves frequently were blamed for *any* stock losses, even when big cats, feral dogs, coyotes, or other predators might have been the cause. Theodore Roosevelt, the first presidential advocate of conservation, spared no affection on the wolf, which he called "the beast of waste and desolation." (He once set off to hunt wolves in a private train of twenty-two cars that carried seventy fox hounds, sixty-seven greyhounds, sixty saddle packhorses, and forty-four hunters, beaters, wranglers, and journalists.)

The imputing of every unattractive human trait to wolves—cowardice, stupidity, rapaciousness, betrayal, viciousness—reminds one of the near hysteria of medieval attitudes. And it is not difficult to find examples of such irrational hatred even today. Lopez records in his 1978 book the treatment three men had recently meted out to an endangered Texas red wolf:

First they rode her down and lassoed her. When she gripped the rope with her teeth to keep the noose from closing, they dragged her around the prairie until they'd broken her teeth out. Then while two of them stretched the animal between their horses with ropes, the third man beat her to death with a pair of fence pliers.

Opposite: Dogs have been bred for thousands of years to socialize with human beings. Although wolves do not identify humans as prey and are innocent of the attacks they have often been accused of, they are still powerful, wild animals, not just big dogs, and they should not be made into pets.

The wolf was taken around to a few bars in a pickup and finally thrown in a roadside ditch.

Given such attitudes, it may not be surprising that no one even pretended to study wolves objectively until 1944, when Adolph Murie published *The Wolves of Mount McKinley*. This was the world's first wolf treatise based on careful observation of the animals themselves rather than on folklore or on the author's own preconceptions. During the past half century, biologists' search for the "real" wolf, as nearly as humans can know it, has accelerated. Extensive fieldwork done by Durward Allen and others on the wolves of Isle Royale in Lake Superior, by David Mech on those of Superior National Forest in northern Minnesota, and by Douglas Pimlott in Algonquin Provincial Park, Ontario, is especially well known. For the first time, separating wolf fact from wolf fiction can begin.

Some of the things ecologists recently have learned are startling; the picture is quite different from that of traditional stereotypes. Wolves are probably the most adaptable of all mammals, except for humans. Before *Homo sapiens* took over the world, wolves ranged from the British Isles in the west, across Europe and Asia to Japan in the east, from Lapland in the north, to Arabia, northern India, and China in the south. They hunted on the tundra, in deep forests, on the grasslands, and in deserts. In America the many subspecies of *Canis lupus* ranged from Vancouver Island to Newfoundland, from the high Arctic of Alaska, Canada, and Greenland, to Mexico's Sierra Madre and the Gulf Coast. Wolves would probably have colonized South America except for the jungles and rain forests that formed a barrier in southern Mexico and Central America. Northern tundra wolves grow larger and heavier than those farther south. (One hundred twenty pounds is large for a wolf, though the record is one hundred seventy-five pounds.) Small, light wolves of the Southwest seldom grow larger that twenty-five pounds, about the size of their coyote relatives. Color varies widely as well, from almost pure white or black in some parts of the North, to more common grizzled, tawny, or rufus mixtures.

Wolves evolved to prey on large ungulates; in North America these have included caribou, musk oxen, bison, moose, elk, pronghorns, and deer. Wolves also eat many beaver during the summer months when these animals feed in the open and are easy to attack. Though the Disney film based upon Farley Mowat's *Never Cry Wolf* stresses that wolves eat mice, small mammals make up only a minor part of most wolves' diets. (Observers mention that pups often catch mice to practice hunting techniques.)

Capable of hunting large and powerful beasts, wolves have developed strong jaws, formidable canines for ripping and tearing, and large, shearing carnassial teeth to cut flesh and tendons. Impressive though this equipment is, a single animal can seldom kill an adult bison, moose, or elk; wolves hunt in packs, like other wild dogs of the world. In turn, working as a group requires cooperation and a social structure to reduce rivalry, sexual aggression, and violence, much as humans find necessary in their own social groups. This is the key to much of wolves' pack behavior.

Pack size varies from three or four to as many as thirty-six, though competition for food, mates, and dominance, as well as environmental factors, tends to break up packs when they exceed about fifteen. A dominant male and female, designated the alpha pair, lead each pack; females have great influence within the group, frequently leading packs and sometimes outlasting several male alphas. They also decide where to den at pupping time, which in turn determines where the pack will hunt for at least six weeks. Lighter than males, the females' speed sometimes makes them better hunters.

The alpha pair is usually the only one to mate, imposing a "birth control" on the group, which must not outgrow the available prey. Lower-ranking females do not usually come into heat, or do so only for a short time. An animal called the beta male often acts as lieutenant to the leading pair and may mate with the female if the alpha male declines. Though a pack's social structure is dynamic, changing over time and circumstance, each animal has a specific place within it. Each wolf is dominant over all lower animals, which are subservient to the higher-ups. Dominant wolves generally move with ears and tails high and may bare their teeth to show annoyance. Subordinate animals carry tails and ears low and make many of the deferential movements of a submissive dog. The pack's underdog leads a nervous life, relegated to the fringes of the group, bullied by dominant animals, which relieve aggressive feelings that way, and is sometimes driven away altogether. Lone wolves are usually these pariahs or young animals looking to find a mate and found a pack of their own.

Wolves show great affection for each other, especially for their pups, which all the pack provide and care for. Adolph Murie commented about the wolves he studied in Alaska: "The strongest impression remaining with me after watching wolves on numerous occasions was their friendliness." This feeling for other pack members,

In 1901 *The Animal Kingdom,* edited by Hugh Craig of Trinity College, Cambridge, offered a plate entitled "Carnivora," showing several members of the dog family. Clockwise from the upper left corner: gray wolf, red wolf, white wolf, black wolf, prairie wolf, jackal, and coyote. The white and black wolves are merely color phases of the gray wolf *(Canis lupus),* and the coyote *(Canis latrans)* is shown here as being nearly equal in size to its much larger and heavier cousin. "Prairie wolf" is a popular name for coyote. The red wolf *(Canis rufus)* is a bona-fide species, though today it is nearly extinct.

evolved over millions of years, is what makes dogs able to respond to human love with affection of their own. Cubs and younger wolves play like puppies, pouncing on elders that tolerate them with great patience, and scaring ducks and other birds seemingly just for fun.

One could argue, though, that wolves' most important relationships are not with other wolves, but with their prey, since everything else—pack organization, care of pups, and even physical evolution—depends on the way they interact with food animals. Wolves and prey evolved together, or as Robinson Jeffers expressed it so elegantly:

What but the wolf's tooth whittled so fine
The fleet limbs of the antelope.

As earlier meat-eaters grew more efficient, so their prey became fleeter, warier, and stronger. Hunters who believe that uncontrolled wolves will wipe out game animals like elk and deer should remember that the animals have lived together for eons, and that wild ungulates are a good match for their pursuers: deer are wary and fast; moose can crush a wolf's skull with one kick; and in the North, musk oxen form impenetrable circles of butting horns to protect the young and weak. Wolves must work hard for their meat: researchers estimated that the Isle Royale wolves killed moose successfully in only one out of ten to twelve serious attempts.

Domestic animals, of course, had *not* evolved to handle wolves, which is why wolves sometimes caused havoc among them. Even that seems to have been much exaggerated. In northern Minnesota, where an estimated twelve hundred protected wolves still range close to farms, farmers submit an average of only about twenty claims a year to the government for animals killed by wolves out of a total of close to twelve thousand farms. Wolves apparently do not form the habit of killing stock unless encouraged by bad farming habits like dumping dead animals in the woods or by serious pack disintegration—such as that sometimes caused by wolf hunting.

Recent field studies have begun to shed light on the perennial controversy over wolf packs' effect on deer, moose, caribou, and other game herds. Only during the past twenty years have researchers confirmed that wolves and other predators actually do not ultimately control the numbers of their prey, but vice versa: just as mouse, lemming, and hare populations determine how many northern owls will survive, numbers of caribou, moose, and deer decide the fate of local wolves. Modern wildlife managers understand that it is food supply and ultimately weather that really determine all animals' numbers. On Isle Royale in the early 1930s, for example, moose outstripped their browse supply. The herd ballooned, then plummeted as the result of disease and starvation. In the late 1960s and 1970s, a similar boom-and-bust process went on, even though a wolf pack had crossed the winter ice to the island in the late 1940s. Biologists believe that wolf predation does not decide numbers of prey, though it may limit the worst population explosions and can contribute to herd decline if other environmental pressures are severe.

On the other hand, preying by wolves does have some very important positive effects: wolves are opportunist hunters. They kill what is easiest to catch, since they must hoard precious energy, especially in winter. Normally they attack individuals that are vulnerable for some reason: these animals may be sick or old; they may be young calves, of which most congenitally defective ones will fall; they may be starving because of over-browsing; they may be hampered by deep snow or slipping on lake ice. This culling of the old and weak actually builds the health of the whole group. So wolves and other predators are in a way conservationists, because they keep prey animals' numbers closer to the environments' carrying capacity and help the group to stay healthy. Recent predator-prey studies also indicate that predators actually stimulate herds of prey to produce more young. Other studies done in Alaska and Minnesota have shown that ranges with wolves actually provided more game for hunters during the study periods than did those with none. The wolves' kills help support many scavengers as well, from gray jays, ravens, and eagles, to foxes, weasels, and bobcats.

Naturalists have found that wolves are perfectly able to live among people as long as they can find prey and are not persecuted to the brink. Douglas Pimlott noted in the late 1960s that heavy concentrations of completely protected wolves had rubbed shoulders with thousands of humans in Algonquin Park, Ontario, for many years without a single serious incident. Minnesota studies also show that wolves prefer their natural prey to farm animals.

Often it is people who refuse to share the world with wolves; their attitudes arise from a complex snarl of history, economics, and politics. The "big, bad wolf" stereotype is still very much alive, though recent studies, books, films, and programs have helped to dispel it. Lopez tells of a grade-school group whose teacher asked them to draw pictures of wolves before one was brought to visit their class. All the portraits featured enormous fangs. After the visit, the children drew more wolves. They all had enormous feet. For years Algonquin Park rangers have conducted evening "wolf howls," taking large groups of visitors to a pack's known range and howling or playing tapes to hear—and participate in—a chorus of wild wolf music that epitomizes the lonely wildness of the northern woods. Many zoos and museums have developed displays and materials designed to present the real rather than the mythic wolf.

Overcoming ranchers', farmers', and hunters' hostility is perhaps the hardest job. Since the wolf wars of the nineteenth century, stockmen, especially sheep ranchers, have been implacably anti-wolf. In 1973, after wolves nationwide had been designated an endangered species, tentative plans were made to reintroduce them into carefully selected areas of New England, Michigan's Upper Peninsula, northern Wisconsin, northwestern Montana, central Idaho, and in Yellowstone Park's back country, where protected elk, moose, and bison were overloading their ranges. But the National Wolf Recovery teams have made little progress, especially in the West, where influential ranchers do not believe wolves will leave their stock alone. So far, the federal government has refused to promise reimbursements for lost stock, as Minnesota's state government does in the Superior National Forest. Commentators also have pointed out that reestablishing protected wolves in western national forests might jeopardize the traditional availability of government lands for grazing and other commercial use—potentially more important to ranchers than fear of losing stock.

Farmers in northern Minnesota also remain hostile to wolves, although the United States Fish and Wildlife Service operates a highly successful wolf control program there: individual wolves that

Wolves evolved to hunt large hoofed mammals, an undertaking that meant hunting in packs: one wolf is certainly no match for an angry moose. Each pack is led by a dominant pair, which is usually the only one to mate. Maintaining harmony in a group of large, powerful predators requires a social hierarchy as well as methods for defusing aggression. Facial expressions and body language are important in maintaining social position and for easing tensions. Adult wolves show great tolerance of puppies' rambunctious behavior.

molest stock are killed (only fifty-six wolves from 1979 to 1984), but others are protected. Farmers' authentic claims for damages are reimbursed. Conservation groups were instrumental in helping to define the program, and it is widely thought to be effective.

Despite studies cited above that clarify predator prey relationships, many hunters still believe that wolf packs are bad for game, when declines are instead due to over-hunting or to changes in the prey animals' food supply. These hunters form powerful anti-wolf lobbies in both the United States and Canada. For example, the government carried out an aerial wolf-control campaign in Alaska in the 1950s because the caribou herd had declined, and the past couple of years have seen heated controversy in British Columbia because the provincial government decided to clear the Ketchika and Muskwa valleys of wolves. In Minnesota, Federal Appeals courts recently struck down a proposed sport trapping season on wolves in agreement with suits brought in protest by fifteen conservation groups.

Finally, economic development sometimes works against wolves. In northern Montana, where a few still stray over the border from Canada, wolves may have a chance at a comeback. But prospecting for oil shale and other mineral deposits has stepped up dramatically in the area's national forests, resulting in much road building and other disturbance. Such activities threaten normal pack formation there. These pressures, population pressures, and others will increase in coming years and will make wolves' comeback road an uphill one.

In all, wolves' future survival chances rest squarely on those other large and efficient predators, human beings. No longer are humans the twins of wolves, sharing lives as closely knit into nature's pattern as are theirs. For better or worse, mankind has followed the teachings of Genesis and has subdued—we think—the world. Our historical prejudices and economic needs often make it hard for us to view the natural world as valuable in itself, aside from its usefulness. Perhaps, with an effort, many of us can learn to see wolves and other living things as Native Americans did, as creatures with a right to share the earth with humankind—to hear their howls not as menacing voices of desolation but as the music of a nature worth saving for its own wild harmony.

ADDITIONAL READING

The Wolves of Minong: Their Vital Role in a Wild Community by
    Durward L. Allen, Houghton Mifflin, 1979.

Of Wolves and Men by Barry Holstun Lopez, Scribners, 1978.

The Wolf: The Ecology and Behavior of an Endangered Species by L. David Mech, The Natural History Press, 1970.

The World of the Wolf by Russell J. Rutter and Douglas H. Pimlott, Lippincott, 1968.

Furbearers

The trade in furs, especially beaver, fueled much of the Old Northwest's exploration. As many writers have noted, a beaver pelt was for a long time the most valuable commodity on the continent. By 1787 beavers had been trapped commercially for nearly a century and a half in the Ohio Country, and already the number of these prime furbearers had dwindled. In 1780 the Moravian missionary David Zeisberger reported that "the beaver was formerly found in great numbers in this region, but since the Indians have learned from the whites to catch them in steel-traps, they are more rarely found." By 1830 trappers and skin hunters had wiped out beavers and the largest game animals, and others had disappeared by the century's end.

Seemingly, eighteenth- and nineteenth-century trappers took out anything that walked, ran, waddled, or swam. Reports are sketchy, with reliable statistics hard to come by, but the numbers of furs were enormous. During the years 1796 to 1798, dealers shipped from Detroit 7,330 bales of assorted pelts, each weighing ninety to one hundred pounds, and many more bales left Michilimackinac, the primary

Page 32: As settlers attacked the primeval forest with fire and ax, the deep woods gray foxes tended to be replaced by the red fox, a beast of more open, brushy country. Farmers long regarded foxes as vermin and killed them whenever possible. Now their services as mouse killers are better recognized. Red foxes' thick fur enables them to sleep in the open rather than denning up. The tail wraps around the nose and insulates it.

Opposite above: River otters have been reported very rarely in Ohio during the twentieth century, and probably no wild breeding population survived. However, the Ohio Department of Natural Resources began trying to reintroduce these large members of the weasel family during the 1980s. In winter of 1988–89, the program released about fifteen Arkansas otters equipped with implanted radio transmitters. Initial results were disappointing: by that summer, researchers were in contact with only one of the released animals. However, further releases were more successful, and these attractive animals now seem to be on their way back in Ohio.

Opposite below: Beaver ceased to be king of furs toward the middle of the nineteenth century, when changes of fashion sent beaver hats out of style and silk hats in. Philadelphia prices fell from $6.00 a pound in 1831 to $2.62 in 1842. In 1793 the North West Company alone had forwarded 106,000 beaver skins from the country bordering the Great Lakes west to the upper Missouri's northern tributaries. Today beavers have returned to Ohio and comprise a modest share of the state's yearly fur harvest.

fur depot for the East. Later, when the major trade in furs had moved farther west, an Indian Department official estimated that the Missouri River basin from 1815 to 1830 annually furnished the following: 26,000 buffalo skins; 25,000 pounds of beaver skins; 4,000 otter skins; 12,000 raccoon skins; 150,000 pounds of deer skins; and 37,000 muskrat skins. In just one month of 1826, John Jacob Astor and Company sold between 500,000 and 550,000 muskrat skins in the New York market at an average price of thirty-six cents each.

Such wholesale trapping and hunting quickly depleted furbearer populations. Black bears, wood bison, and elk were rare or gone from Ohio by 1800. Continued trapping and habitat destruction during the settlement period accelerated the decline. Cougars, lynx, and bobcats vanished by mid-century, as did martens and fishers. Deer lingered until 1900. In 1976 the Ohio Division of Wildlife designated river otters—probably once common in Ohio—an endangered species; no breeding population is known in the wild.

Yet even today a much-altered fur trade still exists in the Old Northwest. From 1968 to 1978 trappers sold many thousands of Ohio muskrat pelts a year, receiving from $0.84 to $4.77 each. Raccoons, although second to muskrat in numbers, became the big moneymaker during the 1970s—at one time commanding up to $20.10 per fur. However, volatile fur prices dropped during the early years of the 1980s. As a result, the muskrat harvest decreased by half and that of raccoons by more than a third.

Besides these two, the Department of Natural Resources lists as Ohio furbearers the badger, beaver, coyote, gray fox, red fox, mink, opossum, skunk, and weasel. Peeled aspen trees in eastern Ashtabula County signaled the beavers' return to this state in 1936 after more than a century of absence. Beavers from Pennsylvania and Michigan, as well as released animals, recolonized Ohio successfully during the following half century. By 1976 nearly 8,000 beavers occupied forty counties, and their numbers have grown since then. In 1979–80 trappers took 4,927 at $24.08 each.

Reintroduced during the early 1930s, white-tailed deer have also made a big comeback, but are now hunted for sport rather than for their skins. The same is true of cottontail rabbits. Though both animals add millions to state revenues through sales of ammunition, equipment, and hunting licenses, they are no longer sought for their hides. And while farmers once classified red foxes as vermin and hunted them as such, researchers have vindicated these beautiful animals, which help to keep rodent populations in check. The state now protects them as furbearers, and their pelts commanded $56.34

An estimated twenty to forty million white-tailed deer browsed the continent in the sixteenth century, mostly east of the Mississippi. Native Americans' and deer's populations were roughly in balance. However, once white traders began offering goods such as knives, cooking pots, clothes, and alcohol for deerskins, an extreme slaughter began. Settlers also shot deer, of course, using buckskin for much of their clothing. Hides were exported to Europe too—in the peak year of 1748, South Carolina traders alone shipped 160,000 buckskins to England. As a result, whitetails dwindled to less than half of their former population by the end of colonial times. Since then, populations have fluctuated as a result of habitat changes and hunting pressures. Today we have too many deer in Ohio for the habitat available.

each during the peak years 1978–79. Mink pelts, on the other hand, bring less today than they did at the beginning of the twentieth century, before entrepreneurs established commercial mink ranches.

Most furbearers from the days of the Northwest Ordinance will probably never return to Ohio: habitat has simply changed too drastically for the big cats, bears, martens, fishers, and others to survive here. Attempts by the Department of Natural Resources to reestablish river otters are as yet inconclusive. However, smaller mammals, intelligently managed, can still support a fur trade at least faintly reminiscent of the richness squandered two hundred years ago.

ADDITIONAL READING

Ohio's Natural Heritage edited by Michael R. Lafferty, The Ohio
  Academy of Sciences, 1979.
Beavers: Water, Wildlife, and History by Earl L. Hilfiker, Windswept
  Press, 1991.

Decline & Recovery

*S*ome animals that disappeared or nearly disappeared from Ohio have made remarkable comebacks. These include beavers, white-tailed deer, and wild turkeys—all of which were completely extirpated from this state—and Canada geese and wood ducks, both at one time in serious decline. All these animals have made their return as a direct result of wildlife management, including control of hunting, though the stage was set by partial recovery of Ohio's cut over forests. Settlers had taken up much land that was unsuitable for farming in the end, especially in the southeastern hill country. Early in the twentieth century, many of these marginal farms failed, due to poor farming practices, inclement weather, and competition from larger farms farther west. Second- or third-growth forests have replaced many of them, providing a variety of habitats for wildlife as they mature.

The animals covered in this section are all those of interest to trappers and hunters: beavers, wild turkeys, white-tailed deer, Canada geese, and wood ducks. Indeed, many successful reintroduction efforts nationwide have involved animals valued for their fur or for outdoor sport. An important exception has been the recovery of Ohio's bald eagle population. From a low of only four nests in 1979, the number of nests today is over thirty, a tremendous management success. The causes of the eagles' return are two: first, the banning of DDT and related compounds in 1972 was essential. These chemicals thinned eggshells and devastated nesting success; as the environment gradually recovers, each generation of eagles contains lower levels of them. Second, a cooperative project involving the Ohio Department of Natural Resources Division of Wildlife, the U.S. Fish and Wildlife Service, and Ohio museums and zoos placed foster nestlings in the few remaining nests to augment those hatched by parent eagles. This was an exacting and difficult project. Young eagles are now pioneering new habitats across the state, especially reservoirs. Other introduction efforts involve peregrine falcons and recently inaugurated osprey and trumpeter swan projects.

The Ohio Department of Natural Resources began releasing beavers into suitable areas in the 1930s, a project which peaked in the 1950s. Their efforts paid off handsomely: by 1989, thirteen to fourteen thousand beavers lived in Ohio's streams and were spreading into new areas. The sight of their lodges, and even of the wary animals themselves, has become fairly common. Beavers' numbers dipped to less than nine thousand in early 1992 as a result of drought, but the animals have recovered well since then. Although they may cause problems when they fell trees near riverside homes or flood roads by damming culverts, their activities can be largely controlled. The pleasure of observing their works and the ecological benefits of the wetlands they create in a state impoverished by ditching and draining make them worth welcoming back.

Wild turkeys survived in Ohio about seventy years longer than beavers, but by about 1900, they were gone even from the southeastern Ohio hill counties. Their decline seems to have resulted more from unregulated hunting than from loss of habitat: they are adaptable birds that make use of a variety of foods and ranges. Efforts to restock them began in 1953. Unsuccessful at first, these measures, combined with hunting regulations, resulted in an estimated 120,000 wild Ohio turkeys in spring of 1996. Numbers shot during spring hunting season have risen from 4,000 in 1990 to about 12,000 in just the past six years; in 1996, hunters bagged 1,251 during a trial one-week fall season in twenty-two counties, as well.

White-tailed deer have undergone an even more spectacular population explosion, one that has recently become a serious problem. Extirpated in Ohio by 1900, deer had to be reintroduced early in this century. Free from the intense market-hunting of the late nineteenth century and lacking natural predators, they began to recover. In this they were aided by their preference for brushy "edge" habitat, precisely the kind that abandoned farms and recovering woodlands offered. Nevertheless, they were still so sparse in Ohio in 1961 that deer-hunting season was closed. Only in the past thirty years have their numbers ballooned: an Ohio Department of Natural Resources estimate projected 550,000 whitetails in fall of 1996, in spite of 180,000 taken by hunters in 1995. Starvation and disease for the deer, impoverishment of forest diversity, increased highway accidents, and destruction of suburban plantings are some results of overloading the range. Virtually everyone realizes that the herd must be thinned, but controversy has arisen over how to do it.

The rise of Canada geese has also caused human conflict during the past decade or so. The giant Canada goose, a subspecies once thought to be extinct nationwide, has been stocked in many places in the eastern states. Introduced in four Ohio locations during the '50s, '60s, and '70s, the big birds have shown a flair for living near people: they are relatively docile and will nest close to each other, unlike some of their relatives. Green lawns provide excellent grazing for them. Their dramatic flights and calls are a pleasure, but their waste products can pollute water and litter the ground, and their aggressive nesting behavior can sometimes intimidate. The spring 1995 count for Ohio was about 69,000, though numbers are hard to estimate accurately.

Canada's small relatives, the wood ducks, are another wildlife success story. Once thought to be headed for extinction, they have recently become the most common duck, after the mallard, in hunters' bags in eastern states. Carefully regulated hunting seasons, nest-box programs, and the regrowth of mature forests that provide needed nesting cavities have all played roles in the return of these pretty little waterfowl.

Amphibious Architect

The Beaver

Preceding pages: Beavers like this one were trapped out of Ohio in the 1830s and were absent for a century. Since the 1930s, restocking and careful regulation of trapping has returned them in numbers. Their dams and lodges, as well as the animals themselves, are becoming familiar to anyone who spends much time out-of-doors. The beaver shown here is towing a willow branch.

Below: Extirpated from Ohio by heavy trapping, beavers were absent from the state from 1830 until about 1934. Since then, reintroduction into suitable areas, as well as strict limits on trapping, has helped beavers make a big comeback here and elsewhere.

*W*ith woodchucks' teeth, monkeys' hands, ducks' feet, and platypuses' tails, beavers seem most curious beasts. The medieval church even condoned eating beavers on Fridays, considering them more fish than mammal.

The animals' history and natural history are also contradictory: millions and millions were slaughtered over the centuries to make perfumes and felt hats. Victims of human fashion, these bulky rodents are nevertheless creatures to be reckoned with. A Cherokee creation myth asserts that the Manitou originally formed a watery world inhabited by giant beavers. The beavers solved his problem of where to put the land animals by obligingly dredging up the continents.

Many know that beavers, through the fur trade, have decided the fate of nations. Fewer realize the extent to which they have determined the shape and productivity of the land itself. Beavers are the only animals besides humans that can alter their environment to suit their needs. This ability, along with their remarkable pelts, has caused the same predators who nearly wiped them out to foster their return to American waterways.

Beavers have always fascinated people, from the Egyptians, who wrote about them in hieroglyphics, to modern students who want to know if they can actually cut down trees—*big* trees. They are thought to have evolved in Eurasia ten or fifteen million years ago and to have migrated to America across the Bering land bridge. Casteroides, an early beaver of the recent ice age, weighed in at about seven hundred pounds but disappeared along with the other huge Pleistocene mammals. Modern beavers, which usually reach about forty pounds, but occasionally seventy or even 100 pounds, once ranged through all of Europe except Ireland and over the greater part of Asia and most of North America. Of rodents, they are second only to South America's capybara in size. Traditionally, taxonomists have classified beavers as European, *Castor fiber,* and American, *Castor canadensis,* but some now believe that the two are so closely related as to be only one species, *Castor fiber.*

Perhaps beavers fascinate because they are so different from us yet apparently so similar to us in their flair for constructive labor and in their social intercourse. Many Native American tribes felt a special relationship with beavers: the Crows believed that people who died came back to earth as beavers. The Flatheads thought that the animals were a race of men and women who had offended the Great Spirit, who transformed them into beavers. Conversely, some eastern tribes said that all ancient beavers had possessed the power of speech, but some bad elements had used such wicked language that Manitou had changed them into human beings as punishment!

To Europeans, projecting their own values onto beavers, they seemed the emblem of Calvinist industry. An early engraving pictures the animals earnestly building a dam at Niagara. It incorrectly shows them carrying mud on their tails to trowel onto the construction and has the beavers, which are very sociable creatures but usually work alone, organized into rather grim work gangs.

Actually, modern observers know that the animals "work like beavers" only when setting up a new dam and lodge, repairing a breached dam, or preparing for winter. They spend much of their time playing, wrestling, cruising around, grooming, and even sunbathing. The first beaver I ever saw was lolling on its back in a summer pond, feasting on water lilies—the picture of indolent self-indulgence. Other authors have noted that since these animals are faced with food shortages less often than many others, they are remarkably easy-going and tolerant about sharing food; in fact, they practice a lifestyle that resembles primitive communism more than capitalist industry or competition.

Beavers' physical and social attributes are more remarkable even than figments of the human imagination. Beavers' digestive tracts can extract nourishment from the bulkiest, least nourishing of substances: the cambium, or inner bark, of trees. Because it must deal with such quantities of low-grade food, the digestive system is immense, which accounts for the beaver's bulky shape and slow, sometimes clumsy movements on land. The senses are very acute, especially smell and hearing. A beaver can also feel the tiniest earth vibrations through its feet, warning it of predators when it grazes or fells trees on land.

The animal's chief tool, its teeth, are ever-growing and self-sharpening. They can cut away the five-inch chips needed to fell trees—big trees, though beavers prefer smaller ones with a higher ratio of bark to wood. Transparent eyelids serve both as swimming and wood-cutting goggles, ears and nostrils shut automatically to keep out water, and lips can close behind the incisors. This permits chewing underwater without drowning and excludes splinters from the mouth when felling trees.

Beavers' forepaws seem so human that observers often refer to them as hands. These are very dexterous, and many have reported

Clumsy and slow on land, the beaver is quite another animal in the water. It swims expertly, forepaws bunched on its chest, with muscular hind legs, webbed feet, and tail providing power. A beaver can probably swim six miles an hour if pressed, faster than a person with swim flippers can chase it.

Beavers live either in bank burrows or in lodges like this spectacular example. They pile sticks into a tipi-like shape, then gnaw out a sleeping chamber within it, complete with underwater entrances, an eating shelf above the water, and a sleeping shelf floored with dry, soft wood shavings. They plaster the lodge with mud, which freezes hard in winter, protecting them from all predators but humans.

watching beavers twirl sticks of wood and eat the bark from them like corn on the cob. The hind feet have five toes and are fully webbed. The second toe's claw is split and serves, along with the forepaws, as a comb for grooming the fur. This marvellous fur, source of many beaver woes, includes a dense, warm underlayer covered by longer guard hairs. It requires constant care, or it will mat and become waterlogged—death to a creature that swims in cold northern waters. Beavers spend many hours caring for their coats, and mutual grooming fosters social bonding. When cleaned, combed, and dried, the fur is waterproofed with oil taken from a gland at the base of the tail.

The beaver's trademark is, of course, its paddle-shaped tail, covered with what look like scales, but which are really only regular depressions in the tough skin. These "scales" are apparently what convinced church fathers to permit Friday beaver eating. Native Americans and mountain men considered the fatty tail a delicacy. Though the tail is not used as a wheelbarrow or trowel, it is a rudder and can aid the powerful hind legs and webbed hind feet to propel the creature through the water at up to six miles an hour. Beavers also slap the water with their tails to warn of danger, or as some observers believe, occasionally just for fun. On land, the tail serves as a tripod, extended either in front of or behind the body. Beavers often carry wood or their kits between their forepaws and chin, walking on their hind legs and using the tail for balance.

Beavers' social organization has always invited comparison with our own. They live monogamously in family groups that usually include two successive generations, in bank burrows or in lodges cleverly fashioned of sticks and mud and hollowed out inside. These are equipped with both eating and sleeping shelves, though not "windows which looked out on the water . . . and balconies for the enjoyment of the sun and air," as Georges Buffon, the eighteenth-century naturalist, believed.

Young animals usually stay with the family until they reach two years, then wander away to find mates and set up their own family groups. If any member dominates, it is the oldest female, around whom the life of the group revolves. In his studies of European beavers, scientist Lars Wilsson observed that females marked territory more assiduously than males did and also showed more aggression. Curiously, however, even modern observers often refer to the generic beaver as "he."

Animals that spend all winter and many daylight hours in other seasons cooped up together in a little lodge must depend on highly evolved social adaptations. Otherwise, few beavers would live to see the spring. Vocalizing, which can sound remarkably like human talk, grooming and body contact, play, and ritualized wrestling to defuse aggression all help the group survive. Students of animal behavior note strong inhibitions against biting among members of wolf packs. The same is true of beavers, which almost never use their wickedly strong and sharp teeth on each other.

Those who have kept beavers as pets remark on their affectionate natures and say they make more expressive companions than dogs. If kits are adopted early, they imprint on human keepers and form lasting relationships with them. In *Pilgrims of the Wild*, the Canadian trapper-turned-conservationist, Grey Owl, said of two young beavers that he raised, "Their utter dependence on our good will claimed all of any chivalry we had. Their little sneezes and childish coughs, their little whimpers and small appealing noises of affection, their instant and pathetically eager response to any kindness . . . all seemed to touch a chord of tenderness for the small and helpless . . . . They seemed to be almost like little folk from some other planet, whose language we could not yet quite understand. To kill such creatures seemed monstrous."

Lars Wilsson, who studied Swedish beavers, was far from being a sentimentalist but also commented on the strong bond possible between beaver and human: "One of them had begun to 'talk' to me. It often came up and nuzzled at me and made a long succession of whimpering sounds, so highly nuanced that it really sounded as though it were talking. It looked at me all the time with what seemed to be an expression of confidence, and it felt quite strange to experience such a personal contact with an animal I had previously had such difficulty in learning anything about."

These authors and others have also commented on beaver's cleanliness and lack of odor. In fact, if the animals did not absolutely need water—they can defecate only in pools or tanks—and were it not for their building and chewing needs, difficult to accommodate in the modern apartment house, Man's Best Friend might have a run for his money. Other observers, such as Hope Ryden in her book *Lily Pond,* document beavers' affectionate relationships among their own kind.

The sterling qualities described above did not, of course, protect beavers from wholesale slaughter by humans or from displacement by agriculture. Although Europeans valued beaver skins, they prized even more castoreum, a musky, pleasant-smelling substance produced in beavers in pockets the size of clenched fists next to both sexes' genitals. Hippocrates, writing about 400 B.C, discussed its supposed medicinal qualities, and later practitioners considered it a miraculous medicine. Castoreum also captures fragrances and releases them slowly in response to body heat, making it useful for perfumes. Needless to say, beavers had disappeared from most of Europe by the sixteenth century, and by 1900 they survived only in small pockets in Germany, Scandinavia, the Rhone Valley in France, and in Russia. American beavers recently have been introduced to Finland, Poland, and Russia.

The opening of North America gave Europeans access to vast beaver country, lands now thought to have supported sixty million to four hundred million beavers. Beavers felled trees from Massachusetts, where the Pilgrims paid the Plymouth Colony's debts with beaver skins, to the West Coast, where John Jacob Astor would later build Astoria in an attempt to capture the fur trade with China. They built dams and raised lodges from Alaska south to northern Mexico and nearly to Florida, where beavers have never lived in historic times, perhaps because of alligators. However, the days of these masses of beavers were numbered: from 1600, when Pierre Chauvin built the first trading post at Tadoussac on the Saint Lawrence, to about 1900, beavers declined almost to the point of extinction.

Although American trappers did sell castoreum, pelts were what really drove the beaver trade. Hatmakers had known for some time that beavers' soft undercoat made superior felt that held its shape well, perfect for the broad-brimmed hats of cavaliers, ladies' chapeaux, and the nineteenth century's tall stovepipe hats. Beaver was in such demand that hats were often referred to simply as "beavers": Shakespeare mentions "young Harry with his beaver on" in *Henry IV, Part I*. The nineteenth-century humorist Edward Lear in *The Quangle Wangle's Hat* says

> On the top of the Crumpetty Tree
>   The Quangle Wangle sat,
> But his face you could not see,
>   On account of his Beaver Hat.

Skins that had been slept on for several months and saturated with human body oil made the best felt. French traders called these *castor gras d'hiver*, or fat winter beaver, and found that tribespeople would part with them for beads, mirrors, kettles, axes, and other trade goods. Alcohol, of course, figured largely in the beaver trade over the years as well.

As early as 1640, the Saint Lawrence Valley had already been virtually stripped of beavers, and traders began to look elsewhere. In 1670 English fur traders founded the Hudson's Bay Company, encouraged by Pierre Esprit Radisson and his brother-in-law Medard Chouart, Sieur de Groseilliers, whose rich haul of prime beaver skins from west of Lake Superior had been confiscated by grafting officials in New France. The French on the Saint Lawrence found themselves increasingly squeezed between the Hudson's Bay Company to the north and the English settlements and hostile Iroquois to the south, whom Samuel de Champlain had defeated and fatally alienated in 1609.

The only outlet for the French was to the west. They developed the famous trading routes of the *voyageurs* and *coureurs des bois* west along the Ottawa River, following the Great Lakes to Grand Portage at the western end of Lake Superior and through the maze of today's Minnesota boundary waters to the headwaters of the Mississippi. Eventually they faced the British and lost to them in the French and Indian War (1754–63). One of the war's important causes was the struggle to control rich fur trading grounds in the Ohio Country.

Many fur companies besides the Hudson's Bay Company, which still trades for pelts today, were founded to exploit the continent's riches: these included the American Fur Company, the Northwest Company, the Columbia Fur Company, the Pacific Fur Company, the Rocky Mountain Fur Company, the St. Louis Missouri Fur Company, and others less well known. They traded for various furs,

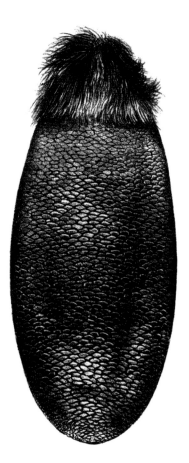

Left: Lewis H. Morgan, the nineteenth-century ethnologist famous for his studies of Iroquois Indians, also published an 1868 treatise on the beaver that has since become a classic. Morgan described the animal's anatomy, bone structure, and other physical characteristics. The neophyte zoologist was utterly fascinated with the creature's distinctively flat, broad tail.

Below: A beaver dam discovered in the Upper Peninsula of Michigan particularly intrigued Morgan: two hundred sixty feet long and slightly more than six feet high, it flooded more than sixty acres. In Morgan's eyes, its siting and design were uncanny examples of animal intelligence.

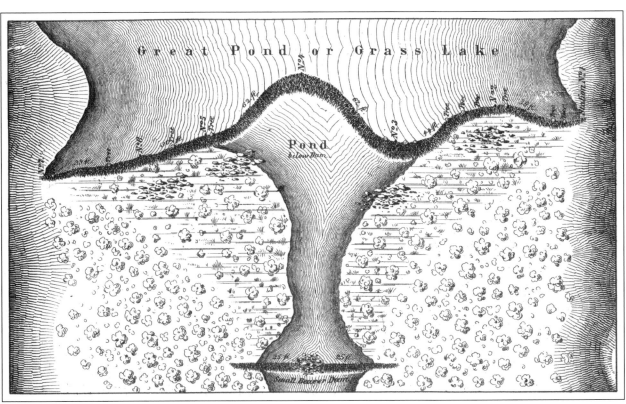

but beaver was king. Volumes were enormous. During the years 1796–98, dealers shipped from Detroit 7,330 bales of assorted pelts, each weighing ninety to one hundred pounds, and many more bales left Michilimackinac, the main fur depot for the East. Later, when the land east of the Mississippi had become nearly a fur desert, an Indian department official estimated that the Missouri River basin from 1815 to 1830 furnished 25,000 pounds of beaver skins alone each year. Profits on these volumes could be even more impressive. During its first twenty years, the Hudson's Bay Company paid shareholders 295 percent on the original price of their shares. About 1800, a trader for the Northwest Company obtained 120 beaver skins for eight quarts of watered rum, two blankets, and a pocket mirror. For an outlay of $30, the pelts earned $400 in Montreal.

In the year 1822, William Ashley published an advertisement in a St. Louis newspaper, "wishing to enlist one hundred enterprising young men to ascend the River Missouri to its source, there to be employed one, two, or three years." The names of those who answered included Jim Bridger, Jedediah Smith, William Sublette, Hugh Glass, and others now legendary for their roles in the brief era of the Mountain Men, rough and ready individuals who trapped the Rocky Mountains and attended rendezvous each year to trade, drink, and generally raise hell. Sewell Newhouse's invention of the steel trap at Oneida, New York, in 1823 ushered in much more efficient trapping: James Pattie caught two hundred and fifty beavers in just two weeks on Arizona's San Francisco River in 1825; a company of twenty trappers took more than five thousand beavers from the Bitterroot Range in 1824 alone. This period, ending in about 1840, was the last great gasp of the beaver trade in the United States, though the Hudson's Bay Company traded over three million beaver pelts in Canada between 1853 and 1877.

This onslaught might have exterminated beavers entirely, but the growing popularity of the silk hat as well as methods of making felt from less expensive furs drove prices down and gave the poor beleaguered animals some relief. However, settlement and the cutting of forests and draining of wetlands also speeded beavers' demise. By the end of the last century, they were completely gone from most of their natural range. In Ohio, beavers disappeared by the year 1830.

Not until late in the century were there signs that help was on its way and a combination of factors began to tip the balance in beavers' favor. Creation of national parks, beginning with Yellowstone in 1872, gave beavers enclaves where they could reproduce unmolested. A budding conservation movement began to grow in the early years of this century, fueled by sentiment against market hunting and plume hunting. Conservation organizations lobbied for legislation to protect threatened species like beavers and also acquired land for restoring habitat. Sportsmen became interested in reintroducing game species like white-tailed deer, wild turkeys, and ruffed grouse that, like beavers, had been wiped out by uncontrolled slaughter.

New York and Pennsylvania were among the first states to begin restoring beavers, in 1904 and 1917 respectively. Wisconsin beavers

Beavers create artificial waterways, which they use to carry wood to their lodges. A three-foot width and depth are common dimensions for these canals, and they can stretch hundreds of feet in length. Beavers usually dig canals when they have lived in one place for some time and are exhausting waterside trees. Canals enable them to tap lumber farther inland without becoming overly vulnerable to predators.

were liberated in Pennsylvania under full protection. Lacking natural predators, they reproduced so fast that only eleven years later, fifteen hundred colonies inhabited forty-nine Pennsylvania counties. A trapping season opened in 1934, and 6,400 beavers were taken. Restoration programs also began in Canada, notably a highly successful one carried out by the Hudson's Bay Company and the Cree tribe on James Bay. Such programs, which sometimes even parachuted beavers into remote areas, have returned them to many parts of their former range. Experts estimate that from six to twelve million North American beavers now inhabit today's more limited habitat.

Adding beavers to a landscape has advantages other than richer trapping or the sight of a beaver contentedly eating water lilies on a sunny summer afternoon. Beavers can alter stream channels and drainage patterns for whole areas because of their lust for damming water. Damming increases beaver habitat and food supply and protects the animals from predators, mainly wolves, both by maintaining water levels high enough to cover entrances to banks and lodges and by bringing water close to trees. Beavers instinctively build dams, triggered by the sound of running water—captive beavers will begin to build at the tape-recorded sound. However, observers note that beavers whose dam is keeping water at proper levels will not build it higher, no matter how much running water they hear.

Thus, much of beavers' behavior raises fascinating questions about boundaries between instinctive and learned behavior. These large rodents' young spend an unusually long time living with parents and watching them at their work. They do not leave home until they are well prepared to meet the demands of their new life. Often they show what observers interpret as prescience: Hope Ryden, for example, recalls a beaver who had been working on a breached dam one evening and returned to the dam the next morning already equipped with wood to resume repairs at once. The interplay between inherited and learned behavior, instinctive actions and those requiring thought, is complex and still little understood, but certainly of interest to our own conflicted species.

Many ecologists have shown that beaver ponds are a boon to other wildlife. They have also noted their important role in what Ryden calls nature's rest-and-rotation plan. These ponds appear and disappear cyclically: by nature they are temporary. A newly built beaver dam creates standing water that serves minks, otters, fish, ducks, frogs, salamanders, turtles, wading birds, and many other creatures. In a country that has lost more than half of its original wetlands, these habitats are valuable. As the beavers cut the trees that, stashed under the ice, provide their winter food, they create brushy forest "edge" conditions that give food and shelter to great concentrations of birds and other wildlife. Spars of dead trees killed by the rising water provide nest holes for pileated woodpeckers, wood ducks, owls, kingbirds, raccoons, flying squirrels, and many others, and branches for great blue herons' nests.

Eventually the beavers eat themselves out of house and home, despite delaying tactics: building the dam higher to raise water levels and digging remarkable canals to reach food supplies without a vulnerable overland trek. They then abandon the pond, which soon drains without dam repair. Eventually a beaver meadow forms, and plants shoot up vigorously, thriving on the rich muck decayed from captured silt, shredded wood, rotted trees, and other nutrients. The meadow supports a new array of animals: meadow voles, deer, and rabbits, preyed on by foxes, coyotes, weasels, and hawks. Eventually aspens, willow, and birch begin to reestablish the old forest, and one day a young beaver wanders in, looking for a mate to start the whole cycle over again. This varied succession, whose motive force is the beaver, prevents soil exhaustion and offers habitat for a varying parade of plants and animals. Beaver ponds also help prevent erosion by slowing down runoff; they replace lost topsoil, help with flood and fire control, and, by forcing more water into the soil, help maintain water tables.

Of course, when the earth's two engineering experts meet, some conflict must follow. As reintroduction programs succeeded, complaints about beaver works began to reach local and state agencies. County authorities are not pleased when beavers flood roads by damming culverts, nor are suburban homeowners when the animals cut down ornamental willows or fruit trees. In the South, where beaver populations have soared, flooding has killed quantities of valuable timber. And once beavers decide to work an area, very little but death or relocation can stop them. Many are the stories of dams torn down by day and rebuilt by the next morning. But where do you relocate beavers when suitable habitat gives out? There is simply not enough room for all beavers in a world crowded with humanity. Most states rely on controlled trapping seasons, based on aerial surveys, to control beavers' numbers and on professional trappers who remove individual nuisance animals.

A few beavers wandered into Ohio from Pennsylvania in the 1930s. They had been absent for a hundred years. The Ohio Department of Natural Resources Division of Wildlife began live trapping and releasing them in suitable areas, an effort that peaked in the 1950s. By

1989, estimates showed a sensational success: thirteen to fourteen thousand Ohio beavers, a population that was actively spreading into new areas. Beavers are especially welcome in Ohio, which has lost a staggering 95 percent of the wetlands that dotted it two hundred years ago. The animals also help to reclaim the ravages of strip mining in the southeastern counties, where they tolerate acid water conditions and help slow erosion, change vegetation, and enrich ponds.

The ODNR controls beaver populations by a trapping season usually held from mid-January through February, the season when fur is prime in this species. The department decides the length of season by doing a fall aerial survey of active beaver lodges. According to Jack Weeks, a wildlife biologist who directs the survey, prices for pelts fluctuate widely, and in some years not enough trapping is done to control beavers' numbers because of low fur prices. Conversely, the season must be shortened in other years to let populations recover from stresses. A skin commanded $24 in 1979 but only $6.71 in 1990–91. Pelts were bringing $12 to $15 in 1992. Weeks believes that fashion, beavers' old enemy, and hard-to-pin-down market forces cause these variations: long-haired fur happens to be more popular right now than short-haired beaver.

Since 1989, numbers of beaver plummeted in Ohio from almost 14,000 to 1992's estimated 8,885. Trapping was not the cause here, but probably recent droughts instead. Beavers suffer from bad water conditions, especially in winter, when ponds may freeze to the bottom, preventing animals from reaching food caches and leaving entrance tunnels exposed. March through June, when the young become active and leave the lodge, is another danger period. Northeastern Ohio, with its shallow marshes, creeks, and rivers has seen a big drop in numbers, but beavers have survived better in the southeastern counties' strip-mining pits. Accordingly, Weeks recommended less trapping in the north in 1992. Fortunately, with such help, beavers can rebound quickly.

For the moment, that anomalous animal *Castor canadensis* and the even more anomalous *Homo sapiens* seem to live in uneasy balance. The drive that sent trappers over the Alleghenies and into the Rockies, over Grand Portage, north to Hudson's Bay, Great Slave Lake, and the MacKenzie River to persue an inoffensive rodent with the bad luck to have a coat that made good felt has dissipated, and with our help, beavers once again build dams and enjoy aspen and water lilies in many of their old haunts. The settlement that beavers helped us pay for with their skins is far in the past. Now, as more of

us look to the land with intent to heal rather than to despoil it further, perhaps beavers can help us again in the process of reclamation.

ADDITIONAL READING

Lily Pond by Hope Ryden, Harper Collins, 1989.
My Beaver Colony by Lars Wilsson, Doubleday, 1968.
Beavers: Water, Wildlife and History by Earl L. Hilfiker, Windswept Press, 1991.
The World of the Beaver by Leonard Lee Rue III, Lippincott, 1964.

Besides eating the inner bark of trees, beavers consume a wide variety of other vegetation. They are fond of water lilies and other aquatic plants and will graze grass on land if the coast is clear. Although beavers today are mostly nocturnal, early explorers' accounts show that they may have taken to the night only as a result of persecution by humans. Their eyes lack the light-gathering crystal, *tapetum lucidum,* that makes truly nocturnal animals' eyes glow in the dark.

A Respectable Bird

The Wild Turkey

*T*he first Thanksgiving, that archetypal celebration of plenty after scarcity, looms large as part of the American myth, even for those who remember little else. At the center of that story, and of later Thanksgivings, steams the brown bulk of the turkey, meaty symbol of nature's bounty revealed to the Pilgrims by Massasoit and his tribe.

Many Americans would be surprised to find out that turkeys were not a new discovery for the Pilgrims. Not only had the colonists dined so often on wild turkey during the preceding months that it was probably less than a treat at that first Thanksgiving, but they had actually brought domesticated turkeys with them from England. Central American or southwestern Indians had tamed a subspecies of *Meleagris gallopavo* centuries before, and Spanish explorers took turkeys to Europe a hundred years before the Plymouth colony existed. They had become common barnyard fowl, the only important domesticated animal introduced from the New World.

Hernando Cortez's 1519 expedition documented the domestic turkey's abundance in Mexico. In that year, when Cortez camped at

Page 58: The wild turkey is a wary, adaptable bird that can survive in fairly close proximity to people. However, relentless hunting by colonists soon thinned the turkey population in eastern states, and by about 1900, these birds disappeared completely from Ohio. They were reintroduced in the 1950s by the Ohio Department of Natural Resources Division of Wildlife, and they have also been reintroduced in many other states. Restoration efforts have been so successful here that in fall of 1997 the Division of Wildlife estimated 150,000 turkeys in the state and increasing. Restocking will soon be discontinued. Control of hunting, as well as habitat protection, are keys to wild turkeys' future survival.

the hill of Zumpango, several Tlaxcalans arrived with five captives, saying diplomatically: "If you are gods who eat blood and flesh, eat these Indians and we will bring you more; and if you are good gods here are incense and feathers; and if you are men here are turkeys, bread and cherries." It is said that five hundred turkeys a day were fed to the meat-eating birds alone in Montezuma's large menagerie. Other carnivores devoured more. Historians estimate that the menagerie and Montezuma's large household consumed some 365,000 turkeys each year, between 1,000 and 1,500 at one human feast alone. The United States today produces more than ninety million turkeys, 40 percent of which meet their demise at Thanksgiving.

Cortez and other explorers took Mexican turkeys back to Europe, where people immediately confused them with several other fowl: the peacock, the capercaillie, and especially the guinea fowl. This African bird was assumed to be from Turkey, probably because it had reached Europe through the Ottoman Empire. Though some suggest that "turkey" derives from one of the bird's calls or from an American Indian name, most believe that confusion with the supposedly Turkish guinea fowl is the origin of the name—or misname. So widely accepted was this erroneous belief about the turkey's antecedents that as late as 1755 Dr. Samuel Johnson's famous *Dictionary of the English Language* defined the turkey as "a large domestic fowl brought from Turkey."

Certainly the early colonists knew that the wild turkey was a New World fowl: accounts of its abundance during the early years of settlement are sometimes unbelievable. Thomas Morton, one of the earliest New England writers, in 1637 commented facetiously: "Turkies there are, which divers times in great flocks have sallied by our doores; and then a gunne, being commonly in a redinesse, salutes them with such a courtesie, as makes them take a turne in the Cooke roome. They daunce by the doore so well." A century and a half later, Benjamin Franklin wrote to his daughter, Sarah Bache: "I wish the Bald Eagle had not been chosen as the Representation of our Country; he is a Bird of bad moral Character, like those among men who live by sharpening and robbing, he is generally poor and often very lousy. . . . The turkey is . . . a much more respectable bird, and withal a true original Native of America."

These respectable birds were big, too, although reports of sixty-three-pound turkeys probably reflect historical variations in the pound weight. And, as a wag commented later, in 1881: "When you kill a gobbler of twenty-five or thirty pounds do not weigh him; they generally resent such a proceeding by falling off from five to ten

The adult gobbler's head and neck sport a gaudy combination of red, white, and blue during the mating season. The caruncles on the neck fill with blood and glow bright red. The "snood," a limp, finger-like appendage between the bill and forehead, changes size and shape according to the gobbler's level of excitement. Fall coloring is similar but somewhat more subdued. The hen, smaller than the gobbler, has a bluish-gray head with a touch of pink on the neck.

pounds." Certainly a twenty-pound wild gobbler is a prize today, though domestic turkeys have weighed in at as much as seventy-five pounds.

Six subspecies of wild turkeys originally roamed the woodlands of eastern and southern North America, being especially thick in the Ohio Valley and extending into a small part of what is now southern Canada. They also lived on the Great Plains along wooded rivers and in the pine forests of the Rocky Mountains. Cold winters and snow cover barred them from northern New England and most of Canada, and they were absent from the Pacific and northern Great

A wild turkey does not approach the weight of domesticated birds, but it is an impressive sight, nevertheless. The wild bird may stand four feet high, reach four feet from its head to the end of its tail, and weigh as much as twenty-four pounds. Its neck and legs are longer than domestic birds', and its feathers show a beautiful metallic sheen. A buffy brown tips the tail feathers of eastern wild turkeys, but western subspecies show whiter markings on tail and body. In all, three subspecies, the Merriam's, the Gould's, and the Rio Grande, inhabit the western United States; and two, the Eastern and Florida, live farther east. Unlike domestic turkeys, which breeding has rendered too heavy to fly or even to copulate naturally, wild ones can fly fifty-five miles per hour in short bursts and regularly roost in tall trees.

A wild turkey hen is very hard to detect as she sits on her nest. She will not flush unless attacked by a predator. If her nest is in good cover, a person may walk as close as eight feet before she will abandon it. Otherwise, she leaves only to feed, which gives her eggs a chance to "breathe," to exchange carbon dioxide for oxygen through their porous shells. The hen may also turn her eggs, said to prevent the embryos from sticking to one wall.

Plains states as well. Deserts and killing by the great Indian civilizations had eliminated them from large areas of Mexico. After settlement, hunting wiped out turkeys from much of their range in the East, Southwest, and Rocky Mountains. During the past half-century, however, wildlife managers have successfully brought back wild turkeys in large parts of their original range and even beyond.

Eastern forest Indians must have eaten a lot of wild turkey, as shown by ancient middens in which turkey bones outnumber all others except those of deer. Tribes also wove feathers into clothing, used wing quills to fletch arrows, and fashioned the spurs on the cock's legs into arrow points. More than fifteen hundred years ago, they made the lower leg bones into awls. Pueblo Indians kept domesticated birds for meat, for making awls and other tools, and for feathers from which they produced capes and ornaments. Some tribes, such as the Cheyennes and Apaches, are said to have refused to eat turkey because consuming a timid creature would breed timidity in themselves.

Common as turkeys were in the woods and meadows of the early colonies, overhunting quickly thinned the ranks of those obliging fowl, observed by Morton to "daunce by the doore so well." In 1672 John Josselyn remarked in *New England's Rarities Discovered* that "I have also seen threescore broods of young Turkies on the side of a marsh, sunning of themselves in a morning betimes, but this was thirty years since, the English and the Indians having now destroyed the breed, so that 'tis very rare to meet with a wild Turkie in the Woods." In 1840 John James Audubon reported that, although un-settled regions were still "abundantly supplied with this magnificent bird," in Georgia, the Carolinas, Virginia, and Pennsylvania, turkeys were sparser. They very rarely appeared in the eastern parts of the

Hens lay from seven to seventeen eggs in a shallow scrape in the ground. If the eggs are viable and are not discovered by predators, they will hatch in about twenty-eight days. Many animals, including raccoons, opossums, crows, snakes, skunks, foxes, minks, and wandering dogs, enjoy turkey eggs.

latter two states, and he almost never encountered one in New York, though he remembered the birds selling for a mere three pence each in Kentucky twenty-five years earlier.

As the nineteenth century progressed, the turkey's decline quickened, and it disappeared completely from many states. Turkeys were last sighted in Massachusetts in 1851 at Mount Tom, named to commemorate the occasion; they were extinct in Connecticut as early as 1813, in Wisconsin in 1881, in Nebraska about 1880, in South Dakota in about 1875. In Ohio, turkeys were scarce in the southwest by 1845 and around Cleveland by 1864. They disappeared from the Toledo area in 1892 and from southeastern Ohio by 1900. Bruce G. Peterjohn, in *The Birds of Ohio*, says that wild turkeys were almost certainly extirpated in Ohio before 1900, although another reference cites an Adams County straggler taken in 1904. By 1941 the wild turkey survived in only 28 percent of its original U.S. range.

Other factors, such as habitat destruction, also contributed to the turkey's decline, but populations plummeted so early in many areas as to indicate that hunting was most important. The wild turkey is a versatile bird that can survive in a landscape considerably altered by

Day-old turkey chicks, more properly called poults, prepare to leave the nest. Chicks cut themselves out of the egg using a temporary egg tooth, encouraged by the sounds of their mother. Unlike baby robins and other songbirds, which the parents must care for in the nest, turkey poults are precocial; that is, they can run about, feed themselves, and freeze at their mother's alarm call soon after they hatch.

human beings. One author comments that an early problem in bringing the turkey back was that naturalists were long unaware of uncontrolled hunting's primary role in its decline. They believed that the remote swamps and forests in which flocks then remained were the only places the birds could survive at all. The turkey's dramatic comeback since 1940, driven by restocking and controlled hunting, refutes this belief. Turkeys have not only returned to large parts of their former range but have taken hold successfully in Pacific and northern Great Plains states where they were previously unknown.

Turkeys are said to consume "anything slow enough to catch and small enough to eat." This flexibility is one reason for their resilience when hunting is curtailed. Insects, especially grasshoppers, make up about 10 percent of the diet. They particularly nourish chicks, or poults, which need protein to support quick growth. Vegetable matter composes the rest of the diet, ranging from green leaves and soft berries to rock-hard hickory nuts, which the birds' tough gizzards can crush in about thirty-six hours. Acorns and other nuts, or mast, are especially important food items in autumn, winter, and into the spring. In a single Virginia study, more than 354 plants appeared in turkeys' diet. They uncover much of their food by scratching with powerful feet.

Fairly high reproductive rates have also helped protected turkeys to recoup their numbers. They are promiscuous birds: dominant gobblers mate with several hens, and hens themselves are believed to mate with more than one gobbler. In spring gobblers begin displaying and gobbling. This is the time when a male looks like the enormous puffed-up picture of the farmyard turkey cock. He struts and gobbles until a female approaches, ducks down, and allows him to tread and mate with her. In this season males are vulnerable to the skillful hunter who can lure them with an imitation of the female's *keuk,* or yelp.

Once mated, females leave the mixed flocks. They lay about seven to seventeen eggs in not more than a scrape in the earth, incubate them for approximately twenty-eight days, and tend their poults as they hatch—all without any help from the males, which eventually calm down and resume life in their bachelor flocks until the next spring. There they jockey to establish and maintain a pecking order, a preoccupation that often involves vigorous fighting. Only dominant gobblers mate, thus ensuring healthy breeding stock. The young, both male and female, stay with their mothers through the summer, often combining with other hens and young in female-headed family groups. During the rest of the year, the birds associate in segregated flocks. In fall and winter, separate flocks are made up of hens that have not managed to raise chicks, hens and their half-grown female offspring, young gobblers that the older hens have recently run out of family flocks, and adult gobblers.

Not surprisingly, most individuals die either in the egg (one study showed 20 to 60 percent nesting success) or as poults. Since turkeys nest on the ground, many animals that like eggs, including raccoons, opossums, crows, snakes, skunks, foxes, minks, and feral dogs, discover and eat the eggs, even though a turkey's nest can prove very difficult to find. Young poults are vulnerable, too, although they imprint very early on their mother and scatter and freeze when they hear her alarm call. Turkey poults are well developed at hatching, leaving the nest within the first day or two after they begin pipping the eggshells. They grow fast, are capable of some flight at seven days, and then begin roosting in trees at about two weeks, an achievement that protects them from ground predators. Cool, rainy weather is actually a greater threat than predators to young poults: their fluffy down wets easily. Exhaustion also takes its toll.

If a turkey can survive from its first spring into late winter, it can deal with all but the largest predators: raccoons, bobcats, and great horned owls—all of which sometimes kill roosting turkeys—eagles, and, of course, humans. Many hunters and some wildlife managers have thought that predators other than themselves should be killed to help turkeys increase their numbers. They say that when trapping of raccoons, minks, and other egg and poult eaters slows, turkeys suffer. Others believe that predator control is difficult, expensive, and, in the long run, may not benefit turkey populations as a whole. Although predators do kill considerable numbers of the fowl, they can also benefit populations by eating sick birds before they pass on their diseases. Also, nests with rotten, unhatched eggs will more likely draw raccoons or opossums than ones with healthy eggs. Destroying these nests removes offspring of hens and gobblers that are not very fertile and, over time, helps keep fertility high. Some predators are beneficial because they eat other predators. For example, rattlesnakes eat rats, which wildlife managers have found can decimate game bird populations in certain areas.

Restoring the American wild turkey to much of its original range, and adding it to other areas as well, has proved one of the major wildlife management triumphs of this century. By 1965 twenty-six states contained enough turkeys to allow hunting, and hunters took almost 100,000 birds out of about 750,000 spread through thirty-five states. Now more than 1,250,000 turkeys live in forty-two states;

Wary wild turkeys have both sharp eyesight and excellent hearing and are slender compared to their domesticated cousins, which are bred primarily for an enormous mass of white breast meat and are literally too dumb to come in out of the rain. The wild turkey is another bird altogether. It is so elusive that hunting it would be very hard without the aid of turkey callers. Some hunters imitate the hen's *keuk* with their own voices, but most use one of a variety of calling devices, usually operated by breath or friction.

thirty-six permit hunting. (Turkey censuses are difficult to make, and all numbers are approximate.) The Ohio Department of Natural Resources has successfully restocked turkeys in about forty-eight counties in southeastern and northeastern Ohio, and about thirty-six are open for hunting. Restocking continues. In 1966, during the first legal season, hunters bagged twelve birds. The total has grown steadily to a high of more than 4,000, although only about one in seven hunters succeeds in bagging the limit of one gobbler, attesting to the birds' wariness.

Restocking efforts began in Ohio in 1953 but failed at first, illustrating a central problem that dogged other earlier programs as well.

Wild turkeys are difficult to raise in captivity. Their wariness and general nervousness cause injuries against fences and other obstructions. Managers tried to compensate by hybridizing wild with domesticated turkeys, usually by penning part-tame hens where wild gobblers could mate with them. However, the very traits that made these game-farm turkeys easier to raise doomed them in the wild. Selective breeding for two thousand years since Indians first domesticated turkeys, some say, had changed their behavior fundamentally. They had lost the edge that extreme wariness gives wild turkeys. Even semidomestic poults failed to freeze at their mothers' alarm calls and were easily picked off by predators. Game-farm turkeys can also infect wild birds with domestic diseases, which some think may even have contributed to early die-offs of wild turkeys during settlement.

The ODNR decided that wild-trapped and transplanted turkeys were the answer. In 1956 Ohio traded with West Virginia for some wild birds. Beginning in Zaleski State Forest in Vinton County, these and other wild turkeys were released during the following five years. They have become the nucleus of other successful restocking efforts since then. Techniques for wild trapping included large drop nets (more often used in the West, where turkeys congregate in bigger flocks); the cannon net, which is fired over groups of birds by projectiles; and tranquilizer-baited food. Sowing of food plants, mowing, or controlled burning to maintain turkey habitat, and occasional winter feeding are all used to manage wild turkeys.

Hunting seasons vary from state to state: some hunters prefer spring turkey hunting, when they can hear the gobbler's exciting call and when the birds' mating urge makes them easier to entice to a hunting blind in response to a hen's imitated yelp. Others prefer fall, saying that a short autumn season tends to move young birds into new areas, mixing the stock and spreading them out. Many states have established spring seasons because hunters can distinguish forbidden hens from gobblers more easily then. Some states, including Ohio, try to set the season for a time when hens have already mated and are out of the way of the guns and bows aiming at their late consorts. Gobblers are expendable: only a few dominant ones mate with the hens, and hunters can kill many males without seriously harming overall populations. Although uncontrolled hunting wiped out early populations, controlled hunting does not seem a central problem for the species' survival today. In the long run, habitat loss will become more important: turkey country now succumbs to suburbs, shopping malls, and industrial parks, types of development that will not revert to brush and forest as abandoned farms did across the state in the late nineteenth and early twentieth centuries, or as disused cotton plantations did in the post–Civil War South.

In Ohio the spring hunting season usually begins the final week in April and continues for three weeks. The limit is one gobbler. Each year more people flock to counties where hunting is legal to experience the ritualized sport that seems a throwback to frontier ways. Each year hunters learn more about how to use blinds and camouflage, about how to locate birds, and about how to simulate the hen's yelp to draw gobblers into shotgun or bow range. They use a variety of turkey calls and sometimes their own voices. Each year, in response, the turkeys themselves become warier.

For the present, the species seems fairly secure; more and more people observe wild turkeys now where fifty years ago none survived. I still remember the thrill of spotting a hen and half-grown poults at a woodland edge in upstate New York for the first time. Later my husband and I watched two adults stride like small dinosaurs across the sandy beaches of Cumberland Island, Georgia, another experience I won't forget. The return of Audubon's "magnificent bird" to country long empty of the wild gobbler's spring call should certainly be celebrated, not only by those who dream all year of the annual hunt but by those who simply enjoy watching these impressive birds, a salvaged piece of lost America, in the woods and clearings to which they have so recently returned.

ADDITIONAL READING

The World of the Wild Turkey by James C. Lewis, Lippincott, 1973.

The Wild Turkey: Its History and Domestication by A. W. Schorger, University of Oklahoma Press, 1966.

Life Histories of North American Gallinaceous Birds by Arthur Cleveland Bent, Dover, 1963.

The Book of the Wild Turkey: Natural History, Range, Management, and Hunting of America's Greatest Game Bird by Lovett E. Williams, Jr., Winchester Press, 1981.

The American Heritage Cookbook and Illustrated History of American Eating and Drinking by Helen McCulley et al., American Heritage Publishing Company, 1964.

The Trouble
with Bambi

*T*hose who see the Disney
movie *Bambi* are often marked by two traumatic events in it. One is
a terrible forest fire started by a hunter's campfire; the other is the
sad death of the fawn's mother at the guns of other hunters. Ironically, after decades of suppressing fires, forest managers today often
decide to let them burn; wildlife managers in many areas, including
Ohio, are also urging hunters to train their sights on Bambi's mom.
Why do state officials resort to what seems such a cruel directive?
The answer lies in the history of our relationships with deer and
landscape and with problems that arise today when deer live and
breed in a world ruled by human beings.

On the whole, the history of the white-tailed deer has been quite
a success story. In spite of the image of fragility shown in *Bambi* and
other sentimental tales, whitetails, though not terribly intelligent,
are tough, adaptable animals with keen senses, flexible behavior, a
high birth rate, and a developed social organization. They can also
sometimes be dangerous. Wildlife writer and photographer Erwin
Bauer points out that of the two hundred people who die each year

Page 72: A half-grown white-tailed deer has not yet lost the white baby spots that camouflage it so well in the dappled sunlight of late spring and early summer. Young fawns lie quietly in hiding and do not move about except when their mothers arrive to let them nurse. At that stage of their lives, they are difficult for predators to detect. Like beavers and wild turkeys, deer were once completely extirpated from this state, but they have now returned in force, and controversy is increasing over methods of controlling their numbers.

in encounters with wild animals in the U.S., by far the largest number are killed by deer, ahead of grizzlies, cougars, orcas, sharks, wolves, or snakes. (Bees are the second most deadly animal.) Many of these deaths result from collisions and hunting accidents, but a growing number involve attacks by injured deer or by bucks that have lost their fear of humans. Bauer calls deer "the most dangerous critters in America." And not only bucks are aggressive. Dominant does keep order over other females and at certain times even over bucks with slashes from their sharp hooves.

Deer's senses of hearing, sight, and smell are incredibly keen. A study reports that a western black-tailed deer can hear a man hidden seventy-five yards downwind clicking his fingernails behind his back. Sight is also strong. Deer have excellent day vision and, unlike most diurnal animals, they can also see very well at night. This means that whitetails, which are normally most active at dawn and dusk, can become completely nocturnal in places like suburbs, where people are abroad during the day. Smell, however, is a deer's most important sense of all. Its uses include finding and choosing food, spotting predators, identifying members of the herd, attracting mates, deciding when a partner is ready to mate, bonding between doe and fawn, and tracking other deer. Deer even have a "sixth sense" called volmofaction, which is a chemical sense like taste and smell and which uses the vomeronasal organ. Volmofaction enables a buck to detect a doe's readiness to mate by "tasting" her urine; this organ apparently has other uses that are still poorly understood.

Alert whitetails are very good at detecting predators—both traditional ones such as wolves and cougars and also human hunters—and they are expert at hiding themselves as well. The fawn that lies completely still while its spotted coat imitates the dapple of sunlight on undergrowth, or its mother, whose reddish summer and grayish winter pelts blend with the colors of those seasons, can elude the notice of the most alert stalker. Deer are escape artists as well, quietly fading away into the trees or, if necessary, bursting into the whitetail's horizontal gallop or the mule deer's stot, a bouncing gait that takes this western deer over and around the obstacles of its rocky habitat. At three days most whitetail fawns can outrun a man, and galloping adults have been clocked at more than forty miles an hour.

Even more important than white-tailed deer's keen senses and evasive actions is their ability to reproduce in a big way. Does can breed at six months, and older females often produce twins or even triplets each year. Deer's response to waning day length times the rut, or mating season, for late fall. This means that in northern lati-

A white-tailed deer fawn shows the big ears and liquid brown eyes that are so attractive to humans. Despite their gentle looks and reputation, white-tailed deer are sometimes aggressive—even dangerous—when they lose their fear of humans.

tudes fawns are born in May or early June when food is abundant and ample time remains for them to grow enough to get through their first winter.

Whitetails' social organization ensures that the fittest bucks sire most fawns. Dominance rituals among bucks establish the largest and presumably fittest animals as sires; analogous rituals among does regulate the matriarchal herds of summer, a time when males live separately from females and their young. Dominance hierarchies disperse does and fawns enough to share browse more efficiently. Herds can even alter sex ratios within themselves to suit population to living conditions—at least to some degree: simply put, when forage is scarce, does produce more male fawns, and when it is abundant, more females, priming for population growth. Experienced does practice various strategies to ensure their fawns' survival as well. As a result of these and other complex factors, whitetails' reproductive potential is huge: a Michigan study of 1979 saw a herd of ten deer grow to 212 in just five years.

Despite deer's impressive resources for survival, the coming of humans to this continent changed the picture for deer drastically, sometimes for better, sometimes for worse. Ancestors of today's white-tailed deer crossed the Bering land bridge from Asia into the Americas about six million years ago. Other deer-family members, such as moose and caribou, arrived somewhat later. Some species of deer died out about eleven thousand years ago, probably in part because of hunting pressure from early Native Americans, but the adaptable whitetail and its western cousin, the black-tailed deer, survived. Twenty to forty million whitetails awaited the first European hunters in the sixteenth century. Since that time, deer populations have swung between extremes as a direct result of the acts of human beings.

Young bucks loaf in a late-summer meadow. Although they may be able to sire offspring, they as yet stand little chance of winning challenges for dominance—and therefore mating privileges—over fully antlered adults.

By the rutting season, bucks have rubbed the velvet off antlers that have grown since the previous winter. Reddish summer coats give way to winter gray. Neck muscles become more massive to support the antlers' considerable weight, and the bucks become more aggressive. October, November, and December, the peak of the season, account for more than half the entire year's collisions with deer on Ohio highways.

By the end of colonial times, whitetails had dwindled to between eight and nineteen million animals, less than half of their earlier population. Evidence for these figures comes from records of the early fur trade. While Indians traditionally used almost every part of the deer they killed, they were now also slaughtering the animals wholesale for hides to exchange for goods such as knives, cooking utensils, clothing, and alcohol. The hides were exported to Europe as well as being used by colonists, who of course hunted deer themselves.

By about 1800 whitetails had recovered somewhat. They were spreading to new habitats and reclaiming others, free from the fur

Deer Types

North American members of the deer family, or *Cervidae*, include wapiti (often called elk), moose, caribou, mule deer, black-tailed deer, and white-tailed deer. Mule deer and blacktails are whitetails' closest relatives. Traditionally it was thought that blacktails, a West Coast species, evolved from whitetails, and mule deer then evolved from blacktails eight to ten thousand years ago. Recent genetic studies suggest, however, that whitetails and blacktails hybridized, and these hybrids then evolved to become mule deer.

The species look mostly similar, although antler shapes, ear size, and light-colored rump patches vary. Behavior has evolved to suit the deer's different habitats, however. Blacktails tend to hide from predators in deep cover; mule deer use a gait called the stot to leap unpredictably among the rocks and bushes of their open, boulder-strewn western habitat; whitetails flee along established trails in the woods and brush, sometimes using stream beds to throw off pursuers. These and other behavioral differences tend to discourage interbreeding or hybrids' survival. Whitetails have recently been expanding westward, and their range overlaps that of mule deer, which may be threatened by this development.

The whitetail, an adaptable species that can live in both open and dense habitat and which eats as wide a selection of food as any herbivore, has been most successful. It lives from southern Alaska to northern Chile and most places in between except for parts of the far West. The first subspecies, *Odocoileus virginianus virginianus*, was described in 1780; since then, a total of thirty subspecies has been recognized, although genetics techniques should probably be used to reevaluate some of them. Twentieth-century restocking efforts have caused hybridization among subspecies in many cases. Ohio's deer are *Odocoileus virginianus borealis*.

trade's intensive hunting, and in 1837 the U.S. Army drove the few remaining eastern Indians from whitetail range. The deer's respite was to be brief, however: from 1850 to 1900, market hunters put more pressure on wildlife than at any time before or since, and the once-growing herds were prime targets for them. We think that by the turn of the century only about five hundred thousand white-tailed deer survived nationwide. In Ohio, deer disappeared completely by about 1890 and had to be restocked early in this century.

During the twentieth century, the picture changed again in this state and across the nation, and populations have more than recovered. This began to happen for several reasons. In Ohio natural predators such as wolves, cougars, lynx, and bears had long since been wiped out, and government also began to control human predation. Hunting seasons were established, as well as limits on the numbers and kinds of deer that could be taken. The slogan "does ain't deer" is still gospel for many hunters, although it has long outlived its usefulness. Modern wildlife management protected deer from poaching and overkill, established refuges, improved habitat, and restocked herds.

Finally, and perhaps most importantly, farmers abandoned many small holdings after the turn of the century, especially during the Great Depression, and the second-growth brush and timber on old farms made ideal habitat. In fact, this kind of range suited white-tailed deer much better than the mature forests of presettlement times. In those days, whitetails were "edge" creatures, searching out the lush browse they needed in zones between deep forest and meadow or prairie. Nevertheless, only in the past thirty or so years have deer populations really exploded, especially in Ohio's southeastern hill country.

I remember well visiting the fenced herd at Oak Openings Metropark west of Toledo in the 1950s and thrilling at the chance to see real live deer. That old enclosure has long since disappeared, unneeded as free-running herds took off, even in the heavily farmed northwestern part of the state. The growth has been truly exponential. As recently as 1961, Ohio deer were so sparse that deer hunting season was closed. Just thirty years later, in 1991, hunters killed a then-record 119,215 deer in Ohio.

In autumn of 1992, Bob Stoll, wildlife project leader for the Ohio Department of Natural Resources Division of Wildlife, estimated the state's deer to number somewhere between 230,000 and 325,000. In fall of 1996, his projected estimate rose to about 550,000, this in spite of more than 170,000 deer taken by hunters in 1994 and almost 180,000 in 1995. Remember that 500,000 is about the same number that are thought to have roamed the entire country in 1900! National estimates of whitetail populations have recently risen to over twenty-five million. Many of these deer are suburbanites. Urban sprawl displaces traditional whitetail range, but replaces it with excellent deer habitat, featuring succulent ornamental plantings, water, and cover.

While we can be glad that Bambi and his family are thriving, the burgeoning herds have caused a range of problems for deer and humans alike. Overcrowding affects deer's health both in the obvious way, starvation, and in others, including psychological stress and highway collisions. During winter of 1995–96, thirty-five deer were found dead in the Cuyahoga Valley National Recreation Area alone, probably as a result of malnutrition. Death rates are higher in areas where winter is more severe and average density exceeds Ohio's ten to fifteen deer per square mile. Overcrowding also leaves deer susceptible to diseases and parasites. Does may abort or reabsorb fetuses and abandon fawns.

Highway accidents are also on the rise. Hemmed in by a thickening network of roads, deer cannot move about without crossing them and being hit by cars. They may also seek out the salt-soaked earth along highways and the shrubby browse found there. In 1994, 25,636 deer-vehicle collisions were recorded in Ohio, 55 percent of which occurred in October, November, and December, the months that span the rutting season. This is a 6 percent increase over 1993 and, aside from injuries to deer and motorists, represents a hefty repair bill statewide.

Whitetails are normally browsers, depending on highly nutritious leaves, buds, berries, and fruit, rather than grazers of grass like cows or sheep. They can eat a ton of plant matter a year. These needs bring them in conflict with farmers, orchardists, and gardeners alike, and farmers are the loudest voices in the state calling for control of the herds. Lyme disease, carried by ticks that live on deer for part of their life cycle, is also spreading nationwide; it can cause flu-like symptoms, crippling arthritis, and in rare cases can be fatal if not treated early. Although Lyme disease is not yet a problem in Ohio, that could change.

Also troubling are deer's effects on the diversity of both plants and other animals. The great naturalist Aldo Leopold noted in his essay "Wilderness" that "the effect of too many deer on the ground flora of the forest deserves special mention because it is an elusive burglary of esthetic wealth, the more dangerous because unintentional and unseen. . . . One is put in mind of Shakespeare's warning that 'virtue, grown into a pleurisy, dies of its own too-much.' Be that as it may, the forest landscape is deprived of a certain exuberance which arises from a rich variety of plants fighting with each other for a place in the sun." Leopold was speaking of Germany in the 1930s, but his words seem prophetic for many parts of America today.

Pennsylvania wildlife biologists Stephen Jones, David deCalesta, and Shelby Chunko note a drop in diversity in forest ground cover and songbirds, slow and incomplete recovery from forest disturbances, and problems restoring commercially valuable species of trees. They say that where deer exceed twenty per square mile, sugar

This young buck has already rubbed the velvet from his small antlers. Antlers differ from horns in being shed and grown again each year—a tremendous energy investment for the animal. They are used in dominance confrontations that decide which males will mate that year. This youngster is still too young to compete in such contests. A successful male will guard a receptive female and then leave her after copulation, playing no role in caring for their fawns.

maple, white ash, yellow poplar, aspen, pin cherry, oak, and hemlock disappear leaving species-poor forests. James Bissell, head botanist at the Cleveland Museum of Natural History, has commented about deer-browsed hemlock trees: "They look as if you could drive a motorcycle under them without ducking!"

Succulent plants like beautiful spring trilliums are also victims, and plants less appealing to deer like ferns, grasses, and sedges begin to dominate the forest floor. Nesting sites for songbirds—some of which are known to be in decline—are lost, as is cover for wild turkey, ruffed grouse, and black bears. The problem is that such changes may be difficult for the general public to appreciate. Some parks, like Sharon Woods Metropark on the northern edge of Columbus, have built deerless enclosures, the inverse of the old deer stockade at the Oak Openings of my childhood. In them, lush trees, shrubs, and flowers contrast with the relatively barren plants nibbled by the deer outside.

Nearly everyone agrees that whitetails need to be thinned. Although some animal rights activists say we should rely on natural forces to regulate the herds, studies using computer modeling show that while deer in bad condition produce fewer fawns, their numbers still rise, although at a slower rate. Deer are no longer living under completely natural conditions, and starvation and diseases are hardly pretty ways to control population. Among other interest groups, disagreements arise about what numbers of deer are ideal and about which methods should be used to reach them. In Ohio, farmers generally favor the lowest levels, while hunters—who spend about $66 million a year on pursuing deer in the state—want the highest. Other citizens, according to Bob Stoll, may love deer one minute and hate them the next when their car whacks one or someone they love comes down with Lyme disease. Foresters point out that biodiversity suffers at even lower levels than those at which deer can thrive and live compatibly with people.

How to get rid of unwanted deer? Doing so is especially controversial in urban areas where citizens want Bambi and his mother out of their back yards but don't want them shot. Many towns and suburbs forbid deer hunting, contributing to ballooning growth. Unfortunately, tranquilizing deer and removing them is time consuming and expensive, $600 a head in 1994. And as time goes on, there are fewer and fewer places understocked enough to welcome newcomers. The idea of birth control for does has been in the air for some time but also poses big problems: feeding them hormones may affect other animals, not to mention deer hunters and their families. Even if nonhormonal methods are used, they must reach an estimated 80 percent of females to be effective—a figure very difficult to achieve—and surgical implants or immunization methods cost $500 to $1,000 per deer in 1994. Finally, if does fail to conceive, they cycle into estrus for as many as seven months. Bucks lose up to 25 percent of their weight in the four weeks of the natural rutting season. Repeated futile attempts to impregnate does in more or less continuous heat could destroy them and throw the sociobiology of herds into disarray.

This leaves culling, especially in urban areas, by professional sharpshooters like the police, and hunting by the general public. The idea of killing off most or all deer in an urban area repels many people, but evidence shows that since deer are quite faithful to home ranges, wholesale culling could be done perhaps only once a decade. Statewide, however, the only effective method so far to control deer herds is hunting, whether we may like it or not.

Hunting must be managed, however, or it can do the opposite of what is wanted. Particularly troublesome is the bucks-only tradition instilled in millions of hunters during the days when deer were scarce. Combined with a "big bucks" mentality that covets large racks of antlers, the "does ain't deer" mindset makes many hunters reluctant to shoot females. A recent editorial in *Deer and Deer*

White-tailed deer are primarily browsers rather than grazers: most of their diet consists of twigs of shrubs and trees. In summer they include weeds and grasses, and in autumn they relish acorns, persimmons, and other kinds of fruit, including apples. Winter deer browse evergreens as well as buds and bark of deciduous trees and shrubs. Each deer can eat a ton of forage in one year.

Hunter magazine admonishes hunters to congratulate a friend who bags a doe: "And most of all, mean it when you say it." Yet it is clear that if most deer killed are bucks, populations will keep ballooning. In other words, the need these days is to get Bambi's mom.

Beginning around 1991 the Division of Wildlife began liberalizing hunting permits to encourage shooting of antlerless deer. As of 1995, individual hunters may obtain a total of five permits a season: two are general permits to shoot one antlered or antlerless deer, the other to shoot an antlerless deer only. The other three are urban permits limited to zones around cities. The three deer taken on these permits must be antlerless. (Every hunter must get written permission from the landowner to shoot deer on private land.) Bob Stoll says this approach appears to be working. According to him, hunters took 3.4 percent more antlerless deer statewide in 1995, in urban areas 28 percent more. Whether this will be enough is yet to be seen. Stoll notes that deer control is more art than science, with many complex variables. Because of the conflicting interests of various groups, control efforts also take place in a politically charged atmosphere. The Division of Wildlife attempts to survey all these groups—farmers, hunters, and general citizens—determine their wants, and set deer population objectives for each of Ohio's eighty-eight counties. The goal is to meet minimum conflict criteria, a difficult one judging by recent controversy over proposed culling in Cleveland suburbs.

Meanwhile, of course, no one polls the deer for their preferences. We dominate the landscape, disrupt deer's natural activities, and skew their life cycles, social interactions, and numbers. When Disney's Bambi and his mother first flee the hunters' guns, she informs him, "MAN was in the forest." Today the problem seems almost the opposite: deer are in the cities, and even those that are not are enclosed in a world defined by *Homo sapiens*. We are the ones who are really the trouble with Bambi and his family, and we need to find better ways to keep those lovely animals in balance with the rest of the natural world for which we are stewards.

ADDITIONAL READING

Deer edited by Duane Gerlach, Sally Atwater, and Judith Schnell, Stackpole Books, 1994.
Whitetails: Behavior, Natural History, Conservation by Erwin A. Bauer, Voyageur Press, 1993.

"Too Many Deer" by George Harrison, *Sports Afield,* July 1992.

"Whitetails Are Changing Our Woodlands" by Stephen B. Jones,
David deCalesta, and Shelby E. Chunko, *American Forests,* No-
vember/December 1993.

Waterfowl Back
from the Brink

Canada Geese &

Wood Ducks

*O*n my way to the suburban campus where I work, I brake at a busy intersection. Above the idling engine a sound, wild and anomalous in this urban area, drops out of the overcast sky. I think of Aldo Leopold, the great naturalist and wildlife manager, who said, "One swallow does not make a summer, but one skein of geese, cleaving the murk of a March thaw, is the spring." When I reach the campus, the Canada geese will probably be there before me, since for years we have hosted a nesting population of the big gray, black, and white birds. I have grown accustomed to these boarders, as has the rest of the college community, whose members sometimes grumble about needing to watch their feet to avoid the geese's leavings.

I've also grown used to seeing smaller cousins of the Canadas as they tip-tilt themselves into the waters of Cleveland's Shaker Lakes searching for fallen acorns and other choice bits of food. These are the wood ducks. Many consider the males' bright breeding plumage the most beautiful of any American duck, although the females' subtle shades of gray and blue appeal as much to me. Occasionally I remember that only a few decades ago, seeing either of these species of waterfowl would have caused an excited shiver, so reduced were their numbers. At the turn of this century, ornithologists feared that the wood duck might be on the brink of extinction. By 1940, Canada geese were also in serious decline, and the giant subspecies that now lounge around the college pond were once thought to have disappeared completely. The recovery of these waterfowl rivals those of the wild turkey and white-tailed deer, and though certain problems remain, their resurgence is considered a triumph of wildlife management.

When European explorers first reached the Ohio Country, Canada geese usually did not nest here but made stops during their spring and fall migrations. There were plenty of resting places since Ohio was a far more watery world than it is today. Most important for the geese were the vast marshes at Lake Erie's western end, an estimated three hundred thousand acres of marsh and swamp forest stretching from present-day Vermilion to the mouth of the Detroit River. During the height of the fall migration, the gabble of thousands of Canada geese and of the many other ducks and geese that stopped there to rest and refuel must have created an ocean of noise.

To the west of the marshes lay the Great Black Swamp, an enormous swamp forest that extended 120 miles to the site of Fort Wayne, Indiana, and covered approximately 1,500 square miles of lake plain.

Pages 86–87: Wildlife refuges have provided Canada geese with important resting and stopping places during migration and, along with control of hunting, have helped their numbers rebound. Migrating interior Canada geese are a common sight at Ottawa National Wildlife Refuge on Lake Erie west of Port Clinton during spring and fall. But today Canada geese seem to be almost everywhere in Ohio. Another subspecies, the nonmigratory giant Canada goose, has been stocked in a number of states and is now often thought of as a nuisance in parks and other human habitats.

Opposite: The male wood duck, with his bright, crisply defined markings, is among the most beautiful of ducks. It has been said that at the turn of the twentieth century there were more wood ducks in Belgium, where they were raised by bird fanciers, than in all of North America. Closely controlled hunting seasons, provision of artificial nest boxes, and the regrowth of forests that can provide nest holes for wood ducks have aided their comeback.

The Ohio Country had no large interior lakes. (Today's Grand Lake Saint Mary, Buckeye Lake, and Guilford Lake were first created as reservoirs for the state canal system in the early 1800s. Many other reservoirs have been built more recently.) However, the land was pocked with small kettle lakes left from the melting of giant blocks of glacial ice, and it embraced a rich system of pristine rivers lined by mature trees of the primeval forest. These swamp forests and wooded river systems were ideal habitats for the wood duck, which nested here in tree cavities, foraging in the water for vegetable matter and invertebrates and on the forest floor for mast. We have no way of knowing how many wood ducks lived here, but given the enormous tracts of preferred habitat, their numbers must have been vast.

These conditions began to change rapidly during the second half of the nineteenth century when both lumbering and drainage surged. By 1850, 9.8 million acres of Ohio forests had been "improved" out of existence, and between 1850 and 1859, when clearing accelerated dramatically, another 2.8 million disappeared. By the turn of the century, only about 15 percent of the land was wooded. The once impassable Great Black Swamp in northwestern Ohio was not lumbered until the 1870s and 1880s, but the area is now one of the most intensively farmed on this continent.

Draining of wetlands nationwide began in earnest with the Swamplands Drainage Acts of 1849, 1850, and 1860. An 1859 state law authorized digging of public ditches, and heavy farm taxes were levied to provide funds. Between that year and 1876, draining transformed the Great Black Swamp, and by the turn of the century, large swaths of the Erie marshes, or "pumplands" as they were called, had been diked and drained as well. Only about fifteen thousand out of the original three hundred thousand acres of marshland remain today. Earlier extermination of beaver had also eliminated the dams that once created many small wetlands. Mill dams, tanneries, sewage, clear cutting of banks, erosion caused by poor farming practices, and stream channelization degraded the once pristine river systems.

Such changes could hardly favor waterfowl. Canada geese lost important resting and feeding grounds on migration. Wood ducks were harder hit. Forest clearing wiped out the mature trees whose cavities were key to their nesting success and which produced mast to support their populations; wetlands' decline further narrowed their food base, especially during the crucial season when new broods needed high-quality protein from aquatic insects and other invertebrates to grow and thrive.

Disappearing habitat is now seen as the most vital threat to waterfowl. However, extreme hunting pressures were also key in wiping out Canada geese and wood ducks earlier in this century. During the early years of statehood, their numbers had seemed inexhaustible, and hunting was unrestrained. Geese were an important food source for pioneer families, especially in autumn, and the wood duck, which nested in such numbers here, could be shot for much of the year. In the 1840s Audubon told of hunters who killed as many as thirty or forty wood ducks in a single evening and of a trapper who trapped "several hundreds in the course of a week."

Nevertheless, the annual kill of Canada geese appears to have had little effect on their numbers for the first two hundred and fifty years of white exploration and settlement, and wood ducks were common into the 1880s. During that decade, however, breech-loading double-barrel and repeating shotguns were developed, followed twenty years later by automatics. Freed from the mechanical constraints of the earlier flintlocks and muzzle-loaders, hunters began massacring waterfowl with a vengeance, unrestrained by any government regulation. Market hunting became much more profitable, and staggering numbers of wild ducks were shot and shipped to the cities, where game and wild fowl padded the menus of fashionable restaurants.

Geese were not so intensively sought by market hunters as ducks were, but many of them were shot as well. About fifty thousand geese from the Pacific flyway were sold in Los Angeles and San Francisco markets alone in 1895–6. Wood ducks were small, inhabited swamps and rivers instead of open water, and gathered in small flocks, and so market hunters did not pursue them with the attention they gave to some other ducks. Still, many wood ducks found their way to market too. In addition, farmers and other hunters shot them constantly because they were often the only waterfowl occurring in large enough numbers near inland homes. Whereas most Canada geese nested far north on the Canadian and Alaskan tundra, which gave them some protection, wood ducks nested in Ohio itself and were shot even while incubating eggs and raising young.

During the early years of this century, it was said that there were more wood ducks in Belgium, where bird fanciers raised them in captivity, than there were in the United States. In 1901 the United States Biological Survey reported that these ducks faced possible extinction, and several eastern and southern states passed laws to protect them, followed by other states in the Midwest and West. Ohio prohibited their hunting in 1913, but enforcement hardly

Canada Geese

About eleven subspecies of the Canada goose *(Branta canadensis)* inhabit the United States and Canada. (Wildlife biologists sometimes disagree about just how many races should be recognized.) These range from the giant Canada goose, which may weigh as much as twenty pounds, to the mallard-sized cackling Canada goose, an Alaskan-breeding race that reaches only three or four pounds. Markings are fairly similar in the different subspecies, but races become duskier in the West and smaller in northwestern Canada and Alaska.

Two subspecies are seen in Ohio. These are the interior, or southern James Bay, Canada goose *(Branta canadensis interior)*, which is migratory and nests around James Bay, and the giant Canada goose *(Branta canadensis maxima)*, which generally does not migrate. Thus, the fluffy goslings seen here in spring are giants, though members of other races may nest farther south than normal if injured and unable to fly north. Since female geese return to their birthplaces to nest, descendants become nonmigratory. However, this is a rare occurrence.

Canada geese—at least in humans' anthropomorphic view—are strong proponents of family values. Mating displays create strong pair bonds which last for life unless one

goose dies early; such a death causes great distress to the bereaved mate, which may stay in the area for some time and be shot itself. Both sexes share in the hunt for a nesting site, although the female selects it and builds the nest. Although the gander does not help incubate the eggs, he is always nearby, guarding the nesting territory with exemplary zeal. Wildlife biologists estimate that the goose spends 98.5 percent of her time on her eggs—the epitome of faithful motherhood.

When goslings leave the nest, which they generally do when only a day old, the gander's defense shifts from territory to family group, and both he and the goose escort their goslings everywhere. Goslings from younger or less dominant pairs may occasionally be adopted—or rather stolen—swelling the family's numbers. The pair remain with their young through summer, fall migration, and sometimes even through return migration in spring. Adults go through their annual molt in July and early August when the goslings are half grown. Unlike other birds, waterfowl molt all their flight feathers at once, so goose parents are grounded, and the whole family is flightless for about three weeks. They are shy and quiet until about mid-August when flight feathers grow in. Canada geese eat a variety of vegetable and invertebrate foods, but they are primarily grazers, nibbling at green sprouts in fields and lawns, sometimes in large flocks.

Autumn geese—even non-migrating ones—are restless and raucous, very different birds from the shy and retiring geese of summer. Extended family units migrate together, usually between one thousand and three thousand feet above ground, though they can also fly over twelve thousand-foot mountain ranges. Anyone who has saved gasoline on the freeway by driving in the wake of a large truck can understand the reason for the familiar V-shaped flight formation: it greatly reduces air resistance while allowing each goose a clear line of sight ahead. Biologists estimate that the pattern allows the birds to fly 71 percent farther than each could do alone. Canada geese winter in many parts of the southern and western states, as well as on the Gulf and Atlantic coasts. They closely follow the melting pond and lake ice north, and they nest early in spring.

Opposite & above: Newly hatched Canada geese have not yet left the nest, but they will do so soon. The goslings are precocial, meaning that they do not need the extended brooding and nest feeding that many other baby birds do. They can walk, swim, and forage for food almost immediately, leaving the nest when only a day old. Their parents will escort them everywhere, and the family sometimes remains together for close to a year.

existed. Also in 1913, the Weeks-McLean Bill offered migratory birds federal protection and forbade hunting of wood ducks. However, the bill was not implemented until the U.S. and Canada ratified the Migratory Bird Treaty Act in 1918. Wood ducks were the only game ducks given complete protection under this act. The nationwide closed season on them lasted until 1941, when hunters in fourteen states on the Atlantic and Mississippi flyways were allowed one wood duck in the bag.

Wood Ducks

The early naturalist Mark Catesby first described wood ducks scientifically when he explored the Carolinas and Florida in the 1730s. He called them "summer ducks," because they were almost the only ones found in the Southeast during that season. They are the commonest breeding waterfowl between thirty and forty-three degrees north latitude, and breeding populations are largely restricted to the United States and southernmost Canada. Wood ducks are uniquely adapted to live in wetlands with fluctuating water levels. One reason is that unlike other ducks (the hooded merganser is an exception), they nest in tree cavities, often in holes chiseled out by pileated woodpeckers.

Wood ducks that breed south of North Carolina, Tennessee, and central Arkansas do not migrate, while north of these three states, almost all do. A few between these populations move south according to the severity of the winter. Drakes and hens begin to form pair bonds on the wintering grounds in the southern states in autumn. They begin moving north in February and reach Ohio in late March or April. The drake follows the hen to her birthplace. Once they arrive, he accompanies her as she prospects for a suitable nest hole in a mature tree or nest box. She does not build

A male wood duck is not a "family man" like the male Canada goose. Although he accompanies his mate in the search for a suitable nest hole, he does not guard her like the gander guards the goose or watch over the young after they hatch. By the time the ducklings leave their nest, the pair bond between their parents has completely dissolved. Drakes spend much time loafing in groups while their mates tend to business.

a nest but plucks down from her breast to surround and insulate her eggs, as do Canada geese. She alone incubates the eggs, and during this period, the pair bond with her mate begins to loosen. Well before the eggs hatch, she is on her own, and unlike the Canada goose, will bond with a new mate if she survives to the next breeding season.

One of the more dramatic moments of a wood duck's life occurs when the tiny duckling leaps from the nest hole to join its mother and siblings below. About twenty-four hours after her offspring hatch, their mother leaves the nest to scout out the route she will take in leading them to water. When she returns, her customary "conversation" with the ducklings becomes more rapid and urgent, and she calls to them from outside the nest. The ducklings respond by leaping and climbing to the nest's exit hole, pausing one by one at the brink, and jumping into the void, spreading their tiny wings and webs. The leap may end in water, but many nests are some distance from it. A landing on the earth may be less comfortable, but few are seriously hurt. Frank Bellrose and Daniel Holm report seeing ducklings drop fifty feet without injury.

The next months are spent in rapid growth. The single mother duck shepherds her young and warns them of danger, but the ducklings can swim and forage for food by themselves. They usually strike out on their own when they are five to seven weeks old. By late summer the mother will have

molted, the young will have developed flight feathers, and they will spend more time loafing and preening, an activity in which the adult males have been indulging since spring. As migration time approaches, the ducks become restless in response to changes in day length and in their own endocrine systems. Body fat increases, fed by nuts and other high-calorie autumn foods. Wood ducks begin leaving this area for the South in late September. They decline here through October and November, with stragglers departing as late as early December.

A female wood duck peers from her nest hole beside the upper Cuyahoga River. When her eggs have hatched and ducklings are ready to confront the world, she will coax them from the nest with excited "conversation." The little fluffballs make dramatic leaps from as high as thirty or forty feet, spreading their webs and winglets to break the fall.

Canada geese's decline was slower, but by 1940 numbers were at all-time low levels. For one thing, settlement had encroached on breeding areas south of the Canadian border. An early ornithologist reported that Canada geese nested abundantly in Wisconsin in 1850 and that foragers gathered their eggs in bushels. Farming, irrigation, logging, and industrial and urban growth had destroyed these breeding grounds by the early 1900s. Hunting pressure, however, and destruction of winter feeding grounds seem to have been more central to the geese's overall decline. Duck populations had also dropped because of hunting, wetland loss, and the droughts of the 1930s, and people, including hunters, began to feel that something must be done.

The first wildlife refuge had been founded in 1903; now the movement accelerated, with more refuges set aside and most being managed for waterfowl. Hunting was also severely restricted. The effect on Canada geese was immediate and dramatic: from 1946, when the season was closed, to 1963, Mississippi Valley populations rebounded from 30,000 Canadas to 450,000. In 1974, about 3,000,000 Canadas were counted nationwide on September 1, prior to hunting, and 2,141,000 remained after most of the hunting seasons had ended. In Ohio, large flocks began wintering in the northern counties. Numbers of migrants that passed through the state also rose dramatically. Managers estimate that 80 to 90 percent of geese killed in the fall are shot by hunters, and the birds' comeback underscores the continuing need to regulate hunting effectively.

Since Ohio hosts two subspecies of *Branta canadensis* that behave differently, management has become more complex over the years. Interior Canada geese *(Branta canadensis interior)* visit in spring and fall on the way to and from their James Bay nesting grounds in Canada. They need resting areas such as Ottawa National Wildlife Refuge west of Port Clinton and several state wildlife areas, as well as control of intense autumn hunting. Giant Canada geese *(Branta canadensis maxima)* nest here in large numbers and winter in Ohio if the season is not too severe. These are the geese that a friend of mine unfairly described as having become "too lazy to migrate."

Giants have never migrated in the way their interior cousins do. Biologists think that at European settlement, their nesting range extended from central Saskatchewan and Manitoba south to central Kansas and Missouri and east to the shores of Lake Erie except for northern Minnesota, Wisconsin, and Michigan. Since, like wood ducks, they nested farther south than tundra-nesting geese, they were more vulnerable to human persecution and declined rapidly.

By the 1930s, many people did not believe that a giant race had ever existed, and most of those who did thought it was extinct. This belief changed when a remnant wintering population was discovered in Rochester, Minnesota, in 1962.

Since then, wildlife managers have reintroduced giants in many areas, and their populations have burgeoned. They are adaptable birds, fecund, tolerant of urban environments, and able to nest in dense groups. Since they resist moving south, they often escape the intense hunting pressure that faces migrating interiors. Giants now nest in all the states and provinces of the Mississippi Flyway; managers estimated their spring 1995 population at one million, though telling them from other subspecies can be a problem and makes

Canada geese begin nesting earlier in spring than most birds do, often choosing the top of a muskrat lodge for a nursery. This location may offer some protection from predators. Although the gander accompanies the goose in the search for a nest site, she is the one who makes the choice of where to lay her eggs.

estimating their numbers difficult. Ohio wildlife managers began restoring Canada geese at the Mercer Goose Management Area, Mosquito Creek, and Killdeer Plains in 1956. In 1967 giant Canadas were introduced at Ottawa National Wildlife Refuge and in 1979 to reclaimed strip mines in Muskingum County in southeastern Ohio. Since that date, giants have spread throughout the state. The spring 1995 count for Ohio was 69,000 plus or minus 26,050.

Ironically, this dazzling success has caused its own problems, epitomized by another of my friends' opinion that Canadas are simply "rats with wings." Urban geese can indeed become problems, like those at my campus that liberally festoon the lawns and walkways with their excrement. Overcrowding creates conditions that exasperate humans, befoul water supplies, and sometimes affect other birds and animals. By 1995, complaints about geese in Ohio had risen to 460, both from city dwellers and from farmers concerned about damage to crops. The surge in giant Canada geese makes counting and managing the migratory interior Canada geese more difficult as well.

Wildlife managers recently formulated a Mississippi Flyway management plan for giant Canada geese designed to control their populations. The most important strategy has been to open hunting seasons for giants that are either earlier or later than the times when interiors are flying through. This combines with other measures designed to deal with urban geese, such as various scare tactics. One strategy that has been tested in other states is to collect geese during their summer flightless period and donate them to food banks. The goal is to maintain a stable and well-distributed population for hunters and wildlife enthusiasts while controlling what managers term "human-goose conflict."

Managing wood ducks has also proved complex. One problem is estimating their populations in order to decide on management strategies and hunting regulations. These ducks are secretive, and their breeding areas along woodland streams and in southern bottomland swamps are fragmented and sometimes remote. Data must be gathered by banding and by counting numbers shot, rather than by making counts on the nesting grounds, as is done with other ducks. However, it's clear that forbidding spring shooting and careful regulating of autumn hunting have been key to wood ducks' comeback, as was the case with Canada geese. Managers also recommend limiting early morning and evening hunting, since wood ducks are especially vulnerable while they are flying to and from their roosts. It took sixty years to bring wood ducks back to their present

levels, though the time might have been less if hunting seasons had not reopened as soon as 1941. This is actually, in nature's terms, a rapid recovery; it is faster than the regrowth of mature forests in Ohio since 1900 or other environmental changes can account for.

Frank Bellrose, the acknowledged expert on wood ducks, writes that three factors are key to good wood duck management: enough nesting holes, whether in hollow trees or nest boxes, adequate food, especially when broods are developing, and cover, the least important of the three. Marshy areas provide the best food base, but they often lack mature trees with suitable nesting cavities. Canoeists in marshes and on streams have grown used to seeing rectangular or conical nesting boxes raised on poles to foil predators such as raccoons and squirrels. Most wood ducks still nest in trees, aided by the aging of the state's forests. But boxes house 4 to 5 percent, a significant percentage. They are especially useful for establishing the ducks in new areas. Gildo Tori, waterfowl biologist for the Ohio Division of Wildlife, estimates three thousand state-maintained nest boxes and another three thousand privately maintained ones in Ohio.

Even though Canada geese are now a familiar sight even in Ohio cities and are sometimes considered a nuisance, "goose music," in Aldo Leopold's words, can still cause a shiver as a "V" of geese passes overhead.

More important than setting up nest boxes is preserving and restoring wetlands. Ohio is second only to California in loss of original wetlands since settlement—more than 90 percent are gone. Fortunately, public attitudes about wetland communities have moved a great distance from the nineteenth-century opinion of them as wastelands; many understand their vital roles in controlling floods, charging the ground water system, filtering pollutants, producing oxygen and nitrogen, and even perhaps regulating the ozone layer, not to mention their importance to myriad species of plants and animals and to those who care about them. The Division of Wildlife has restored about eighteen thousand acres of wetlands to date and has plans for more of these projects. Development pressures, however, are ever expanding, and the future of waterfowl will be intimately linked with our success or failure in balancing competing demands on the land.

As I get out of my car, a family group of Canada geese splashes down in the college pond. The air is filled with excited "goose music," Aldo Leopold's term for their wild calls. I take a deep breath of the chilly spring air and shiver as I ponder the ironies of humans' relationships with nature; we are at once scourges and protectors, and our biggest successes often breed problems we never expected. As I walk toward my office, I keep a sharp eye on the ground before my feet. But as I enter the building, the memory of wood ducks dabbling for acorns and the music of the geese are what stay with me.

ADDITIONAL READING

Ecology and Management of the Wood Duck by Frank C. Bellrose and Daniel J. Holm, Stackpole Books, 1994.
The Canada Goose by Kit Howard Breen, Swan Hill Press, 1990.
The World of the Canada Goose by Joe Van Wormer, Lippincott, 1968.
The World of the Wood Duck by F. Eugene Hester and Jack Dermid, Lippincott, 1973.

Mixed Effects

*U*nlike animals discussed in the previous sections, most Ohio fauna are not game species or "charismatic megafauna," in the experts' term, and our effects on them are not usually so obviously dramatic or so likely to be noticed by the general public. Many are small, retiring, and were long thought to be either beneath notice, like salamanders, or ugly and creepy, like spiders. Only recently have more than a few people begun to appreciate their essential roles in natural communities and to insist on their study and protection. In many cases, we have little information about these groups before 1797, to provide baseline information on changes in their numbers and habits, or even accurate information about their status today. Section 3 includes pieces on owls, *Macbeth*'s "fatal bellman," snakes—irrationally feared by so many—salamanders, frogs, the small fish called darters and shiners, butterflies, and the loathed spider clan. These are fascinating animals and are certainly as worthy of study and protection as eagles or wild turkeys.

Owls are so retiring that we really do not know how many there are. Their shy habits have both helped them to live beneath our notice, and hindered us in our efforts to know which ones are declining and what to do about it. Some kinds, such as great horned and screech owls, are probably holding their own; others, such as the famous spotted owl of the Northwest and the short-eared owl, are not. Shrinkage of wetlands and moist grasslands and use of less diverse agricultural practices have deprived barn owls of prime hunting territory, and they are now considered endangered in Ohio. The Ohio Department of Natural Resources has monitored these owls statewide through a nest-box and banding program since the late 1980s. The idea is to obtain a more accurate idea of their distribution, although it is difficult to determine how many may be nesting in natural cavities. In 1995, twenty-five nests were reported.

Ironically, growing interest in reptiles has put many of them under increasing pressure by collectors. Rare wood turtles (not native to this state) bring $200 each in Europe, and even common box turtles are being shipped by the thousands to that continent. The Ohio Department of Natural Resources' data collection project on snakes is confidential for fear of supplying sensitive information to poachers. The eastern plains garter snake, the copperbelly water snake, the timber rattlesnake, and the massasauga rattlesnake are all listed as endangered in Ohio, and the island and Kirtland's water snakes may soon be declared either threatened or endangered. Once traditional prejudices about snakes are discarded, their beauty, the harmlessness of most, and the value of many as predators of rodents become obvious and their claim on our protection clear.

Certain amphibians, such as redback and two-lined salamanders and green frogs, are quite successful and are more abundant than most of us would imagine. Others, like the green salamander and many frogs worldwide, appear to be in trouble. Frog declines have garnered much attention from the media recently, and herpetologists are attempting to determine how great the threat is and what its causes may be. Here again, we are hampered by scanty information about frog populations historically and by uncertainty about the meaning of the changes being reported. Frogs of the Northeast and the West Coast seem to be under more environmental stress than are Ohio frogs—possibly because of acid rain in the East and ozone depletion at higher altitudes in the West—though cricket frogs seem to be dwindling in the heavily farmed western Ohio counties. Homeowners' growing distrust of lawn chemicals and their developing interest in creating ponds and water gardens have helped certain amphibians like bullfrogs and green frogs and probably have aided small snakes as well.

Darters—small, advanced members of the perch family—and shiners of the minnow family are two of the most successful groups of fish in America. These pretty little animals are often quite colorful, and exhibit fascinating mating, feeding, and schooling behaviors. The secret of both groups' success is their adaptability, which they used to exploit many specialized freshwater niches created in North America as the ice age glaciers withdrew. They became part of an exceedingly rich fish fauna which both Native Americans and immigrants exploited for food. Pollution, channelizing, damming, erosion caused by poor farming practices, and other human depredations have made the history of Ohio's aquatic communities a sad one: a look at the most recent state endangered species list shows the names of twenty-five fishes and thirty species of freshwater mollusks. Some species of darters and shiners—those less picky about clear water and unsilted stream bottoms—are doing well, but others are declining.

Insects and spiders were barely mentioned in early accounts of Ohio's natural history, and researchers have just recently begun to study them exhaustively. The volumes *Butterflies and Skippers of Ohio* and *Owlet Moths of Ohio* appeared only in the early 1990s, and a comprehensive study designed to identify Ohio's spider species was not begun until 1995. Interest in the insecta and arachnida is growing, however, but a great deal remains to be learned about both their habits and their statewide distribution. The Ohio Lepidopterists, located at 4434 Rosemary Parkway, Columbus, Ohio 43214, welcome information about rare Ohio butterflies like the regal fritillary, which has not been identified in Ohio since 1988 and is considered in trouble in the eastern United States. They, the Ohio Department of Natural Resources divisions of Wildlife and Natural Areas and Preserves, the Toledo Zoo, and the U.S. Fish and Wildlife Service are cooperating in a plan to reintroduce the rare Karner blue butterfly, which has not been seen in this state since 1987. The Ohio Spider Survey, still in its early phases, has already increased the list of known Ohio spiders from 308 in 1995 to 511 in 1996. A consortium of Ohio arachnologists is also being formed to study the ecological significance of spiders. For many of the creatures discussed in the following section, building a base of knowledge about them and about their needs is an essential step toward conserving them.

Owl

Sorcerer,

Spirit-Bird, Predator

Sweet Suffolk owl, so trimly dight,
With feathers like a lady bright,
Thou singest alone, sitting by night,
  Te whit, te whoo, te whit, to whit.
Thy note, that forth so freely rolls,
With shrill command the mouse controls,
And sings a dirge for dying souls,
  Te whit, te whoo, te whit, to whit.

*T*he anonymous author who shivered at a tawny owl's cry in some English wood so long ago expressed the mixture of affection, respect, and fear that we have felt for these shadowy birds since earliest times. People have long been drawn to owls for their beauty and supposed wisdom and have feared them for their associations with sorcery and death. Today we also look at owls more scientifically, amazed by their superb hunting techniques and appreciative of their vital role in controlling vermin.

Page 104: The histories of animals such as those in the previous sections, which have supplied meat, hides, and recreation to our own species, are relatively well documented. The fates of many other groups of animals, ranging from birds like the diminutive saw-whet owl pictured here (see also back cover) to reptiles, amphibians, fish, insects, and spiders, are harder to trace. These groups have often been less thoroughly studied, and since settlers tended to consider them beneath notice, there is often almost no information available about their status two hundred years ago.

Left: Fond of nesting in old buildings and church towers, the barn owl has inspired many a tale of the supernatural with its ghostly appearance and hissing screams. Known for centuries as the farmer's friend, the barn owl is a bird of open country and a rodent killer without equal. Unfortunately, this beautiful species has suffered from modern intensive farming, the tearing down of old buildings where it nests, and especially from the use of pesticides, since it hunts over heavily treated fields and pastures. During the past century, the barn owl has nearly disappeared from Ohio but is still relatively common in the South. Some farmers build nest-box entry holes into their barns to encourage this useful owl.

Science aside, however, we can still feel a primal chill when we hear a great horned owl's deep call, a barn owl's shrieks, or the eerie trill of a tiny screech owl quavering through the summer night. The mystery of owls still draws us.

Owls have appeared in folklore and art since the Old Stone Age; it was probably a shaman who etched the clear outlines of a pair of snowy owls and their chicks on a rock wall at Trois Freres in present-day France. Halfway around the world, a rock picture at Balu-Uru in northern Australia depicts a stylized "owl-man," obviously a figure of power. Elsewhere in Australia, owls were believed to protect women's souls. Similar legends regarding guardian owls exist in other cultures worldwide.

But the powers of owls have oftener been viewed as dark rather than protective. These birds, not surprisingly, have been associated with the underworld, witchcraft, and ghosts. Many, though not all, owls are nocturnal, abroad when people huddle next to the fire, listening to things that go bump in the dark. Many of the larger owls utter truly hackle-raising sounds as well: hoots, shrieks, hisses, groans, and maniacal laughter. Experienced woodsmen have confessed to near panic when saluted by a barred, great horned, or barn owl on a dark night. Even the diminutive screech owl is called "shiver owl" in the American South. Historically, owls have tended to nest or roost in old ruins, tumble-down buildings, and church towers, accounting, no doubt, for many a satisfying ghost story.

Probably because they were found in such unsavory haunts and because they ate flesh, Leviticus, in one of the first literary references to owls, admonished:

The great horned owl's size, weight, ferocity, and powerful talons make it the most formidable owl in the world, except for its close relative, the slightly larger Eurasian eagle owl. The extremely adaptable great horned owl ranges from parts of Labrador and northern Alaska to deciduous woodlands, deserts, mountains, and rain forests and all the way to the far tip of South America. With a fifty-five-inch wingspan, it is large and powerful enough to catch a wide variety of prey: rodents, birds, snakes, insects, rabbits, woodchucks, and even skunks, porcupines, and domestic cats. Like other large owls, it is a cannibal that consumes its smaller kinfolk, especially barred owls.

These are they which ye shall have in abomination among fowls;
they shall not be eaten . . . the eagle, and the owl, and the night-
hawk, and the cuckow . . . and the little owl, and the cormorant,
and the great owl. (Chapter II, verses 13–17)

Many other writers through the ages have made slighting references
to owls. Pliny claimed the "The scritch-owle betokenth always some
heavy news, and is most excrable and accursed in the presaging of
public affairs." Chaucer called the owl a prophet of "wo and mis-
chaunce." In Shakespeare's *Julius Caesar,* Casca reported a sure sign
of coming disaster:

And yesterday the bird of night did sit
Even at noonday, upon the marketplace
Hooting and shrieking.

Lady Macbeth heard the owl—"the fatal bellman"—cry and knew
that her husband had murdered his king. In the same play the three
witches added a "howlet's wing" to the contents of their evil pot.
    Many American Indian tribes also associated owls with death,
though often positively rather than negatively. Margaret Craven
built her novel, *I Heard the Owl Call My Name,* around the Northwest Indian belief that the owl is a spiritual guardian, representing
both the dead person and the soul. Another Northwestern Indian
legend describes the proper way to address a guardian owl: "Welcome, Supernatural One, thank you for coming, trying to come to
me that I may see you, long-life-maker. Please, do not leave me and
pray take good care of me that nothing evil may befall me, long-life-
maker." Still other Indian legends recount the owl's origins and
occasions on which owls intervene in the lives of human beings.
    Folklore collected in the Ohio River valley as recently as the 1960s
provides excellent examples of the traditionally mixed feelings toward these night birds. An owl's hoot meant bad luck, or a change
in weather, and whoever heard it must try to stop its noise. In
Fayette County, Kentucky, to halt an owl's hooting you took off
your left shoe and turned it upside down. Or you could pull off
both shoes and cross them or tie a knot in your dress or skirt. In
other areas folkways required that you answer the owl's hoot. The
bird's subsequent refusal to reply might warn of death. Many stories
told of ghosts taking the form of owls. In Kentucky's Green River
country, a slave, brutally beaten to death by a cruel master, returned
as an owl to haunt his murderer.

At the same time and quite in contrast, owls were credited with the power to cure a host of illnesses. In various locations along the river valley, owls' brains were used to treat scurvy, headaches, shingles, glaucoma, sties, and even hemorrhoids. Giblets were used for mumps, jaundice, and gout. Owl's heart was prescribed as a love charm while one report from St. Louis claimed that an owl's claw stimulated passion if used to scratch the person desired!

The mistaken notion that owls are wiser than other birds has long contributed to this positive feeling toward owls. In ancient Greece, for instance, the little owl was associated with Athena, guardian of Athens and goddess of wisdom, and this owl appeared on ancient Athenian coins. In 1875 the English magazine *Punch* published an anonymous verse which has been much quoted since:

There was an old owl who lived in an oak,
The more he heard, the less he spoke;
The less he spoke, the more he heard,
O, if men were all like that wise bird!

Owls often appear in children's books, including Edward Lear's delightful "The Owl and the Pussycat," who "went to sea in a beautiful pea-green boat." A. A. Milne's owl, Wol, is representative of both brain-power and poor spelling in *Winnie-the-Pooh*.

Many of us, regardless of knowing that owls are—well—bird-brained, still cherish them, perhaps stimulated by childhoods of stuffed owls and owl toys. We react more positively, studies have shown, to birds and animals that have human-like faces. Owls' forward-facing eyes, ear tufts, upright posture, and fluffy feathers are anthropomorphic features that we find appealing. Moreover, feathers camouflage a perched owl's slashing beak and cruel talons, letting us forget that these birds are ruthless and effective predators, not cuddly toys. Regardless of the reasons, the owl faces that peer at us from books, cards and posters, and the myriad owl figurines and toys for sale attest to our continuing involvement with these remarkable birds.

The realities of owls' physical characteristics and life habits are as fascinating as the folklore. This is an old order of birds, with a long though incompletely understood fossil record. Owls probably evolved sometime late in the Age of Dinosaurs, perhaps between sixty-five and ninety million years ago. The oldest fossils yet discovered come from Romania; one is appropriately named *Bradycneme draculae*. Familiar types like the great horned, barred, and barn owls probably appeared from twenty-five to twelve million years ago during the Miocene period.

Owls make up one order of birds, Strigiformes, which is divided into two families. The Tytonidae includes the barn owls and their relatives, the bay and grass owls, while the Strigidae includes all other modern owls. These birds are widely distributed around the world, inhabiting every continent and many islands from the Arctic to Australia. The barn owls are especially widespread.

Sizes range from the great Eurasian eagle owl, twenty-four inches from head to toe and capable of killing small deer, to the miniature least pygmy owl of Central and South America, no larger than a sparrow. All are predators. Mice, voles, lemmings, and other rodents make up the largest part of many owls' diets. In fact, the evolution of owls progressed side-by-side with the explosion of the Rodentia. Large owls also may eat rabbits and hares, ptarmigan and grouse, fish, and even frogs, snakes, and lizards. Many small owls eat large numbers of night-flying insects.

From a mouse's viewpoint, an owl is a terrible killing machine that appears without warning and strikes with deadly accuracy, sometimes uttering hideous shrieks. Some victims actually may die from sheer fright. Evolution has indeed equipped these birds with amazingly fine-tuned senses and superb physical control to fill the niche of night watcher and hunter. Small animals, especially rodents, depend on stealth and burgeoning birth rates for species survival; birds of prey must depend on inherited and acquired skills. An owl's lot is not an easy one, especially during winter when rodents tunnel under the snow, or in the spring when there are ravenous young to be fed.

More than any other predators, owls have perfected the union of efficient night sight and extremely acute hearing. Their eyes are enormous tubular affairs—some are even larger than human eyes, despite the birds' much smaller sizes. Because the eyes are tube-shaped rather than round, they cannot roll in the sockets but are fixed staring forward. To compensate, owls' necks are so flexible that they can look almost directly behind them. A special shunt modification of neck arteries prevents cutting off of blood to the head. Contrary to legend, however, the owl's head cannot screw around and around like a twist-off bottle cap.

As with many preying species, the owl's eyes face forward rather than sideways. While a hunted creature, such as a mouse, needs a very wide field of vision to foil attacks from the rear, birds of prey

Clutching a young rat, a short-eared owl pauses in its daily hunt over marshlands. Black feathers around the eyes give it a slightly dissipated look. Like the barn owl, the short-eared is a bird of open spaces rather than woodlands, and it too has probably declined in numbers because of draining and developing of marshy wetlands, its preferred habitat, and because of the widespread use of pesticides. Unlike the barn owl, the short-eared hunts during the day, bouncing and gliding above grassy or marshy terrain on its especially long wings.

need accurate distance and depth perception to pinpoint the tiny game in the grass and follow it through its frantic evasive actions to a successful kill. Like our own, the owl's two eyes focus simultaneously on the same field, creating the stereoscopic effect essential to space perception. The eyes contain not only an abundance of rods—cells that permit the bird to see in the faintest of light—but also of cones, which provide daytime perception of color and detail. While owls cannot see in total blackness, as is sometimes believed, with eyes one hundred times more sensitive than ours a cloudy, moonless

night might seem only moderately gloomy. Owls, contrary to another mistaken belief, can see in the daytime. In fact, although resolution of detail may not always be so clear as ours, owls are able to function in daylight, and the adjustment of their pupils to light is rapid. Surprisingly, about a third of the 133 living species are partly diurnal. Some types, like the short-eared owl, hunt predominantly during the day. Such far northern species as the great gray, great horned, hawk, snowy, and boreal owls naturally must hunt in the light under summer's midnight sun.

The hearing of owls, especially night-hunting types, is even more remarkable than their eyesight. Behind the disc of facial feathers, night owls hide huge ear slits that may cut from nearly the crown to below the jawline in some species. The slits' edges can be manipulated to catch sounds coming from all directions. In the small boreal owl, the two ear openings are of different sizes and are positioned asymmetrically. This allows the bird to triangulate sound stereophonically and thereby pinpoint its source more accurately. At Cornell University, experiments proved that barn owls could capture live prey in absolute darkness by relying upon hearing alone. An owl's hearing is especially tuned to the faint, high sounds that mice make while going about their business. As an owl sits quietly on a tree limb or glides soundlessly above field grasses, tiny, furtive rodent rustles may be all it needs in order to make a kill. In the evolutionary battle, however, the rodent hordes have struck back: some calls, especially those of the young, are made in ultrasound—such high frequencies that owls cannot hear them.

Once the bird has sensed its prey, it must locate and kill it. Recent experiments conducted with barn owls indicate that specialized nerve calls are arranged in the brain to form a map. When a bird receives sounds, its brain arranges them into an exact spatial "picture" of the prey's location. The flying owl, in its final approach, kicks its razor-sharp talons forward and throws its head back; the feet then grab at the spot that the brain mapped out a moment before.

Owls increase their effectiveness—and eeriness—by being able to appear like apparitions—without a sound. Special feather adaptations make such silent flight possible. Any bird that depends on surprise and stealth must be able to pounce unheard, and it must avoid confusing itself with unnecessary noise. Birds with hard plumage make fanning or rustling noises or the whistling sound of mourning doves' wings. Owls' feathers are muffled. Their edges are fringed, and a velvety pile covers the surfaces of the primary flight feathers.

Opposite: Long-eared owls, like several others, have two tufts of feathers that resemble ears but are not. Owls' real ears are long slits hidden by the feathers of their facial disks. When a long-eared owl is disturbed, it raises its ears and elongates its body. The long, thin silhouette is excellent camouflage, enabling the owl to pass for a dead stub. Screech owls commonly employ the same strategy. There are five owls in this picture!

Owls also are very light—the biggest weigh only from six to eight pounds—and their wing area is large compared to the weight of their bodies, so noisy flapping is unnecessary.

Once an owl has pounced on a field mouse, a vole, or perhaps a sleeping grouse or rabbit, its formidable weapons come into play—the gripping talons and the hooked, ripping beak. When an owl strikes, pressure makes its legs bend, causing ligaments to clench and drive the talons into the struggling creature. Since the clutch is involuntary, it is instant and unhesitating. Sometimes the prey suffocates, sometimes the claws pierce its chest cavity. If it does not die immediately, the hunter uses its strongly hooked beak to tear and rend. Like other birds, owls lack teeth, and their food is either bolted in chunks or swallowed whole. Indigestible parts too large to pass through the bird's system are spit up as neat, elongated pellets of fur, bones, and hard insect parts. Captive owls must be fed such roughage to stay healthy.

Nineteen species of owls live in North America. These range from great horned owls with wingspans of fifty-five inches to tiny sparrow-sized elf owls of southwestern deserts. North American owls can be divided roughly into three groups according to where they live: in the Far North, in the Far West, and more generally distributed throughout the United States.

Owls are very private birds and observing their social behavior can be difficult. Every person in this country no doubt lives within a few miles of an owl. Yet, few of us have ever seen one outside of books, museums, or zoos. One reason is obvious: most owls are active at night, when we are not. Except for their hoots and screams, often mistaken for dogs barking or people shouting in the distance, these birds are silent creatures. They also are camouflage experts: feathers of soft browns, grays, and whites with black shadings allow the sleeping or nesting owl to escape notice. A sleepy owl chooses dense foliage to roost in, sitting close to the tree trunk and remaining very still. Some owls, the screech and long-eared in particular, react to disturbances by pressing feathers close to their bodies, stretching tall and thin, and pointing ear tufts straight up. In this position they look exactly like a broken-off branch or stub and usually escape unseen.

Early spring is a good time to locate owls as they begin to court and nest. This may be very early. Larger owls, like the great horned, nest as early as February to give nestlings time to fledge their feathers and learn to hunt before next winter's survival test begins. At nesting time the birds become much more vocal. Males call to warn

Like the closely related short-eared owl and the barn owl, the long-eared owl is one of the most effective mouse predators. Although long-eared owls prefer forests, they hunt over open country as well, and they do so at night rather than during the day. They resemble smaller versions of the great horned owl, with similar feather tufts on their heads, and their hearing is among owls' sharpest. Summer ranges of both the long-eared and short-eared owl extend far into northern Canada.

off potential rivals for territory, and paired birds call and answer each other in courting duets. Courtship calls and rituals—bobbing, sidling, and posturing in various ways—are important to owls' breeding success. With both sexes looking very much alike, dancing rituals let each bird know that it is dealing with the opposite sex. This prevents the cock from attacking a hen that he thinks is a male rival, and it also prevents him from being savaged by the larger female.

Once cock and hen have established a pair bond, they find a nesting location. Owls are not home builders; larger types often take over old hawks' nests while smaller ones nest in woodpecker holes, prairie dog burrows, or other suitable real estate. Their homes, like the owners, are hard to spot. In early spring stick nests high in the trees may be spotted or hole nests found by rapping gently on dead tree trunks. "Whitewash," or droppings, and regurgitated food pellets often decorate the ground near the site of a roost or nest.

As the hen lays her round, white eggs, the cock provides her with food. Most females leave the nest only for water and occasional exercise. Clutch size varies with different species and conditions, but unlike most birds, owls begin incubating immediately, at the same time that eggs are being laid. This means that the young hatch at different times. Thus, the oldest may sometimes be twice the size of the youngest. If prey is scarce, parents will feed the older and more vigorous chicks first, and the younger ones may starve or be devoured by their elder siblings. This seemingly ruthless adaptation ensures that at least some chicks will survive, even in difficult years. The hen owl does most brooding and care of the young, with the cock feeding the whole family during the early stages of child-rearing. Gradually the hen withdraws from the nest as the chicks become able to maintain body temperature without brooding, and both parents then supply the gaping maws of their offspring with food. Owlets depend on their parents for a surprisingly long time after they leave the nest, unlike many young birds which become self-sufficient quickly. Much practice is needed to hone the hunting techniques that must take the young owl through its first winter—the period of highest mortality.

Owls have been able to coexist with human beings partly because they are so private. They live among us without our ever knowing. But as Jonathan Maslow points out, this evasion may actually work against them in the long run. We do not know how many owls inhabit this country, and we have no statistics to help us determine whether they are declining or maintaining their numbers. As a result, few studies have been carried out to discover how the tremendous changes that we have made in North America's natural environment have affected owls. As a result of modern farming practices, barn owl populations have certainly suffered, both in this country and in Britain. The short-eared owl also is probably declining in number. The western spotted owl is rare and getting rarer because of forest clear-cutting, and burrowing owls have declined with the extension of range and farmland. Some owls, like British tawny owls and great horned owls, seem to be holding their own. But no one knows what future use of pesticides or the complex results of habitat destruction will bring.

Owls are well worth protecting, even from a purely economic point of view. They help to control the hordes of mice, rats, and other rodents that chew their way through millions of dollars of crops yearly, ruin forage for game birds, and are especially resistant

The barred owl, a wood owl about three-fourths the size of the great horned, is found in northern forests and southern swamps and river bottoms. It resembles Wol in Winnie-the-Pooh—fluffy and round-headed. Unlike most American owls, the barred owl is dark eyed, which adds to its gentle, sleepy appearance. Like its kin, however, it is an effective and ruthless predator. While the great horned is a "five-hooter," giving several deep *hoo-hoo's,* the barred is an "eight hooter." It sounds like a real owl should and has often been described as saying, "Who cooks for you? Who cooks for you-all?" The barred owl on occasion utters bloodcurdling shrieks, ow's ah's, and guttural moans—enough to scare the daylights out of anyone hearing them in the woods at night. More common in the days of the virgin forests, barred owls must have made the woods seem even more forbidding to early settlers.

This eastern screech owl and its western counterpart are the small, common, eared owls of orchards, riversides, suburbs, and even city parks across the nation. They do not screech. The southern name, "shiver owl," better describes their high, soft, tremulous call, which Henry David Thoreau likened to that of a suicidal lover saying, *"Oh -o -o -o -o that I had never been bor -r -r -r -r n!"* Screech owls are robin-size and nocturnal, catching insects in the summer, small rodents in winter, and some migrating birds in the spring nesting season. While this individual appears in the rusty red color phase, chicks in the same nest may be either red or gray. Ornithologists do not yet agree on the reason for this variation.

to poisons. Many owls are active predators of moths and other night-flying insects whose larvae also damage trees and crops extensively. The occasional sleeping chicken, pet cat, and the song or game birds that some species add to their diets should not blind us to owls' overall value.

Meanwhile, our fascination with owls remains with us: from ancient beliefs in owls as guardians of souls, as harbingers of death, as ghosts and familiars of goddesses, witches, and sorcerers, to modern images of wise old owls and the Forest Service's Woodsy Owl, who tells us, "Give a hoot! Don't pollute!" May we continue to provide owls with a suitable environment so future generations can experience the wild cries of a lover's lost soul sent shivering through the darkness.

ADDITIONAL READING

Owls of the World: Their Evolution, Structure, and Ecology edited by John A. Burton, E. P. Dutton, 1973.
The Owl Papers by Jonathan Maslow, E. P. Dutton, 1983.
Owls: Their Natural and Unnatural History by John Sparks and Tony Soper, Taplinger, 1979.
The Folklore of Birds by Edward A. Armstrong, Houghton Mifflin Company, 1959.

Snakes

One morning not long ago, my sister and I disturbed two small snakes basking on the warm concrete edge of a swimming pool. One was a garter snake, one a milk snake, both common and both harmless. The two crawled hastily away together toward a low thicket. Like all of their kind, they chose to retreat rather than to fight. "Oh," said my sister, "don't frighten them!" What an unusual reaction this was in a culture that has traditionally hated snakes.

The two small creatures aroused a sense of poignancy: they were so unlike us but so perfect in their difference. And the little heads and ribbon-like bodies, superbly adapted to snakes' role in nature, seemed so defenseless against a serious threat from either one of us. Considering how these useful and usually inoffensive creatures are dwindling in Ohio and around the world, empathy for them does not seem overdue.

Perhaps because they *are* so different from us, snakes elicit many emotions in humans, but seldom indifference. Most cultures pass down some kind of snake lore that either venerates or vilifies the animals. Pre-Columbian Toltecs and Mayans worshiped the plumed serpent as god of wind and air, sun and dawn, agriculture and metalworking. Serpents were sacred to Aesculapius, the Greco-Roman god of healing, and were featured as messengers to the gods in Hopi snake dances.

The Bible treats snakes more negatively, and it still influences our attitude about them. Few have forgotten God's curse upon the serpent for tempting Eve. Serpents are mentioned elsewhere in the Bible as agents of God's retribution, as receivers of his wrath, or as metaphors for unattractive human qualities: "They have sharpened their tongues like a serpent; adders' poison [is] under their lips." Unusual is Proverbs' wonder at the uniqueness of snakes: "There be three things which are too wonderful for me, yea, four which I know not: The way of an eagle in the air; the way of a serpent upon a rock; the way of a ship in the midst of the sea; and the way of a man with a maid."

Snakes still fascinate people, but aside from professional herpetologists and hobbyists, the response is often mixed with fear, revulsion, or aggression. (In my family everyone understood that my mother could never be asked to enter the snake house at the zoo.) The recent reaction of one of my friends seems fairly typical: "Ugh, snakes. What an extraordinary woman you are to write about them.

Pages 120–21: The eastern hognose snake is a dramatic bluffer, hissing and striking and then playing dead if these strategies fail to intimidate. The snake, however, is completely harmless. Unfortunately, people have hunted it and other inoffensive snakes with gusto and have thus forfeited the services of many snakes whose main interest in life is devouring mice and rats. Habitat destruction, collecting, and deaths on highways where snakes crawl to warm themselves on the asphalt are other threats.

Left: The many species and subspecies of garter snakes, sometimes called garden snakes, inhabit most parts of North America; garter snakes survive farther north than any other American snake. Related to water snakes, they may bite aggressively if handled and will void a smelly substance from their anal glands when excited. Their skin patterns and colors vary greatly, but one can usually see lengthwise stripes. This is a Butler's garter snake, mostly confined to the northern and western glaciated parts of Ohio.

Massasaugas, named by Native Americans, are also called swamp rattlers because they live in moist habitats. Another common name is black snapper. Mice are a favorite food, but these snakes eat more frogs and other amphibians than do their relatives. Like other rattlers, massasaugas subdue their prey by injecting it with venom through two hypodermic fangs that fold out of the upper jaw. They also wear the rattle common to all rattlesnakes. Massasaugas' rattles, however, are small and seldom heard. These snakes were once common in Ohio's glaciated western and northeastern counties. Endangered in many areas, Eastern Massasaugas today survive mostly in bogs of the north and northeastern parts of their range.

I have been wracking my brain all day, wondering what sort of article it will be and who will read it!"

Unfortunately, many people's opinions of snakes rests on an array of formidable misinformation. Anyone but my mother may remember reptile house visitors commenting on snakes' sliminess (they are, in fact, cool and dry), their "stingers" (their tongues are harmless organs of taste-smell), the deadliness of their venom (you are many times more likely to die from beesting, lightning, or falling in your bathtub than from snakebite), or their habit of chasing victims at high speed (snakes almost always head for cover or a favorite hiding place if allowed to, and the very fastest can travel less than half the speed of a sprinting person).

Myths about snakes, especially venomous ones, have a long and flamboyant history in America. Rattlesnakes, particularly, have starred in some of the tallest tales an oldtimer ever spun for a tenderfoot: about the boot bitten by a rattler that poisoned every man who put it on, about rattlers that avenged dead mates by tracking

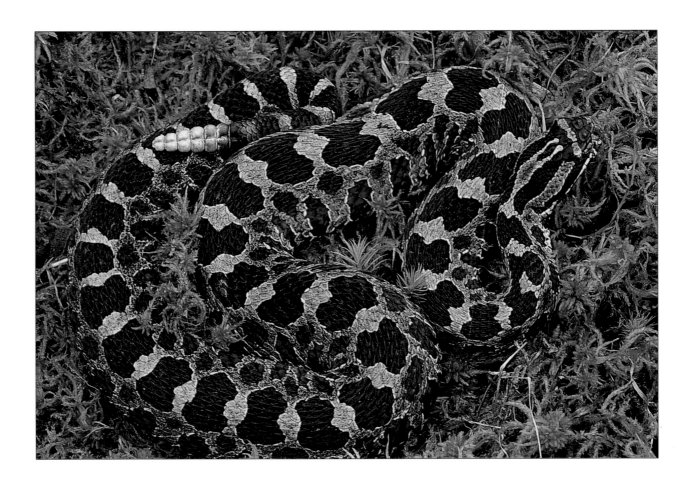

down their murderers, or about the circle of horsehair rope that could protect a sleeping cowboy from a less-than-welcome bedmate. Whiskey was wrongly touted as a snakebite cure, as were mud packs, animal dung, onions and garlic, split chickens, hog lard, and many other useless or even harmful remedies. Carnival sharpers sold snake oil to cure whatever ailed you.

People's much-exaggerated fears of poisonous snakes have routinely extended to harmless kinds as well. If cornered, many snakes hiss and vibrate their tails in a vigorous attempt to scare off their attackers. Many people mistakenly interpret these acts as viciousness rather than self-defense. The eastern hognose snake, one of Ohio's nearly thirty kinds of serpents, bluffs especially well: first it coils, flattens itself like a cobra, hisses, and strikes viciously—but with closed mouth. If these moves fail to impress, it then gives a dying shudder, rolls over on its back, hangs its tongue out, and lies still. One can almost hear organ music in the background. If picked up, the snake remains limp and dead, but if turned on its belly, it immediately rolls over on its back again, giving itself away.

This beautiful Kirtland's water snake, named after early Ohio naturalist Dr. Jared Kirtland, is strikingly marked with a row of conspicuous spots along each side. Living in moist, prairie-like habitats in western and southwestern Ohio, it is secretive and very rare.

Unfortunately for the poor hognose, this behavior convinces many that the snake is poisonous and that they must dispatch it immediately; it has also earned it names like puff adder, blow snake, and hissing viper. Jedediah Morse, in his ambitiously titled *The World and the United States in Particular* (1793), warned that "Of the venomous serpents which infest [western Lake Erie], the hissing snake is the most remarkable. . . . When you approach it, it flattens itself in a moment, and its spots, which are of various colors, become visibly brighter through rage; at the same time it blows from its mouth, with great force, a subtile wind, said to be of a nauceous smell; and if drawn in with the breath of the unwary traveler; will infallably bring a decline, that in a few months must prove mortal. No remedy has as yet been found to counteract its baneful influence." Morse's lurid superstition has survived into this century, as has the belief that nonpoisonous northern water snakes are venomous water moccasins, a species unknown north of Virginia.

Accounts of early snake hunters, scientists or otherwise, could elicit sympathy for the devil himself. Pity the poor boa or python, who, stuffed with a recent kill, was unable to slither off into the bush quickly enough. It would be shot, measured, and often left to rot. Roger Conant describes fairly typical Ohio collecting trips in his invaluable 1938 book, *The Reptiles of Ohio,* updated in 1951: "Dozens of species [of Lake Erie water snakes] were taken in a very short time on many occasions and three collectors obtained 234 of them in exactly four hours on June 1, 1935." The Lake Erie water snake is now one of ten snakes on the state endangered wildlife list. One wonders what role this kind of overzealous collecting has had in this and other snakes' decline. Conant himself called for an end to such massive collecting in 1951, as it became clear that snakes were not inexhaustible.

Attitudes toward snakes are beginning to change, but the war against the serpents still continues, even though they are some of our best allies against burgeoning insect and rodent populations. John Crompton's lively book, *The Snake,* recently reissued in paperback, points out that snakes are especially effective in controlling mice and rats because they can enter the nests themselves and dispose of entire broods of young, rather than having to stalk them one by one as a cat must do. Crompton relates one of his own snake experiences with some frustration: "Snakes are nature's rat and mouse destroyers, but they get little thanks. I once lived in a rat-infested hut in Africa. The creatures even ate the candles. Then a rat snake came along and took up its quarters in the thatch above and the rats disappeared. Unfortunately a visitor also came along when I was away on patrol and spent the night in the hut. When I got back I found a note saying he'd found a snake in the hut and shot it. He wrote as if he had saved my life. When I met him later I found it impossible to make him believe that I did not want that snake shot."

One certainly can understand why many country people have long taken a dim view of snakes. No one would want swamp rattlers or copperheads around where children played barefoot or where threshing and other farm chores were going on, even though their bites are almost never fatal. I'm told that the purpose of picket fences around West Virginia chicken coops is more to keep the copperheads out than to keep the chickens in. However, one feels for both the 106 dead racers in a photo in *The Reptiles of Ohio* as well as the grim but satisfied farmers displaying them. The grain-eating mice and rats those harmless snakes would have killed would have been, as the author comments, "incalculable." Rodents can also make short work of quail and pheasant chicks and otherwise disturb natural balances. The Ocotee hunting preserve in South Carolina has recently limited eastern diamondback rattlesnake collecting in an attempt to control rats and mice.

Looked at dispassionately, snakes are both beautiful and amazing creatures; sometimes the facts about them seem even more fanciful than the tall tales. Snakes, fairly new on the world scene, became common only about sixty-five million years ago during late Cretaceous times. They are highly specialized predators that instead of legs have from one hundred to four hundred vertebrae connected to a complex musculature that is in turn connected to belly scales or scutes. This system accounts for snakes' incredible flexibility and their ability to use the slightest surface irregularities to glide along.

Without claws or beaks, snakes must perforce swallow their prey whole. Their jaws are very loosely connected and can "dislocate," allowing the snake to engulf meals much larger than its head. The jaws' left and right sides also work separately to pull prey items down the throat in alternate tugs. The job of catching and swallowing animals alive without legs to hold them still is formidable, however, and some snakes have developed venom, which subdues prey for easier eating. The venom did not evolve to kill enemies, as some believe, although snakes do, of course, strike in self-defense.

Snakes have also developed a marvelous array of senses. They can see, though in most cases not very clearly; smell; sense vibrations through solid materials and to some extent through air; and can "taste-smell" with the tongue. When a snake flicks its tongue, it is

A blue racer slides through the branches of an oak. This snake and its close relative, the black racer, divide Ohio roughly in half: the blue racer inhabits western Ohio and the black racer the state's eastern half. The two snakes interbreed where their ranges overlap. Although racers are not poisonous, they are nervous and aggressive and may inflict painful bites if handled.

not trying to sting. The tongue gathers chemical particles from the air and deposits them in a sense receptor in the roof of the mouth, called Jacobson's organ, which gives the animal more information about its surroundings. Pit vipers, which include rattlesnakes, cotton-mouths, and copperheads, can also sense infrared rays with heat-sensitive pits located between the eyes and nostrils. A rattlesnake can detect a temperature change of one-fifth of one degree Centigrade from a distance of a foot or two. This "sixth sense" helps in hunting small warm-blooded creatures, the rattlesnake's major prey.

Snakes' other features are also amazing: their often brilliantly colored and patterned skin, which is shed three or four times a year; the single lung, which extends along most of the body's length; the male's forked reproductive organs, called hemipenes; the female's ability to store viable sperm, sometimes for years; and many snakes' birthing of living young, nourished by a placenta somewhat like mammals'.

Although snakes have no feet, they do have a kind of Achilles' heel. Like other reptiles, they are exothermic. That is, they cannot produce heat internally as mammals do, or sweat to cool off. Thus, they must spend much of their time regulating temperature: basking in the warm sun to bring cold-stiffened muscles back to life, as the two small snakes my sister and I surprised were doing, or moving out of hot sunlight into shade or cranny to avoid being literally cooked in their skins. In hot climates, especially in the desert, most

Two subspecies of smooth green snake, the eastern and western, both live mostly in the northern and western glaciated parts of Ohio. This snake, especially the western smooth green snake, is one of those species of concern whose numbers have declined due to habitat destruction and other causes.

snakes are nocturnal hunters. Those that live in temperate climates (none inhabit the far North) must hibernate below the frost line in winter. In fall and spring, great congregations of rattlesnakes come together at the mouths of favored hibernating dens, especially in the West; at these times they are especially vulnerable to hunters.

Being exothermic does offer advantages, however. Since snakes lack mammals' organic furnaces, they don't need to stoke nearly so often, though they do eat more at a single meal. A well-fleshed snake might survive for a whole year without eating at all, and the search for food is a much less urgent affair than it is for warm-blooded creatures.

Horrific as these predators may seem to their prey, snakes pose very little threat to human beings in most parts of the world. Almost universally, they try to hide or flee from humans. They do not perceive us as prey—certainly we would be too large for all but the very largest anacondas or pythons to swallow whole! Almost 90 percent of snakes are nonvenomous, and of those that are, even the dreaded black mamba of Africa prefers avoidance to confrontation. Most people bitten by snakes have stepped on or near them or have otherwise startled them into making a quick strike. In some places, such as Southeast Asia and Brazil, large numbers of poisonous snakes and people live in the same areas, and many people walk or work barefoot. These conditions, as well as the difficulty of getting antivenin, make snakebite a significant killer there. In the United States, however, annual estimates of death by snakebite are only ten to fifteen out of perhaps six thousand bites. Herpetologists estimate that people handling snakes purposely or attempting to kill or molest them account for one-third to one-half of these bites and that even *without* antivenin, only about 5 percent of the bites would prove fatal.

Ohio boasts about twenty-eight species and subspecies of snakes. Some may range over most of the state, like the northern ringneck snake, black rat snake, eastern milk snake, queen snake, northern water snake, brown or DeKay's snake, eastern garter snake, and eastern ribbon snake. For some kinds, Ohio lies at the extreme northern edge of their range, and they inhabit the state only in small, usually southern enclaves. These include the Midwest worm snake, rough green snake, black king snake, northern copperbelly, and eastern smooth earth snake. Timber rattlers also live only in southern Ohio, though more because humans have wiped them out elsewhere in the state than because of natural range limitations.

Another major division corresponds to a line running roughly northeast-southwest, separating glaciated Ohio from the unglaciated hill country of the state's southeastern third. Smooth green snakes, both the eastern and western subspecies, the blue racer, Kirtland's water snake, the eastern plains garter snake, Butler's garter snake, and the eastern massasauga are confined mostly to the northern and western glaciated parts of Ohio. Several of these snakes are prairie species that followed the grasslands when they spread eastward during a warm, dry post-glacial period four or five thousand years ago. A good example is a small population of eastern plains garter snakes in west-central Ohio, disjunct from others of their kind in states farther west.

Other snakes, the black racer, northern copperhead, and timber rattler, largely favor the wooded southeastern third of the state. A few species, the eastern fox snake, the eastern hognose snake, and the northern red-bellied snake, fit less neatly into these geographical categories, appearing in localized areas that suit their various specialized habitat requirements.

Only three of the above snakes are venomous. The eastern massasauga, also called "swamp rattler" or "black snapper," is a shy snake whose small teeth hardly ever deliver a fatal bite and which is now quite rare; it lives in the few undrained wet prairies and bogs left in the state. Much commoner is the copperhead, which inhabits the hills of unglaciated Ohio. Its weak venom fortunately means that it causes very few fatalities. More dangerous are the larger fangs and potent venom of the timber rattlesnake. However, the snake is so retiring, and its range is now so limited, that it too poses little threat to humans. (Anyone bitten by a poisonous snake, incidentally, should not waste time on self-treatment but go straight to a hospital for antivenin.)

On the Ohio Department of Natural Resources' newly adopted list of Ohio's endangered plants and animals, fully ten of the state's twenty-eight species and subspecies of snakes appear either as endangered or threatened, or are termed species of concern—not yet endangered or threatened, but needing careful oversight. Endangered are the northern copperbelly and the eastern plains garter snake, snakes that are at the edge of their natural ranges and confined to small, easily destroyed habitat areas. Listed as threatened is the Lake Erie water snake, a subspecies of the northern water snake. It is menaced by development on the Lake Erie islands, by heavy killing and collecting, and by competition from the northern water snake. Also threatened is the timber rattlesnake for the reasons discussed elsewhere in this article.

Opposite: Though the eastern milk snake ranges throughout Ohio, it is commonest in the eastern counties. Like its relative the black king snake, it is a constrictor. Milk snakes hunt mostly rodents and so would be an asset on anyone's property. Unfortunately, the myth arose that snakes drank milk from cows, and so farmers hunted them. If they had thought more clearly or had known more about snakes, they would have wondered how the snakes reached the udder or how they "milked" the cow without lips that could suck. As one writer has commented, it would have taken chloroform to reconcile any cow to the snakes' small, sharp teeth! Of course, milk snakes hunt mice and rats in barns, not milk.

Related to rattlesnakes but without rattles, northern copperheads are upland snakes of Ohio's southeastern third. The broad, triangular head is typical of pit vipers, whose heat-sensing pits between eyes and nostrils help them to hunt the mice and other rodents that are their prey. The hourglass-shaped, light-colored patches help to identify copperheads. Its venom is weak and causes few fatalities, although anyone bitten by a copperhead should go immediately to the nearest hospital for antivenin.

Several other snakes merit special concern: the eastern hognose snake, the eastern smooth earth snake, the western smooth green snake, the eastern fox snake, Kirtland's water snake, and the eastern massasauga. In most cases, they are beset by combined destruction of habitat, disappearance of prey animals, overcollecting, and death by human hands or by the wheels of cars and trucks. (Countless snakes and other reptiles and amphibians die on roads where they crawl in the night or early morning to soak up heat.)

Protecting Ohio snakes, which are obviously taking it on the chin—in a figurative sense, since they have no chins—is an urgent and complex task. First, we need more and better information, both about existing snake populations and about their needs. The Ohio Department of Natural Resources recently funded a data-collection project. This information has been computerized and at the time of this writing awaits development of software programs so that the department can use it. ODNR has also begun a needed trend of consulting amateur herpetologists who have detailed field knowledge to share and suggestions to make about protection strategies. For example, Chuck Strong of the Northern Ohio Association of Herpetologists suggested that the state mow its land at Killdeer Plains (home of several rare species) in the afternoon, rather than in the morning when snakes are basking and are more vulnerable to the mowing machines. Similar work with amateur herpetologists located previously unknown northern copperbellys on the Ohio-Michigan line. As a result, both states were able to buy land and protect the rare snakes.

Development, pollution, draining of wetlands, and overcollecting, all of which threaten Ohio snakes, pose complex problems that must be tackled as part of an overall environmental game plan. Discussing them adequately here would be impossible. However, concerned

Although it may look superficially like the copperhead, this eastern fox snake is a very different serpent. Like other rat snakes, it is a nonpoisonous constrictor that kills its prey by literally squeezing the breath out of it. Rat snakes are fast, active snakes that may bite unpredictably if handled. In Ohio, fox snakes' range is roughly commensurate to the old Lake Erie marshes before draining destroyed so much of the marshes. This helps us to trace the boundaries of the marshes during settlement times.

individuals can help create and protect living space for snakes. An extra, undisturbed woodpile or brushpile provides crannies for snakes as well as shelter for the animals they hunt. Chuck Strong suggests placing a park bench or other seat near such a pile and sitting quietly to observe the habits of the life in it. Building a compost heap atop loose rocks and branches also creates shelter for snakes and encourages grubs, earthworms, and other food species. If a stream runs through your property, leave some bushes along it; the roots will provide a place for racers or green snakes to hibernate. Don't cut stumps flush to the ground, but leave some wood to rot and give a snake a home. The passion for meticulously shorn lawns and golf courses, chemically treated by lawn companies, is probably one reason for the perceived decline of garter snakes, toads, and other amphibians and reptiles in city suburbs.

Herpetologists report that attitudes toward snakes really have begun to improve rapidly during the past few years: talks about snakes draw sizeable audiences. Many farmers now realize that milk snakes, racers, king snakes, and other species are partners in their efforts to control rats and mice. Collectors report that today's landowners often extract promises that they will remove only a few snakes from the property or even ask if they will release additional ones there.

Ohio snakes' complex problems will not disappear simply if we change our attitudes, if we see them not like the serpent of Genesis—dangerous, disgusting, and just as well dead—but as interesting creatures worth learning about, worth appreciating, and worth protecting. But such a shift in attitude is surely a good beginning. If more of us can learn to look at a snake as D. H. Lawrence does in his poem "Snake," as one of the "lords of life," or as Mary Oliver does in her beautiful poem, "The Black Snake," we may perhaps be on our way to coexisting with them:

When the black snake
flashed onto the morning road,
and the truck could not swerve—
death, that is how it happens.

Now he lies looped and useless
as an old bicycle tire.
I stop the car
and carry him into the bushes.

He is as cool and gleaming
as a braided whip, he is as beautiful and quiet
as a dead brother.
I leave him under the leaves

and drive on. . . .

ADDITIONAL READING

The Reptiles of Ohio by Roger Conant, University of Notre Dame
   Press, 1951.
Ohio's Reptiles by Guy L. Denny, Ohio Department of Natural Re-
   sources, no date.
Reptiles of North America: A Guide to Field Identification by Hobart
   M. Smith and Edmund D. Brodie, Jr., Golden Press, 1982.
The Snake by John Crompton, Faber and Faber, 1963; reprint, Nick
   Lyons Books, 1987.
Their Blood Runs Cold: Adventures with Reptiles and Amphibians by
   Whit Gibbons, The University of Alabama Press, 1983.

Fire Lizard

The Humble

Salamander

$\mathcal{A}$mphibians have long made a virtue of obscurity. Of course, male frogs and toads lose this discretion in spring, forming ribetting, peeping, trilling choruses in their frenzied attempts to lure females. Many of us can also remember the green frog that leapt from beneath our feet with an "urk," catapulting itself into the safety of deep water, or a phlegmatic toad brazenly hopping about in the garden.

But who has enjoyed a salamander chorus? Salamanders have no voices at all, or at most a feeble squeak. How many—aside from those few who spend their time turning over rotten logs or streamside boulders and stalking the rainy woods with flashlights in the dead of night—have ever seen a salamander? Even more than frogs and toads, salamanders live by being overlooked.

We tend to think of amphibians as primitive creatures that lost the evolutionary sweepstakes and inhabit the world on borrowed time. In fact, the three modern orders, frogs and toads (Anura), salamanders (Caudata or Urodela), and the legless tropical caecilians (Gymnophiona) are unlike the ancient amphibians and quite sophisticated, and they have been modestly successful. They arose about 150 million years ago, but their relationship to previous amphibians is still cloudy.

Since the old amphibians lost their ascendancy to reptiles a good 200 million years ago, their descendents have lived in a ruthless world dominated by others: fish rule the waters, reptiles and mammals the land, and birds the air. All eat amphibians. To survive, these animals must resourcefully exploit marginal areas lying between the habitats of terrestrial and aquatic creatures. In addition, their breathable skins and their shell-less eggs must be kept moist, limiting their ranges to water and its margins, damp soils, and rain-drenched woods and, in the case of salamanders, restricting their activities almost completely to cool, moist darkness. Ironically, the name salamander comes from the Latin *Salamandra,* in turn derived from a Greek word meaning "fire-lizard." People apparently associated salamanders with fire because when they threw logs on the hearth, salamanders crawled out of them. Therefore, it was thought, they must be able to live in fire.

Nine salamander families exist worldwide and include about 340 species. More than 100 species inhabit America north of Mexico. These include several aquatic families: the mudpuppies and waterdogs; the giant salamanders, represented in North America by only one species, the hellbender; the amphiumas; and the sirens. The

Pages 136–37: The long-tailed salamander, so-called because its whiplike tail constitutes 58 to 67 percent of its body length, is one of Ohio's most beautiful salamanders. Several other species are also red; the bright color warns would-be predators that these animals exude toxic skin secretions and are not good to eat. Many people have never seen salamanders in the wild because they are so retiring; however, their behavior and life cycles are varied and fascinating.

Left: The spotted salamander is one of the commoner mole salamanders, a family whose members spend most of their time underground. In spring, spotted salamanders emerge from their hiding places and migrate to breeding ponds where males compete intensely for females' attention. After mating, females lay small, jelly-like masses of eggs in shallow water, masses that subsequently swell to the size of a gelatinous tennis ball, visible here.

Overleaf: The red salamander's corpulence and the bright yellow iris of its eye distinguish it from other scarlet Ohio salamanders.

mole salamanders have fashioned a more amphibious life, living in water as larvae, inhabiting the land as adults, and returning to water to court and lay eggs. Newts divide their lives between water and land as well. The most advanced family, the lungless salamanders, began as denizens of mountain streams. Their evolutionary loss of lungs cut down on the excess buoyancy that made it difficult to hold fast in the rushing water, and they now breathe through their skins and the linings of their mouths. Many are completely terrestrial, laying and guarding their eggs on land, passing their larval stage within the egg, and emerging as miniature adults.

There is no typical salamander—some are slender, some are stout; some live in water, some on the land, some in both places; some are drab, some, like the red eft, sport gaudy reds and oranges. However, like most other amphibians, salamanders are alike in having a smooth, moist, flexible skin that lacks scales. They breathe through this skin and through their mouth membranes, and many also use lungs or gills. Unlike frogs and toads, they cannot hear but can feel vibrations through their legs and through water. All salamanders and newts are carnivorous, feeding on insects and other arthropods, slugs, snails, and worms. For most of them, almost any creature they can subdue is fair game, sometimes including other salamanders.

Unlike tadpoles, salamander larvae do not begin lives as vegetarians or shed their tails as they mature. They do, however, go through a metamorphosis to their adult forms that is not so spectacular as frogs' and toads', but nevertheless involves changes in nearly every part of the body: loss of gills and tail fins, growth of bulging eyes and eyelids, change of cartilage to bone, alteration of mouth parts, tongue, and skin, as well as many other transformations. Some kinds, however, are paedomorphic (sometimes called neotenic). This means that physically they remain larval, keeping their gills and tail fins and larval eyes but becoming sexually mature. Mudpuppies are a good example, retaining their bright red gills and other larval features their whole lives. Other species, like the tiger salamander can "choose" to stay in their aquatic larval forms if important nutrients are missing or if life on land becomes too precarious, but they will metamorphose into their adult, land-living forms if conditions are right.

Just as there is no typical salamander, there is also no typical life history. Some are born, live, and die in the water; others live completely on land in moist ravines and woods. Many divide their lives between water and land. Of them, the newts have woven the most complex relationship between these two worlds. Ohio's one species,

Upper left: Although newts are the principal salamander family in Europe, Asia, and northern Africa, only six species inhabit North America; and only one, the eastern, or red-spotted, lives in Ohio. Eggs are laid in water and hatch into aquatic larvae. These metamorphose into a small, lizard-like red eft stage that leaves the water for three to seven *wanderjahren* on land, protected from predators by irritating secretions from its skin glands and its bright red warning coloration. Efts reenter the water to mate and spend the rest of their lives there. The adult form retains only a few red spots from its flashy adolescence.

Upper right: One of the earlier signs of spring is the jelly-like masses of spotted salamander eggs that can cover the shallower parts of vernal breeding ponds. The adults, which may have traveled long distances to reach the ponds, will not return until the following spring. Newts sometimes eat their eggs.

the eastern or red-spotted newt, is completely aquatic as an adult, preferring small, quiet pools. Males and females court in an elaborate water ballet, and the female deposits eggs singly on water plants in spring.

A newt egg hatches into an aquatic larva that in turn metamorphoses into a small land-living form which by late fall abandons the water like a rebellious adolescent. It is called a red eft and is colored a vivid red-orange. Red efts live on land for as many as seven years. Unlike most salamanders, they wander rather boldly through the woods in rainy weather, gorging themselves on insects and other small creatures. They can afford to be bold because their skin glands make poisons that predators learn to avoid; their bright color is an advertisement and a warning. Eventually, the eft's skin, which is rather rougher and drier than most salamanders', smooths and moistens and turns from brilliant orange to drab olive green, retaining several small bright orange spots. The tail flattens, and the animal returns to the water to reproduce and complete its life cycle. Herpetologists call this the second metamorphosis. Newts in harsher or unstable environments may skip the terrestrial eft stage, spending their whole lives in water.

Other salamanders, particularly the mole family, use a simpler amphibious strategy with only one metamorphosis. Born in the water, these change from larvae to land-living adults. Like their namesake, mole salamanders spend most of their time underground and are seldom seen. In spring, however, they migrate to breeding ponds where they court and mate and lay eggs, leaving the water afterwards to resume their mole-like existence underground. Spotted salamanders provide an especially frenzied spectacle as masses of males vie for the attention of egg-bearing females in the breeding ponds. Cars kill many spotted salamanders as they attempt to cross roads to get to the ponds, and park districts often close certain roads in early spring to help them arrive and return safely. The marbled salamander is the mole family's only member to lay eggs on land: the female lays in dry pond beds in autumn and stays with her eggs until rains cover them.

Male salamanders court their mates with a variety of ingenious displays. Many frogs and toads use amplexus, in which the male grasps the female's torso to immobilize her. Some salamanders also use this technique, especially members of the newt family. This enables them to stimulate females with glandular secretions and prevents other males from interfering. However, in species in which the female can move about as she pleases, friendly persuasion is much

Opposite below: An eastern red-spotted newt larva looks superficially like its adult parent (see upper left). However, it sports feathery gills which are absent in the adult, and it lacks the line of red spots visible on its elders. It will undergo significant structural changes as it shifts to the land-living red eft stage, which in turn will metamorphose into the adult form and return to the water.

more important than force. The reason for this is anatomical: rape is difficult for salamanders because although fertilization is internal, the male has no penis with which to insert his sperm into the female's vent. Instead, he deposits from his cloaca a sperm packet, or spermatophore, shaped rather like a bulletin board pushpin, with a broad base and a sperm cap resting on top of it. A consenting female will lower her own cloaca, or vent, over the spermatophore, taking up the sperm. To bring her to this point, males of different species use a variety of rituals ranging in length from a couple of minutes in the relatively uncouth red salamander to a lavishly choreographed dance of up to three hours in slimy salamanders.

A male red-spotted newt adopts an "alert posture" as he scans the surrounding water for prospects. If a willing female appears, the two nudge each other with their snouts. The male undulates his body in what is called the "hula display," and he and his prospective mate change positions in the "wave display." He deposits his spermatophore, and she, following him closely, takes up the sperm from it. If she fails to accept his invitation to the dance, the male abandons finesse and tries to clasp her around the neck with his hindlegs (am-

Here a mudpuppy eats a crayfish, one of its favorite foods. Although it may look malign, it is completely harmless—at least to humans. Mudpuppies retain their bushy red gills throughout life and are completely aquatic. They attach their eggs to underwater rocks in late spring.

plexus). He may hold her for more than three hours, rubbing her with legs and cheeks and vibrating his tail, presumably to waft sexual perfumes to her nostrils. He then deposits his spermatophore, and she rewards him for his efforts, one hopes, by taking up the sperm.

Dusky salamander males nudge and rub females with the so-called mental glands under their chins. Next they approach them with a movement curiously like a butterfly swimming stroke. The male then leads the female around for some time in a tail-straddling walk, her chin pressed against other glands at the base of his tail before he produces the spermatophore. A slimy salamander male's white body flecks turn deep pink with passion, and he executes an elaborate foot dance by raising and lowering his legs alternately in place. His courtship is lengthy and sophisticated. The details, and other secrets of salamander courtship, can be found in Ralph A. Pfingston and Floyd L. Downs' provocative volume *Salamanders of Ohio*.

Salamanders also show considerable ingenuity in defending themselves against the attacks of shrews, birds, snakes, and other predators, which may even include beetles, centipedes, spiders, and other salamanders. Ingenuity is needed—salamanders lack the usual defenses of claws, large teeth, scaly armor, or in many cases, even speed. Their defense mechanisms usually combine unpleasant or poisonous skin secretions and various body movements and postures.

Species like the spotted salamander that have glands at the back of the head often bend their heads down or hold them flat against the ground, presenting their most distasteful body part to the attacker. Other species butt with their heads or lash or undulate their tails if they have poison glands on the upper surface. Efts sometimes undulate their tails too but are more likely to use the "unken reflex" under intense attack: they hold themselves rigidly still with tail and chin elevated, rather like a gymnast touching head to heels. This displays brightly colored underparts to remind experienced predators that newts are inedible. At the same time, efts' stillness inhibits attack reflexes in predatory birds that have not yet tasted newts and learned to avoid them. Many salamanders also can afford to lose their tails to attackers, leaving them with a wildly wriggling piece of themselves while escaping to live another day and grow another tail.

The southern Appalachians, with their unglaciated streams and forests, were a major development center for salamanders, and they remain today the richest area in the world in both species and numbers. Herpetologists estimate that in some forests, the total mass of woodland salamanders is greater than that of all the birds and mammals put together. Twenty-five species of salamanders inhabit Ohio alone; they particularly favor the eastern two-thirds of the state, that portion occupied by the glaciated and unglaciated Allegheny Plateau, scored with cool ravines and offering a variety of other suitable habitats. Another reason salamanders are more common in eastern counties than in western ones is that sandstones commonly outcrop on the surface here. Because they are evenly permeable, these rocks store and release cool water more consistently than do the limestones of western Ohio, protecting salamanders from fatally droughty conditions. The till plains of western Ohio are also so intensively drained and cultivated that salamanders do not find many habitable areas there, except for a few streams and gorges.

Five families inhabit Ohio. The giant salamanders are represented by the hellbender, a large, wrinkled, extremely ugly, but harmless aquatic salamander that needs clear, unpolluted streams to survive. Hellbenders have become exceedingly rare here and appear on the state list of endangered species. The waterdogs also offer one species, the mudpuppy, another large aquatic salamander easily identified by the ruff of bright red gills at its neck. Mudpuppies, although certainly strange looking, are also completely harmless and should be protected. They can tolerate silt better then hellbenders can, but their eggs need clear stream riffles to develop. Mudpuppies have declined in Ohio in recent years but are not yet endangered. The eastern or red-spotted newt is fairly common and widely distributed across Ohio. It is the only member of its family in this area.

Mole salamanders include Jefferson's, blue-spotted, spotted, marbled, silvery, smallmouth, tiger, and Tremblay's salamanders. Some, like the spotted and smallmouth, are fairly common. The blue-spotted is endangered, not because it is particularly rare farther to the north and west, but because its range includes only the far northwestern corner of Ohio. Smallmouth, tiger, and Tremblay's salamanders are unusual in that their ranges cover the western rather than the eastern part of the state.

Identifying some mole salamanders can be very tricky because several of them hybridize. The blue-spotted and Jefferson's long ago interbred to produce the Tremblay's and silvery hybrid species. These species are overwhelmingly female, with three sets of chromosomes instead of two. If two sets come from the blue-spotted parent, the triploid offspring will be Tremblay's; if two sets come from Jefferson's, the offspring is a silvery. These hybrid females apparently need to mate with a male to stimulate egg-laying, but herpetologists still debate whether the male's genetic material enters the mix for

the next generation or whether the offspring are simply female clones of their mothers. The plot has thickened as investigators recognize that smallmouth and tiger salamander males also mate with the triploid Tremblay's and silvery females!

Lungless salamanders offer by far the greatest number of species and individuals in Ohio: the dusky and the mountain dusky, the green, the two-lined, the longtail, the cave, the spring, the four-toed, the redback, the slimy, the mud, and the red. Wehrle's salamander has also been reported once or twice in southeastern Ohio, but many believe that it is not really resident here. Some lungless salamanders are indeed abundant, populating cool ravines, forest floors, seeps and springs, the margins of streams, and other suitably moist habitats. The redback lives in numbers all over the state, while the ravine, the slimy, the dusky, the two-lined, and the long-tailed are common across Ohio's eastern two thirds. Mountain duskies are abundant as well, but their range includes only northeastern Ohio. Red salamanders and spring salamanders are stout species that live in or near springs and seeps. The latter often feed on other salamanders. These two range sparsely on the glaciated and unglaciated

Above: The vivid red cave salamander is endangered in Ohio, partly because southern Ohio is at the far northern edge of its range, partly because its habitat requirements are quite specific: it needs limestone ledges with running water near them to accommodate its larvae, which are aquatic.

Overleaf: This red eft is the juvenile, land-living form of the red-spotted newt. Efts hide under logs, boards, or brush but also often wander through moist woods and meadows or perch on shrubbery after heavy rains. Although glands in their skins produce a rather powerful neurotoxin that defends against predators, gentle handling presents no problems to those who want to study them.

plateaus because of their specialized habitat requirements. The four-toed—so named because it has one less than the usual five toes on its hind feet—is scattered in small numbers across the whole state. It prefers undisturbed or mature forest with bogs, a habitat now rare in Ohio.

Green salamanders, cave salamanders, and mud salamanders are quite rare, primarily because their ranges extend only into small areas of southern Ohio. The green, however, is declining over all its southern Appalachian range, for reasons unknown. Cave salamanders are known in Ohio only in Adams County and in the Cincinnati area. They are salamanders of the great limestone cave systems farther south, where they prefer to live in the twilight zone near cave mouths. Mud salamanders like muddy, swampy lowlands and are mostly an Atlantic Coastal Plain species. The Ohio Department of Natural Resources lists green and cave salamanders as endangered in Ohio.

Salamanders, like other amphibians, are truly valuable members of ecosystems. They live near water where they help control mosquitoes and other insects, and they collectively eat tremendous quantities of these and other invertebrates. They have survived modestly well in a world populated by myriad predators of other animal classes—fish, reptiles, mammals, and birds. If it were not for our own species, their success would be assured for millions of years into the future, probably with increases in their diversity.

Recently, however, amphibians have begun to decline alarmingly. Though most of them, except for the few used for food and education, escape direct persecution from humankind, destruction of habitat proceeds rapidly: we have drained or otherwise lost 95 percent of Ohio's original wetlands, essential for amphibian survival. We have polluted most of our remaining rivers, lakes, and swamps. We are building suburbs, roads, and other installations. Many salamanders and other amphibians with limited ranges will die out. Others that live in rugged, difficult-to-develop areas will probably survive, as will small, common, inconspicuous species like the redback and two-lined salamanders. Diversity will shrink, however, as habitats decline.

Fortunately, people are beginning to realize that we owe protection to whole ecosystems rather than just to game species; to "lower" orders rather than just to mammals and birds, and to those creatures like reptiles and amphibians that are neither cuddly nor conspicuous. The system of state nature preserves founded by the Division of Natural Areas and Preserves of the Ohio Department of

Page 149: Entirely land dwelling, the redback salamander is one of the smaller, commoner Ohio salamanders. Its stripe may be red, orange, yellow, or even gray—the so-called leadback phase. An all-red color phase inhabits northeastern Ohio. The redback female suspends her clutch of eggs like a bunch of grapes from the underside of a fallen log or rock. Like females of several other terrestrial species, she stays with the eggs, keeping them moist to prevent fungal infections and aggressively defending them from predators. This is a woodland species especially typical of beech-maple forests.

Natural Resources during the past quarter century and lands privately purchased by the Nature Conservancy give habitat protection to many plants and animals, but prospects for saving habitats on private lands are much less certain.

Why should we study salamanders? In *Salamanders of Ohio*, Ralph A. Pfingston says, "Those who have tramped Ohio in search of these animals have felt what I've felt; finding the first *Ambystoma* [mole salamander], and the ecstasy known only to those who have found something for the first time; looking west from Stone Hill in Strongsville with the Great Plains in front and the foothills behind; atop Buzzard Roost Rock with the same view that Indians had for thousands of years; walking through the forest with a misty drizzle on the brow and being awed by the incredible silence." Perhaps more of us should seek out the lowly salamanders. They are such unassuming animals, but they are another necessary part of that giant jigsaw puzzle of nature whose pieces we seem determined to misplace, another way of approaching the natural world whose influence can serve to make us more human if we only let it.

ADDITIONAL READING

Salamanders of Ohio edited by Ralph A. Pfingston and Floyd L. Downs, Ohio Biological Survey, 1989.
Ohio's Amphibians by Guy L. Denny, Ohio Department of Natural Resources, no date.
A Field Guide to the Reptiles and Amphibians of Eastern North America by Roger Conant, Houghton Mifflin, 1958.
Amphibians of North America by Hobart M. Smith, Golden Press, 1978.
The Encyclopedia of Reptiles and Amphibians edited by Tim Halliday and Kraig Adler, Facts on File, 1986.

Frogs & Toads
Are Friends

An old pond—
A frog leaping in—
The sound of water.
        Matsuo Basho

*D*uring the past few years, frogs and toads—while neither cuddly nor charismatic—have become TV idols, appeared on t-shirts, posed on restaurant doors, and chased trucks in beer ads. The government recently added Mark Twain's famous jumping California red-legged frogs to the endangered species list. There they join such stars as American eagles, grizzly bears, and condors. A recent *New York Times* article ponders the frog phenomenon that is blossoming at a time when many people think amphibians are in trouble worldwide. The author, Timothy Egan, comments, "behind the frog's popularity is this paradox: it seems that many things human and wild become objects of infatuation just when they are dying out."

Page 152: A gray tree frog lounges in the cup of a pitcher plant. It may be competing with the carnivorous plant for small insects that fall into the cup and which the plant then digests. Two species of tree frog are common in Ohio, although many who hear their trills mistake them for calling birds. Scientists have recently become concerned with apparent worldwide declines in frog populations.

Frogs of the World

Frogs cover the earth, except for Antarctica, the far North above the permafrost line, and the very driest deserts. About four thousand species of the order Anura (sometimes called Salientia) are known, and new ones are discovered yearly. The richest assemblages inhabit the disappearing rain and cloud forests of Central and South America. Anurans are grouped into 303 genera and twenty to twenty-five families, mainly based on fossil evidence, features of tadpoles, and internal anatomy.

According to *The Encyclopedia of Reptiles and Amphibians*, families include tailed and New Zealand frogs (Leiopelmatidae), disk-tongued toads (Discoglossidae), clawed and Surinam toads (Pipidae), burrowing toads (Rhinophrynidae), spadefoot toads, horned toads, and parsley frogs (Pelobatidae), "true" toads (Bufonidae), gold frogs (Brachycephalidae), mouth-brooding frogs (Rhinodermatidae), ghost frogs (Heleophrynidae), myobatrachids (Myobatrachidae), leptodactylids (Leptodactylidae), poison-arrow frogs (Dendrobatidae), "true" tree frogs (Hylidae), glass frogs (Centrolenidae), pseudids (Pseudidae), "true" frogs (Ranidae), Seychelles frogs (Sooglossidae), sedge and bush frogs (Hyperliidae), Old World tree frogs (Rhacophoridae), and narrow-mouthed frogs (Microhylidae).

Frogs that live mainly in water have slender bodies, long heads, and very long legs. These streamlined frogs are shy and leap headlong into water if surprised. Those that live on land or burrow underground tend to be squat, with short legs and spade-like feet with horny edges. We often call them toads. Tree-living frogs' bodies are flattened for resting and balancing on leaves, branches, and trunks. Their toes end in adhesive disks, and their belly skin is loose for pressing against surfaces. Many have sticky webbing between their toes, and some possess extra bones or cartilage in them for better gripping. A few species can even "fly," gliding for as much as fifty feet by spreading the webs between their long toes.

Anurans are tailless amphibians of several families. They are roughly divided into frogs—long-legged animals with moist, smooth skins that leap—and toads—short-legged, warty ones that hop and use skin glands to produce defensive poisons. (The poisons will not hurt humans unless they touch eyes or mucous membranes.) These interesting, useful insect eaters have evoked a bizarre range of responses from peoples of different times and cultures. And why not? Animals that change from fish-like larvae to four-legged land creatures that fill the night with weird croaks, ribbets, and trills, and that

Left: This green frog tadpole is well on the way to metamorphosis. Not only are its hind legs and webs well grown, but its front legs have broken through the skin on one side and through the breathing spiracles on the other. At this stage, tadpoles are sometimes called polliwogs.

Below: Adult bullfrogs are formidable predators. Mary C. Dickerson says, in *The Frog Book*, "He is the green dragon of the pond to the fish, small turtles, the young water-birds, and, alas, to the frogs also." This frog is probably a female: the eardrums, faintly visible behind the bulging eyes, are about the same size as the eyes. In males they are much larger.

materialize in great hopping, leaping hordes when conditions are right, must certainly figure in human story and song. From the plague of frogs that punished Pharaoh in the Bible to Kermit ("It's Not Easy Bein' Green"), we have projected our own concerns onto frogs, just as we've done with many other creatures.

Older cultures' views of frogs and toads and our present fascination with them are different, however. Frogs in some traditional societies were figures of power—for good or evil—which was understandable in a world where people faced nature and mortality ungirded by glazed windows, central heating, or hospitals. In contrast, we moderns tend to humanize anurans, turning them into small green people in frog suits, Disney characters that require little understanding and pose no threat, or as logos for selling products. Neither attitude asks what anurans are really like, explores their history and populations, or inquires what their needs might be. We've only begun to pose some of the complex questions—let alone gather data to answer them. Until we do, we will not know what kind of trouble frogs and toads may be in or what to do about it.

Ancient cultures displayed marked ambivalence toward these animals. In Mesoamerica and South America they were often linked with fertility and rain. Mayan images sometimes show maize growing from their heads. In the Far East, toads were believed to have supernatural powers and were thought masters of escape. The Japanese guru Kosensei, a wart-covered hermit who sometimes changed himself into a toad, was often pictured sitting with his toad companion. More sinister Asian toads accompanied an assortment of demons and goblins, as well as the Woman of the Three Road River, Japan's analogue of the River Styx. In China, the toad, spider, lizard, centipede, and snake represented dark feminine *yin* as opposed to the masculine *yang* forces of light. Eclipses were caused by a giant frog swallowing the moon.

Although the Egyptian pantheon included a frog-headed goddess, Heqt, who collaborated with Khnumu to create other gods and men, Greek and Roman culture apparently paid scant attention to anurans—this despite Aristophanes's famous play *The Frogs*. By the Middle Ages in Europe, however, frogs and toads had evolved into sinister creatures, the familiars of witches and the cohorts of Satan. Witches, it was said, were especially fond of toads, pampering them and dressing them up to celebrate the Witches' Sabbath in scarlet silk and green velvet capes.

The story of one old Englishwoman named Julian Cox, tried for witchcraft in 1663, seems especially poignant. Her biggest mistake

Ohio Frogs

Unlike Ohio salamanders, whose life histories are quite varied, our frogs all follow one basic pattern with slight variations: they lay eggs that are pigmented to soak up the sun's heat and perhaps to protect against damaging ultraviolet light. They lay the eggs in water, fertilize them externally, then abandon them, unlike many of the world's frogs, which provide parental care in various ways. Their voices are well developed, and the males indulge in loud choruses and territorial calling during their breeding seasons. In Ohio, breeding seasons extend from early spring in some species to midsummer in others. Eggs hatch into tadpoles with rounded bodies, long tails, and specialized rasping mouth parts. All metamorphose into four-legged adults with major changes to their bodies.

Four families inhabit Ohio: the spadefoot toads (Pelobatidae), true toads (Bufonidae), tree frogs (Hylidae), and true frogs (Ranidae). There are six genera and fourteen species: The eastern spadefoot (*Scaphiopus holbrooki*) is Ohio's only member of the Pelobatidae, and it is known from only a few

Mountain chorus frogs appear in Ohio only in the southeastern hills, where they are found in woodlands, often at some distance from water. This little frog shows faintly the reversed parentheses on the back and the white upper lip that help distinguish it from its cousin, the western chorus frog. Its voice is also higher and more nasal and has been described as sounding like a squeaky wagon wheel.

locations in southeastern Ohio, on the northernmost edge of its range. It is listed as endangered in this state. These burrowing toads are rarely seen except in their temporary breeding ponds or when they are accidentally dug up. They are not closely related to other Ohio toads.

Fowler's toad *(Bufo woodhousei fowleri)* and the American toad *(Bufo americanus)* belong to what are called "true" toads (Bufonidae). They are the familiar warty toads of the garden and are hard to tell apart. American toads' bellies are usually more spotted; they have an enlarged wart on their thighs and have one, two, or three warts in each of the larger dark spots on their backs. Fowler's toads have three or more. While American toads trill sweetly during breeding season, Fowlers' voices have been described as a "terrible squawking." Fowler's toad is more common in New England and the American toad in Ohio. Ranges often overlap, and the two species sometimes hybridize, just to confuse things further. No toads cause warts in human beings.

The state boasts six species of tree frogs. Gray tree frogs (or tree toads, as they are sometimes called) were long thought to include only one species, the common gray tree frog *(Hyla versicolor)*. Recently, however, herpetologists have distinguished another, Cope's gray tree frog *(Hyla chrysocelis)*. The two are impossible to tell apart in the field, except by their voices. *Versicolor*'s trill is lower and slower than its cousin's. Both can vary from light gray-green to pearl gray depending on the background on which they are sitting. They seldom come down from the trees except to visit ponds during the breeding season. *Versicolor* can be heard on rainy nights in the northern part of the state and may be mistaken for a bird; in general, *chrysocelis* lives south of Columbus.

When I was growing up in Wood County, Blanchard's cricket frog *(Acris crepitans blanchardi)* called in sunny streams and ponds, sounding like someone rapidly clicking two marbles together. Although these warty little frogs are members of the Hylidae, or tree frog, family, they do not climb. Color and patterns vary greatly— lighter in hot, light, and dry places. Like their close relative the western chorus frog, they are prairie frogs that moved eastward with clearing of the forests after settlement. They are still absent in the eastern half of this state. Ohio herpetologists believe that they may be in decline, probably because of intensive agriculture and water pollution.

Three more of the Hylidae family are the spring peeper *(Pseudacris crucifer)*, the western chorus frog *(Pseudacris triseriata)*, and the mountain chorus frog *(Pseudacris brachyphona)*. Peepers, those tiny frogs whose high piping voices mean spring to many of us, were until recently classified as *Hyla crucifer*. Experts have determined, however, that they are more closely related to chorus frogs than to hylas. They like brushy or cutover woodlots near small pools or swamps. The two chorus frogs also have high voices, but they sound more like a thumb running over a comb from large to small teeth: their voices rise at the end of each trill. Chorus frogs often call from the same pools as spring peepers, and people sometimes confuse them with each other. *Triseriata* has three dark stripes on its back, as well as a stripe on each side through the eye; *Crucifer* often—but not always—sports a dark X on its back. *Brachyphona*, a woodland species from southeastern Ohio, has two dark, curved stripes on its back that have been described as reversed parentheses.

Ranidae, called true frogs for no particularly valid reason, form the last group of anurans in the state, with five species: bullfrogs, green frogs, northern leopard frogs, pickerel frogs, and wood frogs. The largest, of course, are bullfrogs *(Rana catesbeiana)*, whose bodies are known to reach eight inches. These big, green aquatic frogs are late breeders, and the males' sonorous bass voices can be heard into July as they defend their territories and advertise for mates. Bullfrogs will eat almost anything that moves and that they can swallow, including other frogs.

Green frogs *(Rana clamitans)* look like smaller versions of bullfrogs, though they have two prominent ridges of skin down their backs, the dorsolateral folds, that are missing in bullfrogs. These are the "banjo frogs" whose voices sound like the plucking of a bass

string on that instrument. Like bullfrogs, they are aquatic anurans and late breeders whose voices enliven summer ponds. Both species are quite common in Ohio.

At first sight, northern leopard frogs *(Rana pipiens)* and pickerel frogs *(Rana palustris)* look much alike. These medium-sized frogs are about the same length and are covered with dark spots. Pickerel frogs, however, tend to be light brown rather than green, and the spots on their backs are squarish rather than round. The insides of their thighs are bright yellow-orange. Leopard frogs are sometimes called "meadow frogs" or "grass frogs" because they wander considerable distances from water. They can be found around lake and river margins and in marshes as well. Pickerel frogs tend to prefer cool streams. They are missing from the former Black Swamp region of northwestern Ohio, while leopard frogs live throughout the state.

Rana sylvatica, the wood frog, is our most terrestrial frog. It is found in woodlands away from water, except early in the spring when it gathers in great numbers at breeding ponds. Wood frogs' calls at these pools are like the quacking of mallard ducks. This is also the most northern of American reptiles or amphibians, extending its range as far as the tundra of Labrador and Alaska. Easy to identify, it is light brown and has a dark bandit's mask over each eye. A northern subspecies found in the oak openings of Lucas County is darker.

was to invite a neighbor in to take a pipe of tobacco with her. At her trial he testified that she then said, "Neighbor, look what a pretty thing there is." Looking down, he saw a "monstrous toad" staring up at him. When he tried to kill it, she told him it would not hurt him. The neighbor, however, decided that the toad was one of the old woman's devilish familiars and reported sundry persecutions by it. These involved the toad's appearing suddenly, to be chased, beaten, and burned by the neighbor. Finally the toad (or toads) desisted, but not soon enough to keep Julian Cox from being hauled up before the court for witchcraft.

Despite their nasty reputations, or perhaps because of them, frogs and toads were used in cures for various ailments. Toads were especially valued for producing within their heads the miraculous toadstone. Its virtue was to change color in the presence of poison and even to cure poisoning and other intestinal, kidney, and bladder problems if swallowed. Some voices of reason questioned the toadstone's existence; other authors described it in imaginative detail and devised fanciful ways of inducing the toad to disgorge it. Toads were also useful in alchemical attempts to transform base metals into gold.

Frogs escaped use in these questionable experiments, saving themselves for twentieth-century lab dissections. However, they did become a sought-after food item, not only by the French (designated "Frogs" by the English), but all over the world. In 1896 alone, 118,000 frogs were killed to supply San Francisco markets. More recently, according to one estimate, the United States imported more than 6.5 million pounds of frozen frog meat each year between 1981 and 1984. Keep in mind that these figures represent legs alone and that these legs came from wild frogs hunted in such countries as Bangladesh—the animals' slow growth, insistence on live food, and tendency toward cannibalism have made frog farming on a large scale impractical. Clearly, since frog's legs taste a lot like chicken, it makes sense to stick with chicken.

Anurans fare better in some folk traditions and fairy tales. The house toad of German tradition lived in the cellar and kept stored food wholesome and the household prosperous, thereby earning the name "treasure-toad." Most children know the story of the frog transformed into a handsome prince by a kiss. Less familiar is "The Three Feathers," a story collected by the Brothers Grimm. In it, a great toad presents Simpleton with one of her offspring when his father, the king, offers his crown to the son who can bring back the highest-quality wife. The little toad, of course, becomes a ravishing maiden; Simpleton seals the bargain with a kiss and claims the crown. In a similar Russian tale, the tsar's clumsy son Ivan must marry a frog princess bewitched by a wicked baba-yaga. He then wins and transforms her through the power of his love. Leaving Freudian sexual interpretations aside, one can see that the theme of these stories is similar: ugliness is not always evil or loveliness virtue, and love can sometimes transform strangeness into beauty.

Certainly, if we want to see frogs and toads clearly, we should have some idea of what we are looking at. Like the salamanders beloved of little boys, and the caecilians, worm-like burrowing animals of the southern continents, frogs and toads are direct descendants of the earliest land-living vertebrates, those that hauled themselves out of the sea about 360 million years ago and made the swamps ring with their grunts and croaks, thought to be the first sounds produced by vocal chords. Like their ancestors, modern amphibians have no scales and breathe partly through their skins, which is why they must keep them moist. Their eggs have no shells. Because of this, they must lay them in water or otherwise moisten them. This tends to tie amphibians to water, although some have become more terrestrial than others. Development of the shelled egg enabled reptiles like dinosaurs and modern lizards and snakes to cut the knot that bound them to water.

Many people think of the Greek-derived word "amphibian," which denotes "two lives," as meaning a life divided between water and land. A more accurate interpretation would be a life divided between very different larval and adult forms. In frogs and toads, the metamorphosis from fish-like larva to four-legged adult is even more remarkable than in salamanders. Tadpoles are almost completely plant eaters, though some will eat dead animal matter, and a few even become cannibals. Adult frogs and toads are carnivorous, devouring insects and almost any other small animals they can get into their mouths and swallow.

To mature, a tadpole must undergo a change as strange as that of the toad princess. As it approaches metamorphosis, back legs bud, and front legs develop beneath the skin, breaking through it in stages. Lungs gradually replace gills. During the last few days of the transformation, the tadpole must float near the water's surface for oxygen; it cannot eat and absorbs its tail for nourishment. Its mouth widens and stretches, losing the horny beak and rasping teeth with which it scraped algae into its tiny maw. It grows a long tongue and real teeth. Its eyes enlarge and protrude, changing from water to air vision, and eyelids develop. Mucous glands form in the skin to keep it from drying out in the air. Bones harden, and the long intestine shortens radically to prepare for an animal diet.

The adult frog or toad is not, as many assume, some primitive evolutionary loser. Arising about 150 million years ago from earlier amphibians, anurans are sophisticated animals and superbly adapted. Tails and ribs have disappeared to make jumping easier (the word *anuran* means "tailless one"); legs have lengthened, and the backbone has shortened to only nine strong vertebrae, the better to cope with the jars of a leaping lifestyle. Leaps may cover a fabulous five to six feet in American bullfrogs. Toads have shorter legs than frogs,

Gray tree frogs' color can vary from a light, mossy gray to light gray-green, according to the backgrounds on which they sit. The patch under the eye helps to distinguish them from other small Ohio frogs. Tree frogs are often stimulated to trill by the approach of rain—or by the sound of propeller-driven airplanes.

and they cannot jump so far. Nevertheless, they can dig backward into the earth quite handily, and their sticky tongues, attached in the front rather than the back of their mouths, can flick out, snag an insect, and flick back in three one-hundredths of a second. Anurans are alert to moving objects, and their hearing is good, as anyone who has failed to grab a green frog at the pond's edge knows.

Male frogs and toads copulate with females by mounting their backs and grasping them around the waist or under the armpits in a grip called amplexus. All except a few primitive species fertilize the eggs externally, the males excreting sperm that are chemically attracted to the eggs. To this basic model, however, is spliced a truly staggering array of strategies for ensuring perpetuation of the many species. These suit various habitats and reduce competition with other kinds of frogs. Many strategies depend on water: frogs spawn in ponds, puddles, streams and torrents, tree-holes and leaf cavities and specially scooped-out pools. Others lay on land and carry their eggs or piggy-back their tadpoles to water.

Most frog eggs are dark with melanin that absorbs the heat of the spring sun and, it is believed, helps protect them from ultraviolet radiation. Here, a leopard frog poses with the newly laid mass of eggs.

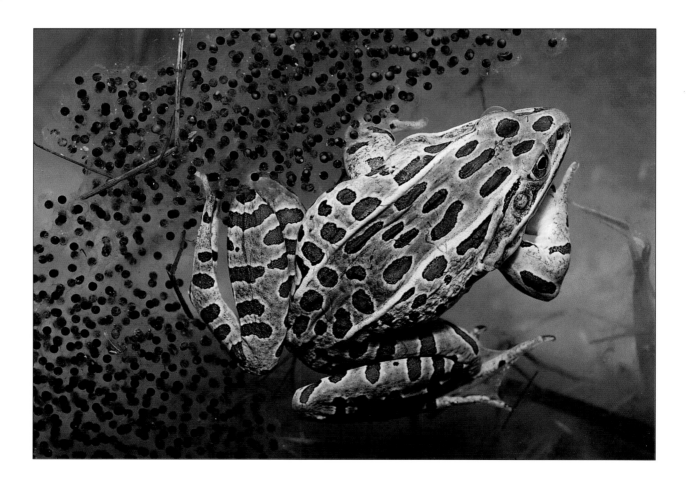

Like many frogs, green frogs may be variously marked—some are greener, some have more pronounced dark mottling. They can be told from small bullfrogs by the lateral ridge shown clearly here. In bullfrogs, the ridge curves around the tympanum, or eardrum, but does not extend down the back.

Still others lay on earth that later floods or deposit eggs in foam nests in trees over ponds or streams, from which tadpoles drop into the water below. Male midwife toads carry eggs wrapped around their hind legs; Surinam toads embed eggs in the skin of females' backs until they hatch; males of Darwin's frog foster young in their vocal sacs and belch them out when they are ready to survive on their own. Tadpoles may mature in mothers' stomachs or in pouches on the back or groin. Poison-arrow frogs—whose skin secretions Amazonian Indians use to tip their darts with death—carry their tadpoles to water pooled in bromeliads' leaves. The mother frogs then visit and lay infertile "food eggs" on which their tadpoles feed. Some frogs lay eggs that hatch directly as tiny adult forms rather than as tadpoles.

Despite the resourcefulness of their cohorts elsewhere in the world, midwestern American frogs are conservative when it comes to making babies. All lay their eggs in water, where they hatch and spend from a couple of weeks to three years as tadpoles before transforming into toadlets or froglets. The main division here is between explosive and extended breeders. Explosive breeders like American and Fowler's toads, spring peepers, and wood frogs converge on breeding ponds *en masse*. Males call frantically to attract females, who arrive singly and stay for briefer periods of time. Males vie hotly for mating privileges and may try to grasp any object of suitable size and shape. I remember watching American toads mate energetically a few years ago in Zaleski State Forest in the Hocking Hills. Several males would try to mount a larger female in passionate free-for-alls. Occasionally females are drowned by the enthusiasm of these would-be mates or succumb to fungus infections caused by skin abrasion from the males' frenzied clasping.

Males of extended breeders like bullfrogs and green frogs stake out territories and defend them for weeks or months. In these species, the females are the ones who choose: usually they select the deepest-voiced, largest males, perhaps because they defend the best territories for offspring's survival. Males of these two species do not usually try amplexus until females approach and touch them. Many female frogs can make what is called a "release call" to notify suitors that they are unready to breed or have bred already; males use this call to discourage other males that may have clasped them in the belief that they are females or in wrestles over territory.

My husband remembers toads as being unexpected creatures, and because of this, magical: they camouflaged themselves so well that when he saw one, at first he didn't believe it. They looked as if they had always belonged where they were. They occasionally fell into basement window wells at my parents' home in Bowling Green without ever losing their amiable composure; they left jellied strands of eggs that hatched miraculously into jet-black tadpoles in the ditches on the way to my school. Green frogs, leopard frogs, and dragonflies animated the waterworks quarry across the street on a sleepy Sunday afternoon. In the Western Reserve, spring peepers and trilling American toads and tree frogs are now my personal measure of spring's birth and passing.

Wild frogs and toads should be part of children's lives and of adults' as well. Mary C. Dickerson, in her 1906 classic, *The Frog Book*, calls bullfrogs the life of the pond. On a more practical note, she observes that an adult toad is believed to eat as many as ten thousand insects a year and says that toads "help to make the home and contribute their share in its work." "We watch their retreating backs until they disappear among rows of beets and lettuce, and we wish them 'good hunting.'" For those who have known real anurans, not simply Kermit or Michigan J. Frog, the Warner Brothers cartoon star, it is sad and unsettling to be warned of their possible silence. We wonder how great the risk to frogs and toads may be.

Unfortunately, definite answers about declines are hard to come by, maybe because historically frogs and toads were at once everywhere and beneath notice. At settlement, the great Lake Erie marshes, the river shallows and oxbow lakes, and the vernal woodland pools must have been full of frogs. Every harrow unearthed a toad or two. Few records were kept, and even that remarkable pioneer naturalist Dr. Jared P. Kirtland described only a few amphibians. Although many herpetologists believe that frogs and toads are declining worldwide, they are starting with very little hard data against which to test their perceptions. Amphibians have always been subject to sudden fluctuations in numbers because of climatic changes and other factors. How to tell the difference between temporary changes and permanent ones? Nevertheless, enough herpetologists became concerned about study subjects that seemed to be disappearing at an alarming rate that by 1990 they began sharing information. Since then, media attention in this country has made their concerns public.

Perhaps as many as one-third of the world's frogs and toads may be affected. Some kinds, like gastric brooding frogs of Australia and golden toads of Costa Rica, have not been found for several years, and it seems unlikely that they will reappear. Whether local conditions like drought or more global threats are to blame is uncertain.

In this country, anurans of the East and West seem most stressed. One informal survey of scientists in the Northeast suggests that as

This male American toad grasps the larger female in a breeding clasp called amplexus. She may lay as many as twenty thousand eggs in long, jellied strands. These hatch into small, black .tadpoles with bulbous heads. Toad tadpoles tend to metamorphose and hop from the water en masse as tiny black toadlets, rather startling to families attempting a waterside picnic. Toads, of course, are harmless to humans and are allies against tent caterpillars and other noxious insects.

many as twelve types of salamanders and eight frogs are decreasing. In that area, acid rain is a suspect. There appear to be limits to the acid levels that eggs and larvae can tolerate. Adults, with permeable skins sensitive to changes in soil acidity, may be hurt as well.

In the mountains of California, Oregon, and Washington, several amphibians, including Yosemite toads, Cascade frogs, leopard frogs, and western toads, diminished in the early 1980s and have not recovered. In California, half the native anurans appear to be in trouble. The California red-legged frog, probably the Daniel Webster of Mark Twain's "Celebrated Jumping Frog of Calaveras County," has disappeared from 75 percent of its range. The reasons for these declines are varied and numerous. One well-constructed study indicates that the eggs of high-altitude frogs and of those in areas closer to the equator are dying because of ultraviolet radiation, possibly as a result of the thinning of the Earth's ozone layer. Midwestern and southeastern U.S. frogs seem to be in better shape. In Ohio, our limy soils are better able to buffer acid rain than are the soils of New England. However, Dr. Timothy Matson, vertebrate zoologist for the Cleveland Museum of Natural History, believes cricket frogs are declining in western Ohio because of intensive agriculture, and other experts share this view.

If we think about the needs of frogs and toads, it seems understandable that our activities have caused them harm. Anurans need wetlands, and 95 percent of Ohio's original swamps and marshes have been filled or drained. Eggs, tadpoles, and aquatic adults need relatively clean water, and we have polluted many streams and lakes. As Roger Conant notes in the Peterson *Guide to Reptiles and Amphibians,* every new housing development, factory, or mall decimates local wildlife. Dumping solid wastes in swamps and marshes, polluting streams with industrial waste and sewage, and spraying the countryside with pesticides all have their effects. Hunting frogs in some parts of the country, stocking nonnative fish, grazing cattle along stream banks, damming and logging, and the capturing and massive transporting of amphibians for pets also must be factors.

On the brighter side, we are finally beginning to notice the plights of animals other than the big, cute ones termed "charismatic megafauna" by professionals. We are beginning to care about what happens to moths and butterflies, frogs and toads, to ask the right questions about them, and to gather data to find the answers, though funding for such efforts is often sadly lacking. Besides contributing money to preservation efforts, there are other things that ordinary people who care about the environment can do. Tim

Matson notes with pleasure the increasing trend for both country and city people to build ponds and water gardens. Although these new wetlands don't help all anurans, they certainly affect some, such as bullfrogs, green frogs, and toads. He also reports that more garden toads seem to be appearing recently, maybe because homeowners are more skeptical now about manicured lawns and heavy chemical treatments. He encourages Ohioans to build backyard ponds and says that these will support toads and frogs and dragonflies even in the city. They also are great for children, who can watch eggs turn to tadpoles and tadpoles to adults; they can be stocked with native fish and are not mosquito breeders if properly planned.

I myself want toads—real toads—in my backyard, and I wouldn't mind a few water lilies, water striders, and dragonflies either. Perhaps we'll invite some in.

ADDITIONAL READINGS

Frogs and Toads of the World by Chris Mattison, Facts on File, 1987.

Ohio's Amphibians by Guy L. Denny, Ohio Department of Natural Resources, no date.

The Book of the Toad by Robert M. DeGraaf, Park Street Press, 1991.

The Amphibians of Ohio: Part 1, Frogs and Toads by Charles F. Walker, 1946.

Tracking the Vanishing Frogs by Kathryn Phillips, Penguin, 1994.

A Field Guide to Reptiles and Amphibians by Roger Conant and Joseph T. Collins, 1991.

"Mr. Froggy Goes a-Courtin'" by Timothy Egan, *The New York Times,* June 9, 1996.

The Frog Book by Mary C. Dickerson, Doubleday, Page, and Company, 1906; reprint, Dover Publications, 1969.

Darters

*S*ay the word *darter*, and you may visualize a small, iridescent bird hovering in a Central-American cloud forest—or perhaps a bright dragonfly hawking for mosquitoes above an Ohio pond. Darters are tiny and quick, but they are not birds or insects; they are small, North American fish. They can often be seen scooting around in clear shallow streams, coming to rest on the bottom on extended fins. Some, especially certain breeding males, sport vivid colors that fade when the fish are taken from water. Because of their diminutive sizes, their vivacious darting behavior, and their bright colors, they are sometimes called the warblers of the fish world.

These little fish are highly evolved members of the perch family. Sports fishers know their larger relatives well: the walleye, the sauger, and the yellow perch. Streamlined bodies, separated dorsal fins, and one or two spines in the anal fin distinguish the perches. The family inhabits both Eurasia and North America but is concentrated in this hemisphere, and darters themselves are strictly American.

Like humans, darters are newcomers on the world scene, having developed during the past million years in the Pleistocene, or Ice Age. They probably began in the Mississippi River Basin. Studies show intricate relationships between their ranges and Ice Age changes in drainage patterns. The advancing and retreating ice probably isolated populations and then allowed them to mingle again. This may have hastened the forming of a wide range of species.

About 150 species are known, organized into three genera: *Percina*, the most primitive; *Ammocrypta*, or sand darters; and *Etheostoma*, the most advanced of these fishes. Because major river systems drained southward in North America—away from the glaciers—many more species of fish survived the long cold here than in Europe, where many large rivers flow northward. Robert Kuehne and Roger Barbour, in *The American Darter*, point out that central Tennessee's Duck River contains more species of strictly freshwater fish than does all of Europe eastward to the Ural Mountains.

Darters have indeed proved very successful. In fact, they are the most numerous fish in North America aside from the minnows. The secret of their abundance seems to be that they have colonized many small ecological niches, mostly in the rather austere environment of stream riffles and raceways. Some live in slab or rock riffles; others inhabit pools with currents. Sand and gravel raceways provide other habitats, and quiet pools yet another. A few have even colonized swampy lakes with muddy bottoms. Within these habitats, species may be midwater swimmers or bottom dwellers that search for food in a variety of specialized niches.

Riffle life offers definite advantages: large predators are barred from these shallow places, and dead leaves and other organic materials catch on the rocks, decompose, and provide food for the microcrustaceans and immature insects like midges and mayflies that form darters' diet. Pool fish must wait for food to wash into their quiet waters; riffle fish can attack it at its source.

Life in fast-moving water is a strenuous matter, however, and darters have adapted accordingly. The lungless salamanders jettisoned the breathing apparatus that made them too buoyant to cope easily with swift-moving mountain streams. Like them, most darters have either reduced the swim bladder that floats many other bony fishes or have abandoned it altogether. Benthic, or bottom-dwelling, forms lack it entirely, and riffle darters also have large pectoral fins, allowing them to wedge themselves in crannies. These outsized fins give the tiny fish a rather comically ruffled look as they dart between resting places.

In general, darters' hues and patterns serve for camouflage. However, many males grow bright between February and June to prepare for spawning. In riffles, where predators are fewer, colors are especially showy. Some species' males establish stationary territories and defend them with spirit. Male variegate darters, rather robust little fish that live in the Ohio River drainage, defend territories around large rocks. They erect their dorsal fins, brighten the horizontal red

Pages 170–71: Male bluebreast darters sport bright red spots on their sides, while females must be content with brown. Breeding males' fins also turn red; bellies are light blue. These darters' specific habitat preferences—fast riffles of large, clear streams at a preferred depth of four to twelve inches—caused their decline as streams were dammed, silted, and polluted with wastes. In Ohio they are now found regularly only in Big Darby Creek west of Columbus.

Right: As its scientific name indicates, the eastern sand darter (*Ammocrypta pellucida)* is partially transparent. Sand darters often bury themselves in sand with only their eyes exposed. This protects them from predators and disguises them from their prey—immature midges and mayflies. The species is steadily declining as silt covers the sandy raceways it requires.

bands on their bellies, thrust out their pectoral fins, and contort their bodies, doing combat by nipping each other's fins until one or the other retreats. Males of other species, such as rainbow darters, define mobile territories around females, who select the oldest, largest, and most colorful suitors.

As to spawning itself, darters use two main strategies. Many females, especially those from the more primitive species, squirm their way into sand or gravel and deposit eggs there, fertilized by attendant males that mount them for the purpose. Others lay eggs on objects such as plants or rocks. Some of the most interesting ones press eggs against the ceilings of rock cavities. In species such as the Johnny and fantail darters, males stay with the fertilized eggs to clean and care for them and to guard them from predators. Male parenting probably confers an advantage on these two successful species.

Declining ecosystems beneath the surfaces of streams and lakes are more easily ignored than those whose destruction confronts us at eye level. It takes a dramatic event like the celebrated lower Cuyahoga River fire of 1969, or the 1970s fight over the snail darter, to rivet attention on the appalling decline of America's aquatic ecosystems. A University of Tennessee ichthyologist, David Etnier, discovered the snail darter in 1973. The three-inch fish was thought to live only in the last thirty-eight miles of the Little Tennessee River and was quickly placed on the endangered species list. However, the Tennessee Valley Authority's Tellico Dam, under construction since 1967 and nearly complete, would submerge the shallow, fast-flowing water the snail darter needed to survive.

A major controversy erupted that involved both conflicting environmental values and the future of the recently passed Endangered Species Act. Proponents of the dam stressed future jobs, recreational values, and production of electricity for twenty thousand homes in poverty-stricken eastern Tennessee. Environmentalists noted that the dam would drown sixteen thousand acres of cropland, inundate two hundred archaeological and historical sites, and destroy a renowned trout fishery. Flood control benefits would be marginal, at best. They took the case to court.

The case went all the way to the U.S. Supreme Court, which ruled six to three in favor of the darter. The fish was an endangered species, the justices reasoned; the river above the dam site was critical habitat; the law forbade operation of the dam. But this was not the end of the story. Congress passed a bill sponsored by Senators Howard Baker of

Tennessee and John Culver of Iowa setting up a board to review requests for exceptions to the Endangered Species Act.

The board promptly ruled unanimously against the dam, arguing that it was economically unjustified, even without reference to archaeological and wildlife losses. Senator Baker then vowed to abolish the panel. Eventually, Baker and other disgruntled members of Congress simply wrote a blanket exemption from all federal regulations, including Occupational Safety and Health laws and workers' compensation, for the Tellico Dam. They attached the exemption as a rider to a public works bill that Jimmy Carter signed into law, admitting that he was bowing to public pressure in an election year. Ironically, Etnier, the ichthyologist who discovered the snail darter in 1973, and TVA divers located three new populations of snail darters in Tennessee by 1981.

For many Americans, the snail darter was the spotted owl of the 1970s. Inevitably, dam proponents reduced the issue to dam vs. insignificant fish. The larger controversy, of course, was over the question of protecting whole ecosystems under siege by development. At

Though a small fish, the logperch is the largest of the darters. Like its bigger relatives, the sauger and walleye, this fish shows the streamlined body and separated dorsal fins of the perch family. Its elongated snout, which has earned it the inelegant common name of "hogfish," is used to turn over small stones in the search for invertebrate food. Female logperch deposit eggs while vibrating their bodies and burying themselves in sand or gravel.

that time, the Little Tennessee was one of a very few free-flowing rivers left in the state. Today, its character has changed completely: it snakes across the map of eastern Tennessee as an enormous, elongated reservoir with relatively impoverished aquatic life. Fortunately, the snail darter controversy may have helped derail the Columbia Dam project proposed for the richly diverse Duck River that still flows in the central part of the state. As Dan Rice, chief zoologist for the Ohio Department of Natural Resources, says, "I like to think that dams are harder to build today than they were back then—at least for the present."

Other darters besides the snail darter have suffered from habitat degradation. For example, sand darters are declining in many places, as the sand substrates that they rely on are silted in by farm runoff. The Tippecanoe darter is diminishing across most of its relatively broad range, and other species that inhabit restricted ranges are especially at risk. Their plight resembles that of many others of the fishes that thronged the Ohio Country's waters at the time of settlement, species that required clear, unsilted, unpolluted waters to thrive.

Milton B. Trautman, whose life spanned most of this century, never finished high school, but his sharp curiosity about fishes eventually netted him two honorary doctorates and a full professorship at Ohio State University. To read Trautman's 1957 classic, *Fishes of Ohio,* is to realize the magnitude of Ohio fishes' destruction. Two hundred years ago, Ohio streams ran in narrow, deep stream banks, well stabilized and shaded by trees and other plants. Fallen trunks and branches provided hiding places for fish. Waters ran clear, and bottoms were mostly clean, unsilted sand, gravel, or boulders. The water table lay near the surface, and many springs fed the rivers year round, keeping flows relatively even.

The waters teemed with food fishes: muskellunge, drum, walleye, sauger, spotted black bass, sturgeon, buffalo fish, carpsuckers, yellow and black cat, and others. One observer related that near Fort Hamilton in Butler County in 1793, he and other soldiers "caught 2500 weight of Fish and about as many on the 4th, which makes 5000 weight in two nights." Another observer described the fishes at the rapids of the Maumee River in 1815 as follows: "So numerous are they at this place, that a spear may be thrown into the water at random, and will rarely miss killing one! I saw several hundred taken in this manner in a few hours. The soldiers of the fort used to kill them in great quantities, with clubs and stones. Some days there were not less than 1000 taken with the hook within a short distance of the fort, and of an excellent quality."

Opposite: Notice the color of the rocks on which this splendidly colored rainbow darter breeding male is resting: rainbow darters' colors may vary according to the rocks beneath them. Adults like swift riffles over coarse gravel or rubble, and they often gather in large numbers there. The young shelter in quieter waters. Rainbow darters' wide distribution—from Minnesota east to New York and south to northern Arkansas, Alabama, and Georgia—may reflect the influence of Pleistocene glaciation. Darters make pleasant, inquisitive little aquarium fish, but the males' colors fade without expertly controlled temperatures and light cycles.

Since then, cutting of trees along stream banks has hastened bank erosion, and rivers have become wider and shallower. Dams have cut off access to spawning grounds. Many streams have been ditched and channelized and the wetlands that fed them drained. Forest removal and bad farming methods have choked the rivers with silt, suffocating many fish and their eggs. Sewage, industrial pollution, farm wastes, fertilizers that cause oxygen depletion, pesticides, herbicides, detergents, and burgeoning trash have all taken their tolls. Aquatic plants have declined greatly. Highways have replaced some streams, and runoff from fields and urban areas has escalated flooding. A lowered water table causes the same rivers that flood during wet weather to dwindle during drought.

These drastic changes have changed the fishes too, thinning their numbers and shifting species composition away from those requiring clear waters and abundant plants to those tolerant of turbid water and silty bottoms. Trautman also noted a shift from large fish of great value for food to types of little or no value for human consumption. By the turn of the century, commercial fishing was forbidden in inland waters other than the Great Lakes; by 1965 the great fishing industry of Lake Erie was no more, and the lake itself was pronounced dead. Trautman's career as witness to these changes could not have been an easy one.

The last decade has seen some improvements. Control of industrial pollutants has started Lake Erie on the road back to viability, though great problems remain. Better sewage treatment has improved water quality in the Scioto River and even in the lower Cuyahoga. Public awareness of wetland preservation, soil conservation, and water quality issues in general has improved. Yet the population pressures increase, and more and more of Ohio is ravaged by suburban sprawl every year.

Darters and other clear water fish do survive in Ohio streams, especially the few whose water quality remains relatively high. Darter and freshwater mussel enthusiasts name the Kokosing, Walhonding, and Muskingum rivers in east-central Ohio, Big and Little Darby creeks in west-central Ohio, and Ohio Brush Creek in the southern part of the state as among the best Ohio streams for aquatic life. Big and Little Darby, soon to join the Little Miami River and Little Beaver Creek in the National Wild and Scenic River System, have received publicity lately for the broadly based coalition that is working to improve their water quality and protect their aquatic systems. Especially threatened is Big Darby because of siltation caused by intensive agriculture, suburban development in Franklin County, and also industrial pollution.

Big Darby Creek is home to eighty-six species of fish, twelve of which are rare or endangered, and to forty species of freshwater mussels, eleven of which are rare or endangered. The 550-square-mile watershed also hosts one hundred seventy species of birds and thirty-four of mammals. About twenty organizations in the Big Darby Partnership are working with farmers to reduce silting of the stream through conservation tillage techniques; they are also encouraging grassed waterways and tree lines along the creek. In 1990, the Nature Conservancy, a more than forty-year-old conservation society that concentrates on saving habitats, included Big Darby Creek among twelve "Last Great Places" in the Americas that it believes should be preserved through broad-based local partnerships of public and private agencies. They chose the ecosystems based on their environmental significance, their uniqueness, the likelihood that they can be preserved, and local interest. In 1994, the national Environmental Protection Agency included the stream in its Ecological Risk Assessment Program, a study of five of the country's best ecosystems.

Like Johnny darter males, fantail darter males care for eggs laid by the females on the bottoms of rocks. Knobs on the first dorsal fin, visible here, are thought to aid in cleaning and caring for the eggs. Ichthyologists also believe that fantails may secrete a protective mucus that kills bacteria and fungi. Milton Trautman reported that fantails were formerly abundant in the prairie streams of northwestern Ohio and in shoals around the Erie islands. They can tolerate low oxygen for a time, which gives them an advantage when water levels drop. These darters are still fairly widespread, preferring shallow riffles but moving downstream to deeper water in winter.

Iowa darters are limited to glacial lakes. This specialization has not served them well in a time of draining, degradation of these lakes by farm runoff, and real estate development. Iowa darters were thought to be extirpated from Ohio until, after intensive study, experts rediscovered them in a few lakes.

Three rare darters—the spotted, the bluebreast, and the Tippecanoe—as well as many others, inhabit Big Darby. They are joined by several rare mussels, two of which, the northern riffleshell and the Club shell, have recently been placed on the endangered species list. Many mussels take advantage of their relationships with fish: their larvae attach to gills and skins of host fish and live parasitically until they transform into their adult forms. Under natural conditions, they apparently do their hosts little harm. Michael Hoggarth, an Otterbein College mussel specialist, reports seeing a female northern riffleshell displaying her soft anatomy enticingly to fool a fish into thinking it was striking at a minnow. As the fish darted toward her, she released a cloud of larvae, some of which must have succeeded in hitching a ride. Though it seems clear that *Epioblasma triqueta,* the snuff box mussel, parasitizes the logperch, largest of the darters, as well as the mottled sculpin, no one knows the host species of the northern riffleshell, although it is almost certainly a riffle species of fish.

We know little about these fascinating relationships and even less of the rich array that have disappeared since settlement. Only recently have ichthyologists turned from taxonomic studies of darters to concentrate on their behavior and their roles in complex aquatic ecosystems. Darters may be called the warblers of the fish world, but they and the other clear water organisms of the few remaining free-flowing streams have also been compared to another kind of bird: the sensitive mine canary that warned of deadly gases by its own death. Darters grew up with us during the million-year trial by ice. Losing these pretty evolutionary companions would be a shame and perhaps a portent of our own demise as well.

ADDITIONAL READING

Handbook of Darters by Lawrence M. Page, TFH Publications, 1983.

The American Darter by Robert A. Kuehne and Roger W. Barbour, University Press of Kentucky, 1983.

The Fishes of Ohio by Milton B. Trautman, Ohio State University Press, 1981 (revised edition).

Bright
Shiners

I am the wiser in respect to all knowledges, and the better qualified for all fortunes, for knowing that there is a minnow in the brook. Methinks I have need even of his sympathy, and to be his fellow in a degree.

—Henry David Thoreau

Pages 182–83: Like the darters of the perch family, little minnows called shiners have successfully colonized many small aquatic niches. Also like some darters, types of shiners that have adapted to very specialized habitats have suffered under pressures of pollution, siltation, and development. Other kinds, like these schooling central striped shiners, have more generalized requirements and tolerate higher turbidity and pollution than can many of their kin. In some places, they are replacing them.

*I*f determined by numbers of species, the tribe of minnows, or *Cyprinidae,* is the most successful family of fishes: 1,500 species wriggle in the bait buckets of the world, about 250 in North America. Though many of us refer to any small freshwater fish as a minnow, some true minnows are actually quite large. They include the Colorado squawfish, a predaceous member of the family that once reached five to six feet long, as well as common carp that sometimes weigh as much as thirty or forty pounds. Large goldfish are also minnows. Nevertheless, most members *are* tiny: the name itself derives from the Anglo-Saxon word *myne,* meaning small.

One branch of the family, the shiners—mostly of the genus *Notropis*—are all small, averaging about two to four inches long. Coloration explains their name: most are silvery little fish, though the males of some kinds display gaudy colors during the breeding season. Like other minnows, shiners have made good in North America. In fact, more than one hundred species of *Notropis* inhabit the *Atlas of North American Freshwater Fishes.* Their secret is adaptability: like the American darters, they have evolved to fit many of the small freshwater environmental niches available to fishes on this continent.

What makes a minnow? Minnows live almost everywhere, eat just about anything available, and behave in a myriad of ways. They are very fertile: a female may produce anywhere from a few thousand to half a million or more eggs in one season, enabling some populations to recover quickly after droughts, oil spills, or other disasters. Minnows have no teeth in their mouths. Instead, they carry pharyngeal, or "throat," teeth that shred animal prey or, in vegetarian species, grind up plant matter.

Another of the family's adaptations involves acute hearing: minnows and a few other fishes possess a series of small bones, the Weberian ossicles, that connect their swim bladders to their inner ears. This linking of a vibrating membrane to the ear gives minnows keener hearing than that of most other fish. Because of this feature, shiners can use sound as part of their courtship rituals, much as birds

do. We humans are oblivious of such watery songs because sound waves travel poorly between water and air. Minnows also secrete "fright substances," chemical pheromones that signal danger to nearby fish of the same species and trigger evasive action.

As the Ice Age ended and the continental glaciers melted, shiners were ready to make their move. From centers of abundance on the Atlantic and Gulf coastal plains, they pioneered northward to claim newly available territory; new niches and frequent isolating of populations created many new species and subspecies. Today, the shiners of Ohio exploit a great variety of watery habitats. Some, like golden shiners, prefer the clear, quiet waters of slow streams, oxbow lakes, beaver ponds, and larger lakes with abundant water plants. Others, silver shiners for example, like streams with higher gradients and faster water with clean bottoms of gravel or boulders. Rosefin shiners choose clear streams with limy bottoms, and glacial lakes are home to blackchin shiners. Emerald shiners and spotfin shiners deal with turbid water better than most of their relatives do and are abundant in a state in which clear streams and lakes are now rare.

Above: These common shiners are breeding males. Like many other minnows, common shiners are gregarious and travel in schools, which may dart and turn as if organisms themselves. Schools confer several advantages: a fragmenting school confuses and frustrates predators. One that spreads out can also locate food, such as patches of plankton, more easily than single fish can. Schooling may also increase breeding success and swimming efficiency. In the eastern United States, several types of minnows may school together, with different species taking various positions. This apparently reduces predation by making schools larger.

Not only have these little fishes developed many substrate, water quality and speed-of-current preferences, but different species tend to feed in their own ways on their own food items in their own areas of streams or lakes. Although a few eat algae and detritus, most shiners are day feeders on small insects, crustaceans, and various kinds of plankton, but they hunt them in different parts of the water. Rosyface, silver, striped, and many other shiners are midwater feeders; sand and mimic shiners forage on sandy bottoms near shorelines, where large predators can't swim; and pugnose shiners are surface feeders. Some may even leap into the air for insects. Small differences in species' mouths indicate these varied feeding habits: emerald shiners have slightly upturned mouths and feed more on the surface; bigmouth shiners tend to feed on the bottom, and their mouths point downward; midwater feeders have straight mouths.

In spring, many males sport breeding colors to rival those of aquarium fish. Some of their names reflect this seasonal gaudiness: red and redfin shiners, bleeding shiner, warpaint shiner, and taillight shiner are examples. Bright colors seem to attract females but may also draw predators. This is probably why only males wear bright colors and only during breeding. Red seems to be especially favored because females can see it well close up in bright light. However, because of the way water absorbs the red end of the spectrum, this color is less visible than others to predators from a distance or when the shiner is in the shade of overhanging branches. Like other minnows and suckers, shiners also develop tubercles—small hard projections on head or fins useful for attracting and stimulating mates and identifying competitors. Whether or not the little fishes use them for combat, as stags use their antlers, is less certain.

Shiners, like other minnows, practice many breeding and egg-laying strategies. Some, like the golden shiner, simply broadcast eggs that stick to underwater plants. Others hide eggs in crevices or, like the spotfin shiner, on the undersides of objects. (This behavior keeps eggs from being silted under, which helps explain why the spotfin tolerates greater turbidity than many of its relatives do.) Various shiners spawn opportunistically in the pebbly nests assembled by other fish, like the hornyhead chub, creek chub, and the stoneroller, or sometimes even in those guarded by largemouth bass. Researchers have found that milt and ovarian fluids of some other fishes stimulate certain minnows to spawn in turn.

Shiners' adaptability once served them well in conquering post-glacial rivers and lakes. Unfortunately, playing specialized roles in particular habitats can harm many, now that we humans have

Opposite above: Spotfin shiners, common across the state, have slightly deeper bodies than many other shiners do. However, they still show features of what ichthyologists call the "rover-predator" type of fish: torpedo-shaped body, widely separated pairs of pectoral and pelvic fins, and forked tail. These tiny hunters' upturned mouths show them to be surface feeders, where they subsist mostly on terrestrial insects that have fallen into the water.

Opposite below: The big eyes of these popeye shiners mark them as sight feeders that need clear water to survive. This species was thought to be extirpated from Ohio until a population was identified in southern Ohio's Scioto Brush Creek in 1983. Observers had earlier thought them to be similar bigeye shiners.

The head of this central striped shiner, a common species in Ohio, clearly shows breeding tubercles, most developed in many males in the spring. Also visible are the gill covers, or opercula. These not only protect the gills, but, along with the mouth, are part of the fish's system for pumping aerated water over the gills in a steady stream. In the gills, oxygen crosses from the water into blood vessels by osmosis, and carbon dioxide, ammonia, and other wastes are eliminated. This exchange system surpasses humans' in efficiency, enabling fish to live on the low level of oxygen found in water. Unfortunately, the gills' efficiency leaves fish vulnerable to pollutants.

changed waterways so drastically. Sewage and farm run-off have wiped out the blackchin shiners that once lived in pristine glacial lakes. Heavy silt in the Maumee River eroding from northwestern Ohio farms has driven the popeye shiner from that river system. Pugnose minnows (which should actually be called shiners) are reduced in Ohio to a single population in Nettle Lake—these little fish require clear water and healthy beds of water plants to live.

Muddy water especially hampers sight feeders like bigeye and popeye shiners, and many others. Ironically, the bottom grubbing of their big cousin, the common carp, is sometimes the reason for muddy water. Carp were introduced from Asia via Europe late in the nineteenth century and are now common. The grass carp, another Asian immigrant, eats water plants voraciously and has been planted in some Ohio lakes to control water weeds. However, it also cleans out beds of plants needed by many other species, both minnows and important sport fishes, and must be used with caution, if at all. Farm clearing of stream-bank vegetation, runoff from shopping malls and highways, and many other factors also heavily influence the lives of Ohio fishes, including shiners, and many have declined.

Most of us do not spend much time contemplating the intricate lives of minnows or the aquatic systems that support them. Learning something about such hidden lives can perhaps nurture in us some of Thoreau's need "even of [the minnow's] sympathy, and to be his fellow in a degree." Possibly, over the long run, such knowledge will modify our destructive human behavior toward all fishes, including the humble shiner.

Below: Emerald shiners are more tolerant of turbid water than are many of their kin, and they are common in Lake Erie. Like other shiners, they play an important role in nature because they consume small invertebrates and, in turn, provide meals for larger fish and for birds such as herons.

ADDITIONAL READING

The Fishes of Ohio by Milton B. Trautman, Ohio State University Press, 1981.

Fish: An Enthusiast's Guide by Peter B. Moyle, University of California Press, 1993.

Fish Watching: An Outdoor Guide to Freshwater Fishes by C. Lavett Smith, Cornell University Press, 1994.

Butterflies

*L*ike other animals, butter-
flies feature largely in human myths, our explanations of the world
and our place in it. Threatening animals, such as wolves and snakes,
howl and slither through our collective nightmares; on them we
project our fear of the dark forces in nature and ourselves. Butterflies, on the other hand, almost always speak to us of pleasant things:
beauty, color, effortless motion, freedom.

Children's stories teem with butterflies, and with their close relatives, the fairies. The insect's incredible transformation from ugly
worm to lovely winged creature appears worldwide as a compelling
symbol of change—either in this life or in one to come. In the
Greek myth of Eros and Psyche, the gods reward Psyche for her
steadfastness by granting her butterfly wings and immortality; death
was sometimes shown in art as a butterfly emerging from the lips
and flying away. The Greek word for soul and butterfly (psyche) was
the same.

Today, butterflies often represent to us pretty, nostalgic aspects of
nature. We remember childhood days chasing them amidst idealized

landscapes gone beneath the asphalt of urban sprawl. We think with nostalgia of sunny afternoons with orange butterflies flickering above alfalfa fields or brilliant swallowtails nectaring on lilac bushes as highlights of our lives.

With such positive images of these insects, one would think we would want to protect them, and many of us do. However, our romanticism about butterflies and ignorance about them can prevent us from understanding their needs, which are often very specialized, and the forces that can cause their decline. Yet the facts about their life cycles—still imperfectly understood—are even more fascinating than human attitudes about these beautiful creatures. Knowing about butterflies' relations with food plants, with predators, with climate and weather, and, of course, with humans, can help us to enjoy them more and to take action for their survival in this age of biological crisis. Since the early 1980s we have seen a significant change in how people think about butterflies in Ohio and an increased activity toward conserving them.

Imagine a common sulphur *(Colias philodice)*—one of those medium-sized yellow butterflies of sunny open meadows, parks, and pastures—laying her eggs on clover. This is the culmination (or the beginning, depending on how you look at it) of a very stylized set of behaviors. Butterflies are not free, as we like to think of them. They live their lives according to instincts formed during a very long evolution, and their lives are enmeshed in intricate relationships with the world around them and with other organisms. Central to that evolution is a complex interplay between species and the plants their caterpillars, or larvae, feed on.

This spicebush swallowtail larva mounts a convincing imitation of a small, gaudy snake with great, menacing eyes. It is all a bluff: the eyes are fake, and the caterpillar is harmless, though swallowtail larvae are great performers, thrashing about, erecting equally fake horns and giving off bad smells if disturbed. Complete metamorphosis, the transformation from worm-like larva to ethereally winged adult, enables lepidoptera to exploit two very different niches: caterpillars browse on leaves; adults live primarily on nectar.

Many large, dark-colored butterflies in Ohio look remarkably alike. This black swallowtail closely resembles the spicebush swallowtail and, more importantly, the pipevine swallowtail. It is an example of what experts call Batesian mimicry: the pipevine swallowtail is poisonous because its larvae feed on toxic *Aristolochia* (pipevine) leaves. Predators learn not to eat these poisonous insects, and the harmless black and spicebush swallowtails fly beneath the pipevine's protective umbrella. Females of the tiger swallowtail also have a dark phase that looks much more like the pipevine swallowtail than like their yellow-marked brothers and sisters. In southern Ohio as many as 50 percent of female tigers are dark, or melanic. Even the unrelated red-spotted purple and female Diana fritillary butterflies have evolved to mimic the pipevine swallowtail. This black swallowtail, covered with dew, will have to bask in order to warm its muscles enough to fly.

This little yellow butterfly lays, or oviposits, only on plants of the legume family, especially clover. These have the chemical properties her larvae need to thrive. The legumes' unique chemical makeup, developed to stave off insects' attacks, would kill most other larvae if they could be induced to eat. This relationship between the common sulphur and clover cuts down on competition from other species for the butterfly. The female apparently identifies the correct food plant by sight and smell, but especially by taste. She "tastes" the leaves or flower buds with receptors in her feet.

These mating buckeye butterflies belong to the Nymphalidae, or brush-footed butterflies. This is a large family, named for their first pair of legs, tiny and useless for walking, and hairy in males. Buckeyes are common in Ohio, inhabiting roadsides, railroad embankments, old fields, and other open places. Like many species, they produce double broods each year, or even triple broods in southern parts of the state. They cannot winter in the North. In October, at places on the East Coast like Cape May, New Jersey, their southward floating numbers rival those of migrating monarchs.

Other butterflies are equally or even more specific in their requirements for larval food plants. The gorgeous blue-washed pipevine swallowtail *(Battus philenor)* lays only on species of *Aristolochia,* or pipevine. Monarch butterflies *(Danaus plexippus)* confine themselves to various milkweeds. These two types of plants confer an added advantage on the butterflies: the larvae absorb chemicals that are extremely distasteful, even poisonous to birds and other predators. A young bluejay generally eats and regurgitates a monarch butterfly only once or twice.

Because birds avoid monarchs, the toothsome viceroy *(Limenitis archippus)*, a distantly related species whose larvae feed on willows, has evolved to look so like the monarch that few predators (or humans) can tell the difference. South of the monarch's range, in Florida, the viceroy changes its spots, so to speak, to mimic the queen butterfly *(Danaus gilippus),* a cousin of the monarch that also eats milkweed. A whole group of swallowtails—the spicebush *(Papilio troilus),* the black *(Papilio polyxenes),* and some female tiger swallowtails *(Papilio glaucus),* as well as other butterflies such as the red-spotted purple *(Limenitis arthemis astyanax)* and the female Diana fritillary *(Speyeria diana)*—are thought to mimic the poisonous pipevine swallowtail, thereby gaining a survival advantage.

Of course, the plants themselves keep evolving defenses to avoid being eaten by caterpillars. Lepidopterists have compared the whole relationship to an arms race played out over eons of time. Through mutation, plants develop new chemical compounds that may repulse insects that feed on them. But this is not the only strategy in their repertoire. Certain passionflowers, food plants of tropical *Heliconius* or longwing butterflies, possess nectar glands outside their flowers. These attract ants that seem to discourage the butterflies from laying or that may attack feeding larvae. Other plants deploy hook-like hairs that puncture and trap the larvae's stumpy prolegs, bleeding and starving them to death. On the other hand, some larvae have apparently evolved methods such as weaving silk over the hairs to subvert these defenses.

Female butterflies inspect leaves carefully to avoid laying on plants that harbor predators or parasites or even eggs of the same species that would compete with their own offspring. The passionflower plants in return have evolved fake yellow eggs to discourage the laying of real ones. A recent issue of the Ohio Lepidopterists' newsletter reports that some mustard family plants in this area also produce small, wartlike growths that look like the eggs of the white butterflies whose larvae feed on them. The above examples only hint at the fascinating relationships played out between butterflies and larval hosts; somewhat less complex ones exist between adult butterflies and the flowers from which they gather nectar and which they benefit by pollinating.

The larva or caterpillar, as many have pointed out, has one essential job: to eat enormously. It is basically an animated gut, with fairly simple senses and body structures. It eats and moults and eats and moults until it has stored enough protein to supply the needs of adulthood, when it will live mainly on the starches and sugars of nectar. We can be thankful that butterflies have chosen this way of supplying protein for producing eggs, rather than the bloodier strategies used by biting flies, mosquitoes, and ticks. A cartoon shows a couple sitting on their porch, surrounded by masses of butterfly wings. She says to him, "The butterflies are merciless today!"

Classifying Butterflies

Butterflies and moths make up the large group, or order, Lepidoptera, with about 165,000 known species worldwide: 150,000 moths and 15,000 to 20,000 butterflies. Moths are thought to have diverged from stoneflies about 215 million years ago, butterflies from moths 50 million years ago. Some people say that butterflies are just a subgroup of moths that evolved to fly during the day. No one feature always tells the two apart, but butterflies' lack of a frenulum, a structure that links moths' forewings to hindwings, and their antennae with small clubs on the ends are the most reliable clues. (Moths' antennae are either slender threads or feathery leaf-shapes.)

Lepidopterists classify butterflies as "true butterflies" (Papilionoidea) or as skippers (Hesperioidea), and they divide these two superfamilies into from four to twelve families. Here is one widely accepted classification: Papilionidae (swallowtails and parnassians, thought to be the most primitive butterflies), Pieridae (whites and sulphurs), Lycaenidae or gossamer-wings (hairstreaks, blues, coppers, elfins, and metalmarks), Nymphalidae or brushfoots (a large, highly evolved family including anglewings, ladies, admirals, fritillaries, checkers and crescents, milkweed butterflies such as the monarch, satyrs, and snout butterflies, among others), Hesperiidae (skippers), and Megathymidae (giant skippers).

Caterpillars are succulent morsels, with soft bodies and limited movement. Many predators—birds, spiders, flies, wasps, ants, small mammals, and others—covet them. To survive these onslaughts, butterfly larvae have evolved many stratagems over the ages. Many rely on hiding and camouflage. Slender green European cabbage white larvae *(Pieris rapae)* are hard to see on green leaves or especially under stems. The viceroy caterpillar artfully disguises itself as a bit of bird dropping. Some larvae resemble flower petals or even twigs.

Others depend on a variety of warning devices and outright bluffs. The caterpillars of monarchs, queens, pipevine swallowtails, and other poisonous species flaunt bright colors and striking patterns: it is to their advantage for predators to recognize them. Some large but inoffensive swallowtail larvae sport big fake eyes to make them look dangerous, and if disturbed raise their forebodies and thrash about wildly. They also extrude hornlike structures called osmeteria and exude smells unpleasant to predators. These bluffs can be impressive enough to scare off people as well as animals.

Smaller organisms such as fungi, bacteria, and viruses also attack caterpillars, as do insect parasitoids—flies and wasps that lay eggs under the larva's cuticle, and whose own larvae eat the unfortunate creature from within. In *The Life of the Caterpillar,* the great French entomologist J. H. Fabre describes tiny ichneumonid wasps' parasitizing of European cabbage white larvae in gruesome detail. Some kinds of caterpillars sport bristles which may help protect them from these attacks, and others feed beneath communal webs. Despite these defenses, few caterpillars complete the chancy transformation to adulthood.

Adults face their own threats from birds, lizards, spiders and insects that lurk among the flowers where they nectar, and others. I once watched a small chipmunk staring at a low-flying swallowtail and leaping at it with clearly murderous intent. Most butterflies' lower wing surfaces sport cryptic patterns that camouflage them when they sit at rest. Eye spots decorate many wings and encourage birds to peck at them rather than at the real head or other vital parts.

Though the facts of these evolutionary battles between plant and insect, predator and prey, take us far from an idealized picture of the carefree butterfly, they describe an infinitely more interesting creature. They also help us understand some of the natural controls on insect populations, rather than relying on insecticides as the only way to protect our flowers, vegetables, and forests. Controlled by natural forces, butterfly larvae seldom become serious pests, though certain moths, especially the infamous gypsy, cause more damage. The growing ranks of butterfly gardeners have learned that in most cases, they can plant enough flowers and vegetables for their own and for butterflies' enjoyment, as well. The general rule is think carefully before you spray.

Weather and climate also limit butterfly populations. Drought can shrivel the succulent plants on which larvae depend. More importantly, wet weather drowns caterpillars and encourages fungi and infections; a cool, wet spring predicts scarcer butterflies the following year. Adults have developed a whole series of interesting behaviors to deal with weather. Most butterflies fly only on sunny days, even when the thermometer reads in the low 70s. This is because, unlike mammals, they are "cold-blooded," or exothermic, rather than "warm-blooded," or endothermic. They must spend a lot of time basking to warm their flight muscles. Storms kill many fragile butterflies, and they are acutely aware of weather changes. A landscape busy with seemingly carefree butterflies can empty in a trice when a cloud passes over the sun, as the insects drop like stones and take cover beneath leaves and stems. Arctic butterflies burrow into tundra mosses and lichens for shelter.

The Baltimore gains its name from the first Lord Baltimore, because its orange and black colors match those on his heraldic shield. Its distribution is localized, since it sticks close to its wetland host plants. The bright markings, typical of those on other checkerspots, as the group is called, warn that the insect is toxic. Actually, only Baltimores whose larvae feed on the preferred food plant, turtlehead, are poisonous. Plantain and white ash, other hosts, do not confer the same protection—but who's to know?

Temperate zone species, not to mention arctic butterflies, must also cope with long, cold winters. Most enter hibernation, or diapause, and they do so at all stages of the life cycle. Some overwinter as eggs. Larvae of viceroys, red admirals *(Vanessa atalanta)*, red-spotted purples, and others of their group roll leaves around themselves like sleeping bags, securing them with silk. The leaves both protect and camouflage. Many butterflies, including swallowtails, winter as pupae in the chrysalids from which they will later emerge as adults. These chrysalids themselves sport many forms and cryptic patterns to hide them from predators active even in deep winter. Anglewing butterflies like the comma *(Polygonia comma)* and question mark *(Polygonia interrogationis)* crawl beneath bark or seek shelter in sheds or hollow trees and hibernate as adults. So do mourning cloaks *(Nymphalis antiopa)* and other tortoiseshell butterflies. This is why you can see the rich maroon and creamy yellow of

The "eyespots" on the forewings or hindwings of butterflies like this common wood nymph are among the several "tricks" that can fool predators. Although the fake eyes may sometimes intimidate, their more important function is to induce a bird to peck at what it thinks is the insect's head and to miss its real vital parts. Butterflies can sometimes be seen flying with beak-shaped wedges clipped out of their wings.

mourning cloaks wafting between the still-leafless trees of the very earliest warm spring days.

Monarch butterflies both migrate and hibernate. They make their famous journey to the volcanic mountains of Mexico each autumn, where they gather in the millions and hibernate in groves of evergreens. West coast monarchs winter in coastal Californian eucalyptus groves. Other butterflies, such as the handsome orange, black, and white painted lady *(Vanessa cardui)* and the clear yellow cloudless sulphur *(Phoebis sennae),* make one-way migrations. They cannot survive northern winters, so they fly north during the warm months, sometimes in large masses. Their offspring may or may not return south before the next winter.

Of the approximately 700 American butterfly species, 144 have been reported in Ohio, so far. Some, like the eastern black swallowtail, the great spangled fritillary *(Speyeria cybele)*, the monarch, and the European cabbage white, have appeared in all eighty-eight counties. Others, like three very rare butterflies that feed on lupine in the oak openings west of Toledo, may inhabit only one. People's perceptions that there are fewer butterflies than they remember as children are partly correct: air pollution, asphalt, and pesticides can be as unfriendly to these insects as they are to other plants and animals.

However, though some butterflies are definitely in trouble, others have actually increased and extended their ranges. These are often the generalists, whose larvae can eat a wider range of food plants, or species well adapted to brushy waste areas and old fields. If we leave our own asphalt jungles and explore grassroot jungles, as naturalist Edwin Way Teale called them, we find many of our childhood butterflies waiting for us there. Butterflies meet many survival challenges with great success. Their reproductive strategy of many eggs in multiple broods pits high production against high mortality, as do the strategies of many other insects. Such behavior can even mitigate some of the effects of the millions of tons of pesticides we dump on the land every year. Nevertheless, the masses of butterflies and moths in unsprayed parts of the Appalachians, such as Great Smoky Mountains National Park, testify to the harm concentrated agriculture and massive spraying do to butterflies in Ohio.

The destruction of habitat is a bigger threat to butterflies than spraying is. Those Ohio butterflies most in danger of extirpation are the specialists: the ones dependent on larval food plants that grow in places like wetlands, most of which have been drained or developed. Ohio has lost 90 to 95 percent of its original wetlands, a sad record second only to California's. Several of Ohio's rarest butterflies, the swamp metalmark *(Calephelis muticum)*, the purplish copper *(Epidemia helloides)*, the silver-bordered fritillary *(Boloria selene)*, are wetland species. Mitchell's satyr *(Neonympha mitchellii)* and the mustard white *(Pieris napi)* have already been extirpated in Ohio. Protecting rare butterflies and other endangered species means protecting and managing rare habitat, two complex and demanding tasks.

The larvae of another group of endangered butterflies, the Karner blue *(Lycaeides melissa samuelis)*, the Persius duskywing *(Erynnis persius)*, and the frosted elfin *(Incisalia irus)*, depend on the lupine, a plant that is itself threatened in Ohio. They are known only from the oak openings, a sand-barren community stretching west of Toledo on the old beach ridges formed by glacial lakes. Lepidopterists now believe that the Karner blue, first scientifically described by the famous writer and lepidopterist Vladimir Nabokov, has disappeared from the state, and survival of the other two species is precarious. Their story illustrates the delicate balance between organism and biological community and the need for our informed management of habitats.

Much of the oak openings is now developed or in parkland, and the wildfires that once kept areas of country open were vigorously suppressed during the past fifty years. Trees began to invade. Lupine requires sun, and the Karner blue even more so. When shrubs and small trees began to shade out lupines, the little blue butterflies refused to lay eggs on the plants, and their numbers plummeted. The Toledo Metroparks and The Nature Conservancy, which administers nearby Kitty Todd Preserve, have worked out controlled burning strategies that may save the Persius duskywing and the frosted elfin. There are also plans to reintroduce the Karner blue from a nearby, genetically similar population in southern Michigan.

Two more rare butterflies, the grizzled skipper *(Pyrgus centaureae wyandot)* and the Olympia marblewing *(Euchloe olympia)*, fly in

Members of this gorgeous "puddle club" of tiger swallowtails are probably not just replenishing their supply of water. Largely male, puddling butterflies may be sipping organic matter supplied from urine or feces, which offers amino acids absent from their usual diet of nectar. In fact, butterflies enjoy tree sap, rotting fruit, and carrion as well. Masses of butterflies are commoner in areas without heavy spraying, such as Adams County.

small clearings on ridgetops in the oak-hickory forests of southeastern Ohio. Their isolation in these small areas makes them especially vulnerable to the other major threat facing native Ohio butterflies and moths: gypsy moth control efforts. Also at risk is the rich brown and orange-colored regal fritillary *(Speyeria idalia)*, a threatened species whose numbers are falling for reasons we do not completely understand—probably loss of tallgrass prairie habitat combined with other factors such as air pollution.

The gypsy moth *(Lymantria dispar)*, introduced into Massachusetts in 1869 from abroad, is infamous for the swaths of denuded trees, especially oaks, that major outbreaks leave behind. Those who have seen such stripped trees in Pennsylvania and other eastern states don't soon forget them. Small infestations have existed in Ohio for at least twenty years, and cars and campers constantly bring cocoons into Ohio from eastward.

The two major agents used to "control" the moths—true control has never been achieved—are Dimilin and Bt (Bacillus thuringiensis). Dimilin has been called by one entomologist a "doomsday" insecticide. It kills all kinds of insects and other organisms such as spiders and centipedes, members of the Arthropoda, the largest and most diverse phylum in the animal kingdom. Massive spraying could devastate native butterflies and moths and many other small creatures that are important pollinators and nutrient recyclers in the forest food web. And yet, Dimilin is touted as a narrow-spectrum pesticide because it affects "only" arthropods.

Bt is a bacterium that attacks just Lepidoptera, not all insects or other arthropods. Unlike Dimilin, which remains lethal all summer, Bt's effects last ten days at the maximum, less if it rains. With it, sprayers can pinpoint gypsy moth outbreaks without killing other arthropods all season. Used sanely, it offers a much better means of control than Dimilin, and it costs about the same. Nevertheless, wholesale spraying, even with Bt, could wreak havoc with native butterflies and moths. And wholesale spraying has never managed to control the gypsy moth effectively.

Though gypsy moths cause a great deal of damage, especially in oak woods, they never affect all trees, and forests do recover. After all, the moths have munched their way through the East since 1869, and forests still survive. Natural regulating forces always eventually cause moth populations to crash, and evidence even suggests that insecticides extend outbreak periods. The key is clear-sighted choice of limited spraying targets: nurseries, street trees, groves of century oaks that have less resistance to moths than younger trees do. But-

terfly lovers and other Ohioans need to understand these facts and convey to legislators and agencies that wholesale spraying, particularly with Dimilin, is unacceptable if major outbreaks happen.

Efforts to conserve butterflies and moths have made great strides in this state during the past ten years. With money from the Ohio Department of Natural Resources' Division of Wildlife, the Ohio Lepidopterists in 1991 were in the seventh year of a statewide butterfly and moth survey that has covered all eighty-eight counties. The reasoning is that to understand the status of lepidopterans today, you must know what existed in the past and how that has changed. The present is invisible without a longer-term context. Most of the survey's work is complete, and a large database of information now exists. Such is not true for most other states. The Division of Wildlife now recognizes butterflies and moths as nongame species to study and conserve. Their strategic management plan for lepidopterans has two goals: to give the public opportunities to study and enjoy native butterflies and moths, and to conserve native endangered species.

Named for their quick, skipping flight, skippers can be distinguished from "true" butterflies by their proportionally larger bodies, smaller wings, and other details. Their antennae are hooked, and they look somewhat like moths. Pictured here is one named the yellowpatch skipper for obvious reasons. One of the commonest skippers in the East, it was formerly named Peck's skipper.

Opposite: **Opposite:** A northern pearly eye sits on its favorite tree beside a forest path or clearing. If disturbed, the insect will fly, but it will return to the same spot before long. These butterflies are territorial and will defend their property from other insects and even from dogs and people. They are not attracted by flowers but prefer willow or poplar sap, carrion, and scat.

Below: This painted lady and its close relative the American painted lady, or hunter's butterfly, range widely over North America. Aptly nicknamed the "Cosmopolite," the painted lady is found throughout Africa, Europe, Asia, and many islands as well.

Increasing numbers of park districts now give programs on butterflies and moths, conduct butterfly walks, and cultivate butterfly gardens to educate people about the insects and their conservation. The Nature Conservancy and the Ohio Lepidopterists sponsored the first Ohio Moth and Butterfly Conservation Conference in summer of 1989; it informed public land managers, educators, and others about techniques for managing habitat and protecting moth and butterfly diversity. That such a conference should even be considered shows an important shift in thinking: recognition that we need to conserve insects and their habitats, as well as birds, mammals, and plants.

As with any conservation effort, the specialists need the backing of an informed public, sensitive to lepidopterans' needs. There are signs that general interest is rising. Attendance is high at park presentations and butterfly walks, and the Ohio Lepidopterists, whose

membership has burgeoned, receive more requests for talks than they can fill. Butterfly gardening is also becoming more popular; although these gardens cannot save rare species with specific habitat requirements, they do provide other butterflies with feeding and nectaring oases. They also increase neighbors' butterfly awareness by making the insects active parts of their lives. Honda of America worked with David Parshall and the Ohio Lepidopterists to save wetland habitat when they planned their East Liberty facilities a few years ago. As a result, a population of the two-spotted skipper *(Euphyes bimacula),* one of Ohio's rarest butterflies, as well as the largest known Ohio population of the northern hairstreak *(Euristrymon ontario),* survived. Positive developments like these give hope for the future.

Native butterflies and moths are worth preserving. With other insects, they pollinate plants, primary producers in a food web whose complexity we are only beginning to understand. As herbivores, butterflies and their larvae also process plant material into animal protein that feeds many other creatures in the web in which we ourselves are entangled. The title of a poem by Wallace Stevens puts it succinctly: "Frogs Eat Butterflies. Snakes Eat Frogs. Hogs Eat Snakes. Men Eat Hogs." This survival web is losing diversity at an alarming rate, and we are finally realizing the extent of what we stand to lose.

Of course, aside from practical concerns, butterflies also add to our lives' aesthetic and emotional richness. In his memoir, *Speak, Memory,* Vladimir Nabokov expressed eloquently the transcendent feelings that involvement with butterflies and their lives can bring:

> I confess I do not believe in time. . . . And the highest enjoyment of timelessness. . . is when I stand among rare butterflies and their food plants. This is ecstasy, and behind the ecstasy is something else, which is hard to explain. It is like a momentary vacuum into which rushes all that I love. A sense of oneness with sun and stone. A thrill of gratitude to whom it may concern—to the contrapuntal genius of human fate or to tender ghosts humoring a lucky mortal.

ADDITIONAL READINGS

The Audubon Society Field Guide to North American Butterflies by Robert Michael Pyle, Knopf, 1981.

Familiar Butterflies by Richard K. Walton, Knopf, 1990.

The Lives of Butterflies by Matthew M. Douglas, University of Michigan Press, 1986.

Butterflies and Moths: A Companion to Your Field Guide by Jo Brewer and Dave Winter, Prentice Hall, 1986.

The Audubon Society Handbook for Butterfly Watchers by Robert Michael Pyle, Scribner, 1984.

Butterflies East of the Great Plains by P. A. Opler and G. O. Krizek, Johns Hopkins University Press, 1984.

The Butterfly Garden by Matthew Tekulsky, The Harvard Common Press, 1985.

Spiders

Laying for
Flies & Bugs

As Earth's top predators, we humans have usually regarded other hunters with deep distrust, and our attitudes toward spiders are no exception. Edwin Way Teale called them Ishmaels of the insect world, universally abhorred and hated, and others have described them as nature's Jekylls and Hydes, inspiring both admiration and fear in us. A dew-covered orb web is an exquisite work of art until one blunders carelessly into its viscid strands.

From the beginning of human time, we have told stories about spiders that reflect what we perceive to be their dual nature. These small hunters appear in cave paintings in France. They inhabit West African folk tales where they are celebrated for their wisdom. In some cultures, they embody ancestral spirits, or their webs carry dead souls to the center of the earth. In many, it is bad luck to kill them. If found on clothes, they may be measuring the wearer for new ones.

The Greeks told the story of Arachne, changed into a spider for her hubris in challenging Athena to a spinning match. A spider frightened Miss Muffet (the daughter of Dr. Thomas Muffet, an eighteenth-century British naturalist) away from her tuffet. In a modern children's story, *Miss Spider's Tea Party,* Miss Spider spends her time in a sincere effort to convince her insect guests that she eats only vegetable matter. On the other hand, no one who has read Tolkien's *The Hobbit* or *The Lord of the Rings* will ever forget the giant spiders that can snare and suck a hobbit dry.

E. B. White's *Charlotte's Web,* first published about fifty years ago, is an unusual effort to portray spider nature more realistically. In it, Charlotte the barn spider informs Wilbur the pig that she *does* eat flies: "Flies, bugs, grasshoppers, choice beetles, moths, butterflies, tasty cockroaches, gnats, midges, daddy-long-legs, centipedes, mosquitoes, crickets—anything that is careless enough to get caught in my web. I have to live, don't I?" She adds, "All our family have been trappers. Way back for thousands and thousands of years we spiders have been laying for flies and bugs."

Of course, there is the matter of poison. All but a very few spiders are poisonous, but as the naturalist J. H. Fabre notes, there is quite a difference between killing a midge and harming a man. Most spiders harm only their insect prey and can inflict mere pin pricks upon us. This has not prevented the growth of a flourishing body of myth about spiders' menace. An Old English word for spider was "attercop," or "poison head," from which the word cobweb derives.

Pages 208–9: A creature fit to inhabit anyone's nightmare, this burrowing wolf spider shows its enormous hairy fangs and its four large and four small eyes. About fifteen hundred to two thousand species of wolf spiders are known. They are hunters rather than trappers, with better eyesight than most spiders have. The fangs of more advanced spiders like this one move from side to side in a scissor-like motion, while those of mygalomorphs that include the spiders called tarantulas move up and down, rather like parallel, curved ice picks. We have so little information about spider populations that it is difficult to tell what their problems may be.

Above right: This handsome six-spotted fishing spider is the most truly aquatic American spider. Like other fishing spiders, it eats mainly water insects. In England, spiders of the genus Dolomedes are called raft spiders because people wrongly believed that they built rafts for themselves. This photo shows clearly the thorax and abdomen, the eight walking legs, the palps, and the multiple eyes typical of spiders.

Right: Since jumping spiders have relatively good eyesight, their mating rituals are full of color and motion. This male waves his legs and palps and displays his beautiful blue jaws to his mate. Scent pheromones also must play a part in courtship, since male spiders will keep displaying even if the female is removed. Through these ritual dances, males inform females of their identities and intentions and begin to coax them into the proper mood for mating.

Opposite: Drops of morning dew turn a web into a shining mesh of pearls. Spiders use at least seven kinds of glands to produce silk for many uses— for lining burrows, silken tubes, and retreats, for trapping and wrapping prey, for constructing egg sacs, and for "balloons" that carry spiderlings aloft and disperse them to new areas.

Arachnids

Although many think of spiders as "bugs," they are not insects. Both groups are arthropods, but spiders belong to the class Arachnida, more closely related to scorpions, pseudoscorpions, harvestmen (also called daddy longlegs), mites, and ticks. Their bodies are divided into two parts rather than insects' three, and they have no antennae or wings. Insects digest their food internally; spiders bathe it in digestive fluid outside their bodies and then suck the resulting liquid. Insects have three pairs of walking legs, spiders four. Spiders carry large fangs to inject their prey with poison, whereas insects have none. Although many insects are plant eaters, all spiders eat meat. Most importantly, they spin silk from

spinnerets on their abdomens, while spinning insects produce silk strands from mouthparts.

Within the Arachnida, spiders make up the order Araneae, of which more than 3,800 are known in North America and about 37,000 worldwide. Many more remain to be discovered. They range from tiny species smaller than a pin's head to the tropical bird spiders whose legs can span a dinner plate. Spiders and scorpions probably evolved from a common, very ancient sea-dwelling ancestor. Although soft-bodied spiders rarely form fossils, a nearly complete, relatively advanced spinneret has been found in rocks formed in the Middle Devonian, about 380 to 385 million years ago. This suggests that spiders may have been pursuing

ground-dwelling arthropods for some time before that, well before flying insects appeared on the scene. Their long evolution has produced tremendous diversity and many fascinating behaviors.

Arachnologists divide the Araneae into three suborders: the Liphistiomorphae, primitive spiders that live only in Asia; the Mygalomorphae; and the Araneomorphae. Mygalomorphs include several families, among which are trapdoor spiders, purseweb spiders, and the large hairy spiders popularly known as tarantulas. Araneomorphs are the most advanced spiders, comprising two groups of families, the cribellate and ecribellate spiders. With the calamistrum, a comb-like structure on each leg of the fourth pair, cribellate spiders comb fine silk tendrils from the plate-like cribellum on the abdomen to make characteristic hackled bands of trapping silk.

Ecribellate spiders lack the cribellum; arachnologists have long debated whether it evolved separately or whether it was a feature of primitive spiders later lost in many families. This theory seems to be favored presently. Functionally, spiders can be sorted into those that hunt and those that trap: wandering hunters include the day-hunting wolf, lynx, and jumping spiders and the night-hunting gnaphosids, or ground spiders, among others; cellar spiders, cobweb weavers, sheet-web weavers, and orb weavers are among the best-known trappers.

An orb weaver of the family Araneidae exhibits clearly the spinnerets on its abdomen. It also shows the clawed grip that allows it to run surely along the lines of its web. Spider webs come in many sizes and shapes, from the messy, irregular masses of cellar and cobweb spiders; to the sheet webs of grass spiders; to the delicate dome shapes of basilica spiders and the exquisite webs of orb weavers like this one. Many more variations exist as well.

This small jumping spider of the genus *Phidippus* is one of our most engaging spiders. Since jumping spiders have large eyes, it is easier to project human faces and characteristics onto them than onto most spiders. They often appear quite friendly, sitting on a finger and cocking their "heads" as if sizing one up. They are efficient and active little predators.

In Italy, the only cure for the bite of *Lycosa tarentula,* a large wolf spider since proved to be harmless, was said to be frenzied dancing of the tarantella. Some believe that tarantism began as rituals of the Dionysian Bacchae driven underground by Christianity. Whatever the origins, by the eighteenth century Oliver Goldsmith noted sardonically that the frenzies of the bitten roughly corresponded to the size of spectators' fees paid by tourists.

In this country, as well as in the warmer parts of the rest of the world, black widows and their cousins in the genus *Laterodectus* are viewed with justified fear and respect. However, these and the few others dangerous to human beings, such as the brown spiders *(Loxoceles sp.),* are really very minor menaces. Several reasons explain this fact. First, except for the free-ranging wolf and jumping spiders, most spiders' eyesight is minimal, though they are quite sensitive to

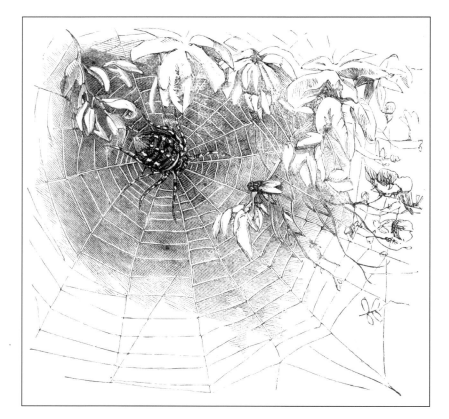

"Come into my parlor . . . ." Silk is absolutely central to spiders' existence, especially to the ones that depend on webs to trap insects and other small prey. Orb weavers may hang upside down in the center of the web or wait in a silken retreat until they feel the vibrations that tell them flies or other small creatures have entered their "parlors." Spiders' digestion is external rather than internal: once its prey is immobilized, a spider injects digestive enzymes into it and sucks the resulting fluids.

"What?" I said. "You don't mean to tell me you don't care about spiders?"
—Bram Stoker, *Dracula*

vibrations. Some jumping spiders can see for ten to twelve inches, but they are very rare exceptions. Spiders do not stalk human beings. Second, they are the prey of many other animals, and their instinct is generally to run when confronted by anything larger than their own prey species. Third, spiders such as widows must be provoked to bite. Even when resting on a human body, they apparently perceive skin as nothing more than a walking surface.

Spider bites generally happen when the animal is squeezed in a shoe or in clothing or is sat on in an old-fashioned privy and bites in self-defense. Widows and brown spiders and a few tropical spiders are venomous indeed, but their jaws are small, and their bites are usually fatal only to the very young or the very old. In the United States, one is much less likely to die from spider venom than from snakebite or a lightning bolt. Although both the black widow and the northern black widow *(Laterodectus mactans* and *variolus)* and brown and red recluse spiders *(Loxoceles reclusa* and *rufescens)* inhabit Ohio, especially the southern part, very few bites are reported.

Aside from the issue of poison, spiders may be hard for many of us to love because they are so different from us. In fact, studying them is an exercise in understanding the alien: What to make of an animal that has eight jointed legs and usually possesses eight eyes on a fused head-thorax attached to a bulbous abdomen, whose large jaws hang outside its mouth, and which digests food outside rather than inside its body? True, a lobster properly viewed is just as strange as a spider, but most of us see it as a desirable food item, whereas few in this culture feel the same about spiders, aside from the zoophagous Mr. Renfield in Bram Stoker's *Dracula.*

However, it does seem that more of us can appreciate these little animals today than may have been true in the past. The arachnologist Dr. Richard Bradley says that, in his experience, spiders now fascinate more people than they repel. Their bizarre forms and amazing range of behavior are hard to convey adequately in a short article. Trapdoor spiders lurk in tunnels lined with silk and leap out from their doors upon hapless insects. Purseweb spiders spin elongated silk tubes on tree trunks and bite through them to grab small creatures. There are spiders that "fish" for insects and minnows, and bolas spiders that fling silk lines tipped with sticky droplets to snare night-flying moths. Spitting spiders shoot gummy material from their mouths to pin down flies and other insects. Pirate spiders invade other spiders' webs and cannibalize them, and cellar spiders whirl like dervishes on their long legs as a defense against attack.

The Spider has a bad name: to most of us, she represents an odious, noxious animal, which every one hastens to crush under foot. Against this summary verdict the observer sets the beast's industry, its talent as a weaver, its wiliness in the chase, its tragic nuptials and other characteristics of great interest. Yes, the Spider is well worth studying, apart from any scientific reasons; but she is said to be poisonous, and that is her crime and the primary cause of the repugnance wherewith she inspires us. Poisonous, I agree, if by that we understand that the animal is armed with two fangs which cause the immediate death of the little victims which it catches; but there is a wide difference between killing a Midge and harming a man.

—Jean Henri Fabre,
The Life of the Spider

Some crab spiders can change from yellow to white to match the flowers on which they wait for the bees, flies, and beetles that are their prey; in self-defense, others are camouflaged to look like bird droppings. Female wolf spiders carry their egg cases attached to their spinnerets and bus offspring on their backs for the first week or so after hatching. Nursery web spiders create silken retreats for their babies and guard them; many female spiders guard egg sacs, and some spider mothers even feed spiderlings with regurgitated food, or spider milk, and hunt for them after they hatch. Certain females eat their mates, although less commonly than many people believe; others live amicably with males in the same webs, and a few spiders even live cooperatively in big communal webs.

For many of us, the creations that denote "spider" are the marvellous orb webs fashioned by, among others, the Araneidae, the largest family of spiders. These beautiful traps demonstrate only one of many uses of silk, an amazing substance central to the lives of all spiders, especially the females. Students of spider evolution believe that silk originated as waste matter that spider ancestors excreted to protect their eggs from drying out and probably from predators as well. Another early use for silk was for lining burrows, a practice still common among the primitive liphistiid and mygalomorph spiders and among burrowing wolf spiders. Abdominal silk glands produce the silk, which is then drawn from several spinnerets. These are flexible and, magnified, remind one of stubby fingers as they manipulate the silken strands.

At least seven types of glands make different kinds of silk for various uses. No spider possesses all seven; web-weaving spiders generally have more silk glands than do the vagrant hunters that depend less on silk. Females sometimes have more than males, since they must produce egg sacs, while the males' duties are finished after courtship and mating. Some silk is sticky, and some is not. Ampullate glands produce the dragline that all spiders except the liphistiids leave behind them as they move about. Draglines enable spiders to drop to safety when threatened by enemies or by hostile mates. They also aid in hunting: jumping spiders, for example, often leap off the sides of buildings after prey like tiny bungee jumpers. Male spiders also follow females' draglines to track down prospective mates.

Other glands manufacture silk for attachment disks from which to suspend webs; still others secrete silk for wrapping prey or for making egg sacs. Spiders in the cribellate group have special glands that produce fine, slightly sticky silk through the pores of the cribellum on the abdomen. Combed out by special

Above: This crab spider waits for its dinner on a black-eyed Susan. Over a period of a day, it can change from yellow to white, matching the color of its background. The insect it has seized is a fly, not a bee, as evidenced by its one rather than two pairs of wings.

Left: A splendid black and yellow argiope hangs head downward in the center of her large orb web. Argiopes' webs hang on shrubs and plants along roadsides and in meadows, marshes, and gardens. Although many flying insects are caught in the sticky strands, grasshoppers are a particularly favorite food.

hairs, this silk combines with normal dragline silk to make the fluffy hackled bands used to entrap the feet of small creatures on which these spiders prey.

Prey-trapping webs come in myriad forms. Orb webs rely on sticky spiral lines to trap flying insects. The proprietor of the web may hang in its center or may lounge in a silken retreat with one leg resting on a signal line that transmits the vibrations of trapped insects from the web. The triangle spider makes a pie-shaped web that it pulls taut by a single thread, then releases like stretched rubber bands to further entangle small insects that hit it. Grass spiders produce sheet webs connected to a silken funnel from which the spider dashes to pounce upon insects that fall on the nonsticky but yielding silk of the sheet.

These and other uses for silk, such as nursery webs, sacs for resting and hiding, and the ballooning threads that waft small spiders into the air for dispersal to new homes, are made possible by silk's amazing fineness, strength, and elasticity. Silk will stretch one-fifth of its length before breaking; its tensile strength is second only to that of fused quartz, and it is much stronger than steel. The finest silk is about one millionth of an inch thick and is invisible to the naked eye. Spider silk's fineness has made it useful as a marker in laboratory and surveying instruments; its strength has led to its use in the Pacific islands for small fishnets and bags.

During the eighteenth century, attempts were made to weave spider silk into cloth. These were successful, producing a pleasant, silvery-gray material. However, plans for commercial production had to be abandoned. The problem was not so much with the silk, but with the nature of spiders themselves. Feeding and maintaining the huge populations of small, sometimes cannibalistic predators needed for silk production proved much harder than raising silk worms on mulberry leaves. However, a recent Associated Press article reports that a pharmaceutical scientist is studying spider silk's molecular structure in hopes of developing a synthetic form to use in surgical sutures.

Male spiders put silk to yet another curious use. Spiders do not have external copulatory organs on their abdomens, and so they have evolved a strange and complex method of reproduction. When a male is ready to mate, he spins a tiny sperm web and squeezes a drop of semen onto it. Sperm webs vary in shape, and in some species may consist of only one strand. The spider next uses the appendages on each side of his mouth as eyedroppers to suck up the

Opposite: A large fishing spider can eat small fish and tadpoles, as well as aquatic insects. If disturbed, it will run over the water and hide among water plants and may even climb beneath the water's surface on plant stems, where it can remain for several minutes. The European spider *Argyroneta* is more completely aquatic, constructing a remarkable, domed, underwater web to live in, which it fills with air bubbles carried on its abdomen.

liquid. It is these two palps that he will insert into the female's genital opening if he is successful in courting her.

The process of charging the palps takes from thirty minutes to three or four hours, depending on the species, and the males, it is reported, seem to enjoy it. In many spiders, the palpal organs are very ornate eyedroppers indeed, consisting of a bulb, a protective sheath, and strange spurs and knobs. Like a key that fits into only one lock, the palp of the male of one species is likely to fit only the genital opening of his female counterpart, and mutual courtship rituals further reduce his chances of choosing a bride of the wrong species.

His palps fully charged, this miniature hero embarks on his quest, one in which his lady and the dragon may be one and the same creature. Since the death of a single male has far less serious consequences for the species than that of the potential mother of many spiderlings, it is he who must risk wandering in search of a mate. If he is lucky, he may find her at random or may track her down by following her pheromone-scented dragline. When he locates her, he faces his final test. The problem is this: How are two predators, each programmed to pounce on any small moving shape, to recognize that the other is a lover and not an especially fortuitous meal? Again, the male is more expendable because he will neither birth offspring nor care for them in any way. The arachnologist Willis J. Gertsch has termed him "a luxury item, developed for the single purpose of transferring the sperm." Thus, it is he who must approach the future mother of his spiderlings and convince her to let him insert his palps.

Courtship tactics vary greatly according to the type of spider involved. Long-sighted hunters like wolf spiders and jumping spiders rely heavily on visual signals. Once in sight of the female, the male begins moving his legs and palps, which are often large and beautifully colored. These "dances" convince the female that he is not prey and allow him to approach, but much stroking and caressing may be needed before consummation. In mygalomorphs and near-sighted hunters, touch is much more important than visual cues, and the correct sequence of caresses persuades the female to mate. Males of some kinds signal with sound: they drum with their palps on the surface beneath them. The European "buzzing spider" stands on a leaf and vibrates his abdomen quickly against it. Even bondage and cradle robbing occur in some types of spiders. Crab spiders of the genus *Xysticus* bind the female's head and legs with silk during courtship; some fisher spiders behave similarly. Certain orb weavers

Crab spiders are so named because of their stout forelegs and scuttling gait. They wait patiently on flowers for the arrival of nectaring insects and can kill creatures quite a bit larger than they are with their poisonous bites. This one has captured a large moth.

move into the webs of immature females, wait until they molt for the last time, and mate with them before their jaws harden.

Courtship is most fraught with danger for males of the trapping spiders. Orb-weaving females are often much larger than their mates and short-sighted and irascible to boot. Males may approach the female's web and pluck it rhythmically to distinguish their movements from the erratic struggles of trapped insects. If their inamoratas rush them, they may drop from the webs on their draglines and thus escape the terrible jaws. Other species have developed ways of locking jaws while mating, or males may induce females to clamp their jaws on variously shaped bumps on their mates' cephalothoraxes. Some, like grass spider males, are much the same size as females and apparently have little trouble approaching them.

On the other hand, male silk spiders of the genus *Nephila* may be only a thousandth the size of their mates, and bolas spiders show a similar imbalance in size. In these species, the females pay little attention to the males at all, since they are far below the size of normal prey. Nevertheless, for many spider seducers, the post-coital embrace ends with a convulsive leap backward to escape the female's jaws. If this expedient fails and the male is eaten, he loses his chance to mate with other females, but his protein increases the number of eggs laid by the female he has mated and thus increases the number of his offspring. Such is the economy of nature!

A great deal has been learned about spiders' biology and behavior, although there is still much more to find out. Much less is known about their distribution, ecological significance, and conservation. Certainly, spiders are everywhere: under stones and leaf litter, on plants and in trees, on walls and buildings, in dark cellar corners, and inside our houses. Over 11,000 spiders per acre were counted in an eastern U.S. woodland and 64,000 in a meadow near Washington D.C.; researchers have estimated 264,000 per acre in a Canal Zone forest and over 2¼ *million* per acre in an undisturbed grassy area in England. Two-thirds of the British spiders were minute dwarf spiders of the subfamily *Micryphantinae.*

These millions of tiny predators "laying for flies and bugs," as E. B. White put it, must have major ecological effects. However, it is difficult to know exactly what they are, since we know little about many spiders' feeding habits. Certainly, spiders and other arachnids, such as harvestmen, are our allies in insect control. Our knowledge of how insecticides affect spiders is also fragmentary: some scientists theorize that spraying favors insects because spiders lay fewer eggs and take longer to mature. Others point out that spiders physically resist insecticides better than insects do. To answer some of these questions, biologists at Miami University are experimenting to find out what effect conservation tillage would have on soybean ecosystems, including weeds, soybeans, insects, and spiders. However, their work is still in its early stages.

Knowledge about exactly which spiders live in Ohio today and how their populations may have changed since settlement is also quite limited. We are dramatically ignorant about many creatures that inhabited the Ohio Country two hundred years ago, knowing very little about invertebrates and nothing about spiders. When the

Moravian missionary David Zeisberger described the natural history of the Tuscarawas Valley in the 1770s, he mentioned various trees, mammals, birds, and reptiles; however, the only invertebrates noted were clams, snails, mosquitoes, ticks, "great and small gadflies," wasps, bees, bedbugs, and fleas. Many kinds of spiders have probably disappeared since then. Others, such as house and cellar spiders, have almost certainly increased, but we cannot be sure of the details without more information about the natural communities of past and present.

Only in the last few years has it seemed vital to biologists to make detailed surveys of invertebrate Ohioans in order to refine our knowledge of their numbers, kinds, and the health of their communities. The Ohio butterfly, moth, and dragonfly surveys are very recent efforts. Work on spiders, even more hampered by lack of historical information, is even farther behind. William Barrows, professor of entomology and zoology at Ohio State University, compiled a checklist of Ohio spiders in 1918 and revised it in 1924. It included 306 species, perhaps one-half the number that actually inhabit Ohio today. Between 1924 and 1994, the list was never revised, and some parts of the state, especially the northeast, lack collections and are described as unknown territory. In 1994, Dr. Richard Bradley, an arachnologist at OSU, Marion campus, proposed that the Ohio Department of Natural Resources support an Ohio spider survey to gather information about their distribution and to identify critical habitats. He has since expanded Barrow's checklist to 493 species, simply by combing printed sources and museum collections. Now underway are field surveys of spiders in varied habitats, and Bradley expects the checklist will reach 500 to 600 species when field studies are completed. The spider survey's goal is to lay the groundwork for future databases to aid in spider conservation.

Certainly, it behooves us to learn all we can about these small spinners, because they are fascinating for themselves and also because they are humans' allies in our perennial war with flies and bugs. Some old beliefs about spiders—that they could influence the weather, for instance—were mistaken. Others, like this saying from the north of England, seem as true now as they did in the old days:

Kill a spider
bad luck yours will be

Until of flies
you've swatted fifty-three.

ADDITIONAL READING

Spiders and Their Kin by Herbert W. Levi and Lorna R. Levi, Golden Press, 1968.

American Spiders by Willis J. Gertsch, Van Nostrand, 1949.

The Book of Spiders and Scorpions by Rod Preston-Mafham, Crescent Books, 1991.

The Opportunists

As anyone who's deplored the raucous mobs of house sparrows at a bird feeder knows, certain species are all too ready to thrive in environments changed by human beings. These include species imported from Europe and elsewhere like house sparrows, starlings, and pigeons that compete aggressively with native species. They also number opportunists such as coyotes that have moved in from other parts of the country in response to habitat changes and human pressures, or natives like raccoons that have adapted so cannily to our altered landscape.

Experts are not certain whether coyotes even lived in Ohio before settlement: they are not deep-wood creatures, and they do not compete well with wolves. They have experienced the same persecution that wiped out timber wolves in the United States except for Alaska, northern Minnesota, and northern Michigan, but they have withstood the human-wolf wars with brilliant success. Gradually they have extended their range east, with young animals relocating to areas where they are less likely to be hunted, trapped, or poisoned. Today coyotes inhabit every Ohio county and every other state except Hawaii as well. Individual animals may become problems if they learn to kill sheep, but coyotes are not a major threat to Ohio's livestock. They are beginning to be hunted and trapped here, and as a result, red fox populations seem to be increasing. The ODNR Division of Wildlife has radio collared some coyotes to discover more about their populations and patterns.

Since raccoons will eat nearly anything they can catch or find and have adapted readily to human food sources such as field corn and garbage, they have thrived, not only in the countryside, but in cities as well. When students at the University of Cincinnati studied raccoons in the Clifton area of that city in the 1960s, they found that while in the country, maximum densities were one raccoon to every ten acres, in the city the maximum could reach one to every two acres. City raccoons often sleep in attics and other human structures, traveling to and from rich garbage sources by way of sewer systems. Nuisance raccoons are often relocated out of cities and suburbs, replenishing those hunted or trapped in rural areas; while the state used to maintain a raccoon farm for restocking, it became unnecessary and some time ago was closed.

Honey bees represent perhaps one of the most fascinating symbiotic relationships with human beings of all. Although many species of solitary bees are native to North America, the familiar honey bee arrived with the earliest colonists on the eastern seaboard. People have kept bees for thousands of years, but the insects themselves have resisted domestication, able to survive just as well in the wild if displeased with their human accommodations. Feral swarms preceded the settlers across America and were dubbed "white man's flies" by Native Americans. The invention of the modern Langstroth hive in the last century set the stage for today's large beekeeping industry, which not only markets honey but is essential for pollinating a wide range of agricultural crops. When parasitic tracheal and Varroa mites, arriving through bee importations from Europe and Asia, combined forces with the hard winter of 1995–96, they wiped out 95 percent of feral honey bees in Ohio and in one year "domesticated" these useful insects: bees can no longer survive except in hives treated for mites. Experts believe that a human lifetime may pass before honey bees develop enough mite resistance to colonize the wild again. Meanwhile, it will be interesting to observe the effects of their plight on native pollinators, and, needless to say, on agriculture. The two mites have also radically slowed the advance of Africanized honey bees in Texas, the so-called "killer bees" of several lurid movies.

The silence of the bees is only one dramatic example of how human actions, both intentional and unintentional, can affect other species. Some consequences, like this one and like the chestnut blight and Dutch elm disease of the twentieth century, can be quick and all too obvious; others, like gradual degradation of the environment can seem less clear but are even more devastating in the end. We have learned much about how to manage game species through hunting regulation and intelligent management. However, the number one problem for us and for many animals in the twenty-first century will be the conservation and restoration of the ecological communities needed for plants' and animals' survival. As a people, we are now a good deal more aware of both the complexity and the finiteness of the natural world around us. We are making strides in amassing the information we need and in supporting measures necessary to conserve the richness that still remains. Yet pressures for development continue to mount, and the endangered species lists grow steadily: the struggle to balance human needs and wants with the needs of the biosphere is only just beginning.

Coyote Arrives

*A*mong the Navajo and other western Indians, Coyote spun a skein of myth as bright as the Milky Way, that big sky river that he was said to have created himself. Devious, greedy, and lecherous (maneuvering his own daughter into marriage), he was the primeval Trickster, seeking to fool Porcupine, Skunk, and the others around him, but just as often foiled by his own gullibility.

Coyote also partook of divinity. Tales from the Algonquin, Yuma, Jicarilla, and other groups insist that Coyote, like Prometheus, stole fire from its supernatural guardians and gave it to the suffering people. His punishment was a singed tail that to this day carries a black tip. Many Native Americans considered him the creator. Navajo stories recount how he stole the water monsters' children, causing a great flood, how he later made vegetation from turkey feathers and traveled the world naming things. His mishaps taught humans the folly of all abnormality, and thus he added Teacher to his many *personae.*

Though Coyote often died when his schemes went awry, reincarnation was another of his specialties, a handy skill in a world where most folk had it in for him. When Tingling Maiden said she would marry him only after she had killed him four times, he begged her to begin; he eventually married her, moved into her hogan, and, shameful to say, smelled it up with coyote urine.

Many other stories end with Coyote resurrected. One, recorded in Father Berard Haile's *Navajo Coyote Tales,* says that Coyote "was again restored to life. From beyond the skies—Spotted Thunder, Left-handed Thunder, (Spotted Wind), Left-handed Wind—all these had come upon him from there, and by these he was returned to life. He never was left killed (but), whenever he would die, he had those above restore him to life. . . ."

Coyote has not lost the knack of resurrection. During the last century, humans have waged implacable war against the Trickster; according to one estimate, we have killed upward of twenty million coyotes, at a present cost to taxpayers of twenty-five million dollars a year. Yet coyotes not only survive in their original habitat on the western plains, but have extended it: to Central America in the south; to Alaska in the north; and to New England, the middle Atlantic, and the Gulf coasts to the east. In fact, Coyote now skulks through all states in the union except for Hawaii. In Ohio, numbers have ballooned since the early 1980s, and coyotes now hunt in all eighty-eight counties.

Canis latrans is a smallish wild dog that stands about twenty-three to twenty-six inches at the shoulder and weighs anywhere from twenty to fifty or more pounds, about the size of a border collie (eastern coyotes tend to grow bigger than western ones). The scientific name means "barking dog"; the common one, pronounced variously coy-ote, coy-o-tee, ky-ote, or ky-o-tee, stems from the sacred Aztec word *coyotl.* Other names include brush wolf, bush wolf, prairie wolf, steppen wolf, and moon dog. Hope Ryden entitled her 1975 book on the coyote *God's Dog,* after southwestern Indian practice. *Canis latrans* is closely related to the other eight canid species, which include the gray wolf, red wolf, dingo, domestic dog, and four species of Old World jackals that resemble coyotes in many ways. All nine species can interbreed.

Female coyotes usually breed at two years and produce litters with an average of about six or seven pups in the spring. Recent research shows that the image of the solitary coyote wailing at the moon is less than accurate. Coyotes are thought to mate for life, though lives in the wild are generally short—snuffed out by poisons,

Page 230: Coyotes, members of the canine family, generally have narrower muzzles, more slender legs, and smaller feet than do gray wolves or many dogs. However, measuring skull dimensions may be the only way to tell whether an individual is a wolf, a dog, a hybrid, or a coyote. While gray wolves were hunted nearly to extinction in the United States, the coyote has actually expanded its range to include every state except Hawaii. It has been able to do this because it is a generalist omnivore, because it is very intelligent, because the more powerful gray wolf was wiped out, and because many of the habitat changes brought about by *Homo sapiens* have suited the coyote's needs.

traps, guns, and other predators. The male hunts for the nursing female and also for the pups, once they are weaned.

Parents have other help as well: coyotes that are not unduly persecuted form small packs. These usually include a mated pair, their puppies, and offspring from the previous year's litter. These older offspring help care for the pups, hunting for them and watching out for them. Like other canids (and humans), coyotes are social predators that must find ways to control conflict within the group, and their ritual behavior firmly establishes a dominance hierarchy in the pack. A subordinate animal acts much like a submissive dog to ingratiate itself with more aggressive members, and coyotes show the

Many farmers blame coyotes for sheep kills that are probably the work of dogs, but others recognize their positive services: control of fast-breeding mice and woodchucks. Even young gray wolves hunt mice, though adults usually concentrate on large hoofed animals like moose, caribou, and deer. Coyotes hunt a large range of smaller animals and will eat vegetable matter as well.

adaptive tolerance and affection that have suited domestic dogs to exchange love with humans.

Coyotes' larger relative, the gray wolf, evolved to hunt big grazing animals like elk, moose, deer, and bison in packs, and in normal times eats little small game. Coyotes, on the other hand, are real omnivores. This flexibility helps them survive human persecution much better than their larger cousins have done. Rabbits, mice, and, in the East, woodchucks are dietary staples, but coyotes turn up their noses at very little. Carrion and garbage are acceptable, as are grasshoppers and other insects, as well as the malformed young and the very old of deer and other grazers. Coyotes appreciate birds, fish, snakes, garden vegetables, nuts, and fruit, including berries and peaches. Watermelon is a special favorite, which earns them the enmity of melon growers.

Coyotes sometimes also kill domestic sheep, which are not adapted, as are wild ungulates, to resist their attacks. Sheep ranchers are the most implacable coyote enemies, and their organized pressure on the government fuels federal control efforts. How many sheep coyotes actually kill and how much this killing costs are issues that stockmen and friends of coyotes debate hotly, as are strategies for controlling them.

Settlers who landed on America's eastern seaboard carried with them a whole dark constellation of attitudes toward the gray wolf. These stemmed from centuries-long competition with the powerful predators over wild game and domestic animals in Europe and Asia Minor. Emotion-laden myth and reality became entangled to the point that a clear picture of this impressive animal is hard to come by even today. The settlers had no such history of contact with coyotes, and for a long time they viewed the brush wolf fairly tolerantly. Unlike the gray wolf, which once ranged over all of North America, the coyote lived in the West, and so it posed little threat to early pioneers' stock.

This picture changed dramatically during the second half of the nineteenth century when ranchers began running sheep and cattle on western ranges swept clear of the mighty bison herds. Some wolves and some coyotes, too, learned to attack stock, particularly when their natural prey populations crashed or when humans wiped out their normal food sources. Neither, however, became the indiscriminate sheep killers that ranchers portrayed. Nevertheless, the wolf wars began, and, curiously, intensified after the turn of the century when most gray wolves had been exterminated or survived only in the mountains.

By the first decade of this century, the war had also decimated the other big carnivores, particularly mountain lions and bears. Suddenly Coyote was promoted to most-hated varmint and has headed the list ever since. In 1915 the federal government officially joined the conflict. It funded the Bureau of Biological Survey (later the U.S. Fish and Wildlife Service) to take the field against "nuisance" animals. Since that year, the feds have provided stock owners with a free predator control program, which operates today under the name of Animal Damage Control in the Department of Agriculture. Coyotes are the main mammalian target. Private citizens and state and local agencies kill many more.

What a war it has been! We have laced carrion with powerful poisons: strychnine, thallium sulfate, and sodium monofluoroacetate, also known as Compound 1080. We have used triggered poison devices, poison-filled sheep collars, leg-hold traps, and high-powered rifles from helicopters. We have burned litters of pups in their holes and chased adults to death over the drifts with snowmobiles. And yet Coyote survives.

Coyotes remain because they are such versatile predators. They also survive because, as with many other animals, their reproductive rate rises when populations are thinned out. Litters can vary from three to nine or more depending on how thick coyotes are on the ground and how much competition for food exists among females. So killing coyotes does not automatically trim their numbers.

Coyotes survive, too, because they are among the most intelligent of mammals, capable of observing, learning from experience, and teaching their young. Many learned to distrust carrion when bait stations were widely used and also to avoid traps and other devices. Unfortunately, many other birds and mammals did not, and the wholesale poisoning in the West killed innumerable bobcats, foxes, badgers, wolverines, raccoons, skunks, weasels, dogs, magpies, ravens, and crows. It also wiped out many coyote prey species and made sheep killing more attractive, especially for breeding animals with hungry pups to feed.

The past thirty years have seen outspoken criticism of government and private killing. Informed in 1972 that Compound 1080 and other poisons killed much other wildlife, including endangered eagles, President Richard M. Nixon barred their use on public lands. The EPA then withdrew these poisons from all use in predator control. Subsequent years have seen the erosion of Nixon's order. Compound 1080 may now be used in sheep collars that coyotes bite into, but which supposedly leave other animals unaffected. Even this more selective use of a lethal poison leaves the door open for widespread abuse, however. An array of other killing methods besides poisons is also still used.

Juvenile coyotes claiming new territories are more likely to kill sheep, it is said, and young adults raising litters may be the most likely of all to hunt livestock. Wholesale persecution, which keeps coyote populations young, may actually boost stock killing rather than lowering it. Environmentalists recommend better husbandry instead. Building lambing sheds, keeping fences repaired, disposing of dead sheep from the range, and training guard dogs, they say, are methods humane, ecologically sound, and effective. They point to successful, low-cost, state-run programs in Kansas and Missouri that concentrate on good stock management and selective removal of offending coyotes rather than on wholesale killing.

High coyote populations, like those in Kansas and Missouri, do not have to mean high sheep predation. Coyotes can, moreover, keep down rodents and destructive insects like grasshoppers. The labor-intensive methods mentioned above may not appeal to large-

Coyote pups are as engaging as any babies in the dog family. In Ohio, they arrive in April, May, or June, after sixty-three days of gestation. Both parents help care for them: the male hunts for his nursing mate, and both parents regurgitate food for the young ones after weaning. Young coyotes spend much time playing and testing out dominant and submissive roles that help control conflict within the family pack.

scale western ranchers who run sheep over vast public lands for minimal fees. However, rising public sentiment against predator control and also against wholesale overgrazing of public range land by big ranchers will keep this and related issues alive.

Meanwhile, Coyote, that grand opportunist, has kept moving. He followed the miners as they mushed north to the Yukon gold fields in the 1890s, scavenging dead horses, mules, and cattle as they dropped beside the long trail. More recently, however, "Go east, young pup," has been his refrain. Coyotes, as one writer puts it, are intelligently inclined to get out of areas where they are under heavy pressure from controllers. As persecution mounted in the West, young animals moved east as they sought home territories.

They advanced from Texas, Oklahoma, and Kansas into the Gulf Coast and up the Ohio River Valley. They reached the Northeast by a longer route, by moving through northern Minnesota, Wisconsin, and Michigan's Upper Peninsula and into Ontario and New York. From there, some pushed north into New England, and others moved into the Mid-Atlantic states. It is now believed that during their journey through eastern Canada, coyote pioneers met and bred with the last remnant gray wolves, producing larger offspring. As a result, eastern coyotes tend to grow considerably bigger than western ones. Farming and lumbering had "prairified" large areas in the East, making them more than suitable for the prairie wolf; extermination of gray wolves, bears, and mountain lions had left a roomy niche for another, more versatile predator. The Trickster made himself right at home.

In Ohio, Coyote was first sighted in Logan County in 1919. He eluded notice from 1921 to 1934, with scattered reports from that time through 1978. Then the population exploded: from 1982 to 1988, the Ohio Department of Natural Resources Division of Wildlife collected specimens in seventy-one counties as part of a research project. A band of counties in central Ohio, from Mercer County eastward to Harrison County, yielded the highest densities. Statewide densities, however, are still relatively low compared with those in western states.

Of the ODNR's 438 specimens, skull analysis showed that 87 percent were coyotes, 2 percent were coyote-dog hybrids, or coydogs, and 6 percent were feral dogs. (Approximately 5 percent were too damaged to analyze.) The low coydog percentages convince some biologists that a few coyotes have roamed Ohio for longer than the past seventy years. Breeding between dogs and coyotes is most common when the latter are just entering an area. Coyotes ordinarily accept dogs as mates only when proper ones are lacking. Thus, the few hybrids in Ohio show that contact may have begun many years ago.

Even when coyotes and dogs do breed, the cards are stacked against survival of hybrid lines. Both male and female coydogs are ready to mate in the autumn, three to four months earlier than purebred coyotes are, so they cannot easily breed back into pure stock. Also, while male coyotes hunt for their nursing mates and supply weaned pups with food, male dogs and coydogs go their merry ways soon after mating, leaving females without enough food to nurse and feed a litter that may appear months too early—in deep winter. This drastically lowers pups' chances of surviving. There were no grounds for the occasionally hysterical claims some years ago that a race of coydogs was taking over New England. There are also none for believing that such a thing could happen in this state.

A modest coyote backlash seems to be mounting in Ohio. Over a two-year period in the late 1980s, 231 sheep kills were blamed on the brush wolf, although Jack Weeks, a wildlife biologist for the Ohio Department of Natural Resources, estimates that free-ranging dogs account for three times more livestock damage than coyotes do. A small collie or German shepherd can look very much like a coyote. Indeed, there are advantages in blaming Coyote for Dog's crimes: As one commentator put it: "Cry 'coyote!' and the game protectors come running with compensation money. Cry, 'Dog!' and you can take it up with your neighbor."

You may kill coyotes freely (in fact, Coyote is the only animal hunted every day of the year in Ohio, including Sunday). You may not shoot a dog unless a dog warden deems it vicious or it is directly threatening life or property. Little wonder that many accept reports of sheep killing by coyotes uncritically. A recent *Columbus Dispatch* article pictures a farmer with a wounded sheep, displaying "where medication coats the belly of a coyote's victim." He is quoted as saying: "When you go out there and see a lamb that is all torn up, it is just disgusting. It makes tears come to my eyes to see something like that." Unfortunately, the report did not mention that coyotes bring down prey by the throat. When stomach or hindquarters are lacerated, it is usually dogs' work.

It is hard to say exactly how serious sheep killing by coyotes is in Ohio. "It's such an individual matter," says Weeks. "One coyote may learn to kill sheep, but many others don't. The toll varies greatly from place to place." For those farmers who are hit, the Department of Agriculture provides compensation and a list of trappers who remove nuisance animals. They also recommend the good management practices.

Most experts believe that in the East's relatively small fields, these practices make more sense than large-scale hunting, trapping, or poisoning. However, pressure is rising for use of Compound 1080: Governor Celeste vetoed a bill in summer of 1990 that would have allowed stock owners to use the poison sheep collars. The bill is dead for now, but it is almost certain to be introduced again. Many wildlife biologists and trappers rightly worry about abuse of a poison slow to degrade, having no antidote, and lethal to humans as well as other animals, and they advocate good animal husbandry and selective trapping instead.

Whether we favor or anathematize Coyote, we are going to have to learn to live with him. No one claims that even the most stringent control efforts will wipe him out. His supernatural mentors, Spotted Thunder, Left-handed Thunder, Spotted Wind, and Left-handed Wind will resurrect him again, no matter how we persecute him. Like starlings, house sparrows, raccoons, woodchucks, gypsy moths, Queen Anne's lace, and other opportunistic species, Coyote has actually benefited from changes humankind has brought to the world—whether we like it or not. The Trickster, who displays so many of the qualities that we like to think of as human—intelligence, enterprise, flexibility, loyalty to family members, musicality— is here in Ohio to stay. He is a remarkable animal, and perhaps his soulful howls are not a bad addition to the varied natural sounds of an Ohio night.

ADDITIONAL READING

God's Dog: The North American Coyote by Hope Ryden, Lyons and Burford, 1975.

The Wild Dogs in Life and Legend by Maxwell Riddle, Howell Book House, 1979.

"Outfoxed, So To Speak, by the Wily Coyote" by Bil Gilbert, *Smithsonian*, March 1991.

"A Howling in the Night" by Jay Paris, *Ohio Magazine*, January 1989.

The Raccoon

Nature's Artful Dodger

*R*accoons wear their black masks to remember unicorns, claims poet Katharyn Machan Aal. When Noah abandoned the unicorns to the Flood, raccoons hung back from the Ark in protest. Taking them by surprise, Noah's sons clapped hands over their eyes and dragged them in.

But "coons" are a flexible lot, and that early pair learned an important lesson. Certainly, if their grandchildren have anything to say about it, they'll be aboard the second ark now building against the flood which is making unicorns of so many other modern species. Early up the gangplank, raccoons will be sighted making dens in storage cupboards, staring down the mast with ruby eyes at dusk, and tipping over garbage cans in the ship's galley. Most estimates speculate that even more raccoons live in North America now than in 1492. They have survived as a direct result of adapting so well to a human-dominated environment.

The first settlers did not know what to make of the bear-like little beasts with grizzled fur, striking black facial markings, and ring tails. Raccoons were a New World breed, never seen in Europe. In 1612

Page 240: Raccoons live in the woods and on river banks, in trees and in rock crevices, and sometimes in holes in the ground. City coons use attics, crawl spaces, and chimneys. They eat virtually anything they can find. Garbage troves, pet food, and gardens are major sources of nourishment for them. Because raccoons are so adaptable and because pelt prices have declined in recent years, the Ohio Department of Natural Resources reported in autumn 1997 that their numbers in Ohio had grown by 800 percent over the previous fifteen years! Local ordinances forbidding hunting and trapping are also a boon to raccoons.

Captain John Smith described a strange new creature of the Virginia colony, "a beast they call *Aroughcun,* much like a Badger, but useth to live on trees as squirrels doe." *Aroughcun* or *arakun* was an Indian name meaning "he who scratches with his hands." The English eventually shortened it into raccoon or coon. The French were equally confused—an early Louisiana account calls the raccoon le *chat sauvage* ("the wild cat") with an accompanying picture that looks a little like an anemic house cat.

However, the settlers did not remain at a loss for long. They learned to relish the dark, sweet, fatty flesh, to cure and clean prime hides for clothes, blankets, and caps, and to find sport in listening to the bell-notes of coon dogs tracking and treeing their quarry through the hard frosts of early winter. They greased their boots and lit their lamps with raccoon fat and cleaned their pipes with the males' hooked penis bone. In the currency-poor backwoods, coonskins were money: the short-lived state of Franklin, founded in East Tennessee in 1784, paid the governor's secretary five hundred coonskins a year, the clerk of the house of commons, two hundred, and each member of the assembly three skins a day. No one got rich—the fledgling commonwealth collapsed four years later.

But the settlers were not the only ones who learned from European-raccoon encounters. If the intruders cut down coon-denning trees, they also provided attractive sheds and crawl spaces to take their places, and raccoons moved in. Table scraps couldn't match today's McDonald's discards, but were not spurned. Settlers' axes created open, brushy places along stream and field edges that offered excellent forage and cover. And farmers grew raccoon ambrosia—tender, young sweet corn dripping with irresistible milk. Raccoon eyes shone softly as the little masked faces moved closer to the lights of human habitations.

As small, unspecialized omnivores, raccoons were ideally suited to make the most of the new regime. They are extremely intelligent and very adaptable in diet, habit, and behavior. Raccoons *(Procyon lotor)* are not closely related to otters, bears, badgers, or cats, as pioneers speculated. The procyonids, to which raccoons and other small foragers like coatis, ringtails, cacomistles, kinkajous, and olingos belong, probably separated from the dog stem during the early Oligocene period, about thirty-five million years ago. Bears diverged from dogs about ten million years later. Procyonids all inhabit the Western Hemisphere except for Asia's greater and lesser pandas. Scientists still argue about whether pandas are more closely related to raccoons or bears.

Raccoons will eat anything edible, and flexible hands and sensitive fingers are their main foraging instruments. Though their distance vision is poor and their hearing is inferior to dogs', their tactile sense is incredibly finely tuned. Their hands contain as many tactile nerve endings as humans' do. They begin foraging at dusk, taper off during the night, and usually end by dawn. Ambling through a woods or along the banks of a stream, they keep their hands perpetually busy—patting, scratching, rolling, feeling. They are attracted to water, partly because of the succulent crayfish and minnows there, but also because their sense of touch works better under water. Raccoons' feeling, dabbling, and dousing have given rise to the myth—still believed by many—that they compulsively wash their food. In fact, much of it is eaten dry; and the supposedly fastidious animals show no inclination to remove dirt clinging to earthworms and other favorite dry-land foods.

A list of raccoon food could well be made into a Gilbert and Sullivan or Tom Lehrer patter song—long, exhaustive and varied:

Raccoons eat—
  Crayfish, salamanders, toads, and water turtles
    bullfrogs
    green frogs
    tree frogs
    and pickerel frogs
  Catfish, sunfish, bullheads, and buffaloes
  With a stop along the shoreline to dig a clutch of
    turtle eggs.
Raccoons love—
  Grasshoppers, cutworms, millipedes, and
    centipedes
    angleworms
    caterpillars
    wasps, hornets, honeybees
  Slugs, snails, clams, and oysters on the half shell
  And even an occasional copperhead or rattlesnake.
They'll take—
  Pokeberries, shadberries, juneberries, hackberries
    strawberries
    ground cherries
    pin cherries
    partridgeberries.
They love—
  Corn and sugar cane, sweet potatoes, peanuts

acorns

pecans

beechnuts

and hickory nuts.

They like—

Meadow mice, moles, and cottontail rabbits.

They'll eat—

Nestlings, eggs, and fresh meat on the roads.

In short, in matters vegetable, animal, or mineral, the raccoon is the model of a gustatory generalist. Adding garbage, the staple of modern urban raccoons, has not been a difficult step.

They are also quite unfussy about where they live. There are southern raccoons and northern raccoons. Length of winter defines their northern limit in Canada. There are marsh raccoons, island raccoons, prairie raccoons, and raccoons that live and scavenge along ocean beaches where crabs are a favorite food. Raccoons live in the woods and on the river banks, in trees and in rock crevices, and sometimes in holes in the ground. The ideal habitat contains some woodland and some water. And of course there are raccoons that live in attics, crawl spaces, or chimneys, traveling through culverts and backyards to the ever-flowing garbage can. A subspecies haunts state park campgrounds, seizing leftover steak bones and disappearing with them into the darkness, uttering warning growls if challenged by the owners.

The raccoon year begins around February when males emerge from their dens, usually in tree holes, to wander through the woods in search of a mate. When the male locates a denned and friendly female, he may spend a week or so with her, then abscond, never to be seen again. Mother is now solely in charge. When the babies are born, fifty-four to sixty-five days later, they are tiny, pink, with a bit of fuzz, and blind. At six to nine weeks, when eyes have opened, fur has grown, and motor functions have developed, their parent moves then to a ground nest on the woodland floor or in a marsh. Cubs follow the mother through that summer, playing and learning, gradually growing more independent. Mother is a firm disciplinarian. Observers have seen females get their cubs in line by slapping their rears, accompanied by loud squeals of contrition from the babies.

By fall the family group has loosened, with young ones striking off alone or together for days at a time. When cold weather comes, however, the group coalesces again and often dens together for the winter to conserve heat, often in sizable numbers. Naturalist Era Zistel tells of a gang of at least thirty-five wild raccoons that spent one winter camped out under her house floor. The din during the February mating season was truly awesome. Like bears, raccoons eat mightily during the late summer and fall, concentrating on high-calorie foods like nuts, especially acorns, to build up fat. Unlike bears, they are not true hibernators, in which body functions almost completely halt, but they do sleep for weeks at a time, metabolizing fat to satisfy food and water needs. The yearlings, which must allocate more calories for growth than for fat, often starve before spring provides new food sources. Weak, young coons can sometimes be seen in April's broad daylight, eating whatever they can find, including leaves and buds.

As befits them, raccoons do not insist on following a strict behavioral pattern. Southern coons remain active all winter, and diet varies according to habitat. Ranges—the bounded areas raccoons patrol in search of food and which they protect from rivals—also vary in size according to whether the animals are living in marsh or woods or city. In marshes, populations as high as nearly one animal per acre have been recorded; more usual is a maximum of one raccoon for every ten acres to a minimum of one for every fifty acres. Like other wild animals' populations, raccoons' vary a great deal over time. When numbers peak, disease and starvation eventually drive them down.

Ranges are usually smaller and numbers denser among urban and suburban raccoons than among their country cousins. Students at the University of Cincinnati studied raccoons in the Clifton area of that city from 1963 to 1969. They found no differences in body weight or sexual characteristics between the Clifton raccoons and country animals, but did discover important variations in density and habits. Densities ranged from one raccoon for every two acres to one for every nine acres, well above normal expectations. The little beasts had appropriated trees, sewers, dumps, attics, garages, chimneys, and even an old sofa as dens. They used storm drains for travel and feeding. Instead of foraging randomly, these animals went straight from their dens to feeding areas, rather like human commuters going back and forth to work. They relied almost exclusively on garbage and handouts to fill furry bellies.

Though it may appear that raccoons have discovered the bona fide good life, a raccoon's lot is often not a happy one. True, humans have killed off most of the larger predators—wolves, cougars, bobcats, and bears—that in the past relished raccoons. Coyotes,

Opposite: Raccoon babies are born tiny, pink, and blind. At six to nine weeks, their mother will move them from this tree hole to a nest on the ground. Although their father abandoned the family before they were born, their mother stays with her offspring all summer, and they learn much about survival from her. The group may also den together in winter to conserve heat.

hawks, foxes, and especially owls sometimes eat babies, but adult animals have few natural enemies. However, men, motors, and dogs account for the death of millions of raccoons each year. In 1971 the Michigan state highway department reported 445 raccoons killed on a single 114-mile stretch of highway. Males wandering in search of mates in early spring and females foraging for their babies are often hit; when a mother dies, the little ones usually starve.

Coon hunting and trapping are still widely popular, especially in southern and mountain states. In southern Ohio and in counties like Ashtabula and Trumbull, residents often hear coon dogs belling across the frosty fields and woods. Old raccoons can sometimes trick the pack and escape, but many, especially young ones, are treed and either shot or knocked down for the dogs to dispatch. Most states set strict early winter killing seasons. For example, Ohio's 1985–86 trapping and hunting seasons ran from November 15 to January 31. But both trappers and hunters, using any opportunity to train their dogs, kill many raccoons out of season.

Some idea can be gained of the sheer numbers of coons hunted and trapped from statistics on trapping permits and skins sold to fur dealers. According to the Ohio Department of Natural Resources Division of Wildlife, the state of Ohio alone issued 35,464 permits to trap small animals including raccoons in the years 1980–81. By 1983–84 the number had dropped to 21,307, probably in part because the going price for a good raccoon pelt had declined from about $20 in 1979 to $11 in 1983–84. A whopping 410,785 coonskins were sold to dealers in Ohio in 1975–76, 267,000 in 1981–82, and 197,494 in 1983–84. Again, the decrease in sales likely reflects the decline in price per skin.

Diseases and parasites take a further toll and are important in controlling populations when they rise too high. Raccoons can contract both the canine and feline distemper, often fatally. The Clifton raccoons declined from 145 to 51 animals in 1969, largely as the result of canine distemper, a foe second only to dogs themselves. Other diseases include tetanus, leptospirosis, and rabies. These diseases plus parasites, among which are fleas, mites, ticks, and lice, and a galaxy of roundworms and flatworms, would make a much less pleasant patter song than do raccoon food items.

Raccoon rabies has caused special concern during the past few years. Beginning in Florida in the 1950s, it has been spreading north increasingly fast. Observers believe that raccoons transplanted north by hunting clubs may be an important cause. Skunks, foxes, and bats get rabies more often than raccoons do, but coons are a bigger

Although young raccoons are engaging little creatures, they do not make good pets, becoming more and more aggressive and destructive as they mature. Wild raccoons should not be approached because they can carry rabies. The Division of Wildlife warned in 1997 that "Cases of rabies in raccoons have been confirmed in northeast Ohio during the past year. For protection against rabies, have all of your pets vaccinated and do not let them roam unattended. Do not feed, touch, or adopt wild animals as pets, and immediately report all animal bites (wild or domestic) to your county board of health."

threat because they live so close to humans and because people often perceive them to be cute and friendly. As a result, raccoons come in contact with people. To control rabies, vaccinating dogs is essential.

All this suggests that approaching a wild coon—and even cute babies are definitely wild—is a bad idea, especially if the animal looks sick, is abroad during the day, or seems unusually tame and fearless. Although few cases of raccoon rabies have been reported in Ohio, the danger is always present. And raccoons carry at least twelve other diseases and parasites that can attack humans.

Nor do raccoons make good pets. An acquaintance who has kept young ones says: "There's nothing cuter than baby raccoons, but at about three months, they begin getting aggressive. They're demanding and possessive, and they want their way. If they don't get it, they go after whatever they want, and they get into everything. I've still got a jade tree that has raccoon toothmarks on it." Raccoons' intelligence, unquenchable curiosity, and dexterity can wreck a house in a matter of hours. George Laycock, writing in *Audubon,* tells of a student who got permission to bring her raccoon to college with her and keep it in the animal lab at night. In a feat worthy of Houdini, the animal picked its cage lock, released hordes of bouncing experimental rabbits, and terrorized an early morning faculty meeting, whose members fled or took refuge on chairs and tables. The raccoon was summarily expelled from school. Older animals can become quite vicious as females go into heat or males feel the urge to set up territories and mate.

Meanwhile, the uneasy *entente* between *Homo sapiens* and *Procyon lotor* holds. Country coons ramble, dabble in streams, and raid sweet corn patches with a sharp ear cocked for the voices of hounds in the distance. City coons trot purposefully from their attic dens through the storm drains that protect them from dogs and cars toward the nightly, noisy feast at the garbage can or dumpster. Humans tolerate their audacious neighbors with a mixture of affection, sheer exasperation, and sometimes even fear, as testified by newspaper and magazine headlines like "Invading Raccoon Horde Tries Suburban Patience," "Battling the Animals in Wild Suburbia," "A Sure-fire Coon Chaser," and "No Need to Panic Over Rabies."

States that license private trappers have spawned a thriving cottage industry of "wildlife removal specialists" who capture the squirrels, opossums, skunks, and raccoons that ordinary exterminators usually refuse to deal with. Ohio licenses two or three such enterprises in most counties. Those authorized to remove raccoons from Cleveland alone take away several thousand a year. Many release animals into the countryside where they replenish the pool for coon hunters and trappers. These burgeoning city-raised beasts have outmoded the old state-run Milan State Raccoon Farm, which raised and released coons from 1934 to 1951 in Ohio.

So despite hunters, trappers, automobiles, dogs, and diseases, raccoons continue to prosper. On the modern ark—provided the ship itself doesn't founder from an atomic war or escalating chemical pollution—it seems that raccoons will be aboard in numbers.

ADDITIONAL READING

"The Cincinnati Raccoons" by Darrell L. Cauley and James R.
    Schinner, Natural History, November, 1973.
"Adaptable Arakun" by George Laycock, *Audubon*, September 1982.

Nature's Confectioner

The Honey Bee

*F*rom the sight of a furry golden worker rummaging in a yellow crocus to the equally golden honey dribbled on slices of toast or stirred into hot tea, honey bees sweeten human lives. In the days before cane, beet, and corn sugars, they gave us our only sweetener aside from fruit. How we craved it! For millions of years, our ancestors plundered bees' colonies in rock crevices and hollow trees. For thousands we have enticed bees to take up residence in hives for their gifts of comb and honey. Most recently we have learned to appreciate their role—even more important—as pollinators of our crops.

Beekeeping is a venerable and exacting profession that requires considerable knowledge of these most complex social insects. For all our efforts, we have never domesticated bees as we have other farm animals. Many more colonies still exist in the wild than have consented to live in hives, and bees swarming from a hive have as good a chance for survival on their own as those issuing from a cavity in a hollow tree. The history of beekeeping, as beekeepers are the first to admit, is not one of domestication but of humans learning to satisfy

Page 250: The honey bee is not native to North America but came from Europe so long ago that we are not sure when. Some even believe that the Vikings brought the first beehives west. The bee has thrived here until very recently. Humans improved bee culture to provide a better supply of golden honey and to pollinate crops, but bees could very well survive in the wild if displeased with their accommodations. In 1996, however, two parasitic mites and a hard winter wiped out virtually all feral honey bee colonies, and the long-term effects on crops and on native pollinators are still unclear. Sadly, it will be a long time—some say a human lifetime—before many honey bees develop enough mite resistance to live in the wild, like this bee shown pollinating a wild rose.

honey bees' needs and wants for our own advantage. As Sue Hubbell muses in *A Book of Bees*, "Strictly speaking one never 'keeps' bees—one comes to terms with their wild nature."

The willingness of people to brave angry bees attests to the extraordinary attraction of honey. Rock paintings as much as fifteen thousand years old celebrate daring raids, whose methods were probably much older than the paintings themselves. Some pictures show hunters bearing torches—they had discovered the use of smoke for calming bees, still the beekeeper's best method. Egyptian tombs and monuments display our earliest records of hiving bees, in cylindrical pots stacked on their sides. Tradition has it that the Egyptians were also the earliest migratory beekeepers, following successive blooms down the Nile with hives on rafts. Whatever their methods, they were effective enough that in about 1180 B.C. Ramses III could offer the Nile god about fifteen tons of honey as tribute.

People were curious about bees of course, and over the centuries a body of bee lore collected, again witnessing to the lengths people would go to obtain bees and honey. One old recipe, first recorded by Virgil, called for bludgeoning a fat ox to death and laying it on a bed of thyme in a sealed building. A month and various manipulations later, clusters of bees should have replaced the rotted ox. Aristotle approached the subject of bees more scientifically, yet repeated the improbable theory that bees gathered up their larvae from plants, an account reminding one of the story about human babies coming from cabbages.

Aristotle also believed that the queen of the hive was actually a king, that drones were female, and that workers were male. Nature, he reasoned, never arms females, so the drones, the only members of the hive without stings, must be the females. We know now that human logic, inevitably influenced by culture, led him to make the wrong deduction in each case: queens and workers are female, and drones are male. The medieval church proved no less confused about bees' sexuality. Bees were seen in analogy to a community of chaste monks and nuns ruled by a bishop, and beeswax was especially prized for church candles because of the belief in the purity of its origins. A hymn dating from the fifth century praises the bees that provide the candle wax "who produce posterity, rejoice in offspring, yet retain their virginity." The information that the queen bee, who produces all the hive's posterity, is actually impregnated by ten or more drones in a riotous nuptial flight would probably have distressed the pious.

Such inaccurate beliefs proved quite tenacious: not until 1609 did an Englishman, Charles Butler, assert in *The Feminine Monarchie, Written out of Experience* that the king bee was no male and must instead be crowned queen. In 1670 the Dutch Swammerdam determined the queen bee's sex beyond doubt through dissection. However, according to the *ABC and XYZ of Bee Culture,* he too misunderstood bee sex, believing that queens were fertilized by "a seminal exhalation of 'odoriferous effluvia'" whose production required many drones in attendance.

Down the centuries, people devised hives of many shapes: among them hollowed out log sections, various pottery vessels, and the traditional domed straw hive, called a "skep." In northern Europe, bee trees were treasured. Laws forbade them to be cut down even when temporarily empty of bees, and they often belonged to individuals other than those who owned the land beneath them. Forest beekeepers fashioned doors opposite the bees' entrance holes for removing honey, carefully camouflaged the doors to prevent theft, and also set traps to catch foraging bears.

Removing honey from beehives usually meant killing the bees. In colder climates, the hives heaviest with honey and those deemed too light to overwinter were traditionally held over holes containing

Nineteenth-century inventions revolutionized bee culture. The movable-frame hive enabled beekeepers to remove frames easily for accomplishing a variety of tasks, such as collecting honey, checking on bees' health, and discouraging bees from swarming. It gave keepers more control over their bees than ever before. Guidance also became easier to find. In his magazine *Gleanings of Bee Culture,* founded in 1873, and the book *ABC and XYZ of Bee Culture,* Amos I. Root of Medina, Ohio, was prominent among those offering practical advice to beekeepers.

Honey Bee Basics

Bees arose from wasps sometime during the Age of Dinosaurs. Unlike wasps, most of which are predators, bees are vegetarians, gathering flower pollen and nectar. They and flowering plants evolved together. The world contains at least twenty-five thousand species of bees (mammals boast only about thirty-five hundred). Many are solitary; many others show varying degrees of social organization. Bee fossils are scant, but honey bee colonies evolved into their present form sometime between fifty and twenty million years ago.

Worldwide, there are four species of honey bee: *Apis florea*, or the dwarf honey bee; *Apis dorsata*, the giant honeybee; *Apis cerana*, the Indian honey bee; and *Apis mellifera*, the temperate-zone honey bee. The first three are largely restricted to Asia. Various races or subspecies of *A. mellifera*, however, have colonized the more temperate areas of Asia, all of Europe except the far North, and all of the Middle East and Africa. Though none of the honey bees were native to the Americas, European settlers brought *A. mellifera* here, and the species is now naturalized in the temperate regions of North and South America. Most bees raised commercially today derive from the Italian race, *A. mellifera ligustica*.

A colony of honey bees is made up of one queen, a female whose only function is to lay eggs, about two hundred male drones, responsible only for inseminating the queen during one nuptial flight early in her life, and about fifty thousand workers. These are females whose ovaries are atrophied and which cannot, except in extraordinary circumstances, lay eggs. Workers fill all the other jobs in the colony: cleaning the beeswax brood cells in which eggs, larvae, pupae, pollen, and honey are kept; tending brood; building comb from wax produced by glands in their abdomens; capping cells; evaporating nectar to make honey and packing pollen; guarding the hive; and foraging for pollen, nectar, and water. Each worker bee usually executes the above tasks in order according to her age. Field bees, the ones we usually see, are the older bees.

The success of the temperate-zone honey bee lies in its habit of storing enough honey and pollen to survive cold winters. A successful colony begins the winter with combs full of pollen and honey. The bees huddle together in a mass at the center of the hive or nest, with the queen in the middle. They eat high-energy honey and generate heat by shivering their wing muscles. In late winter, the queen begins to lay eggs, which hatch into white larvae. Worker bees feed the larvae royal jelly, more accurately called "bee milk," a secretion of their hypopharyngeal glands. The few bees destined to become queens are kept on this rich diet, while future workers and drones are switched to pollen and honey. It is this early diet that forms queens.

Drones hatch from unfertilized eggs that the queen lays in response to the stimulus of larger-than-normal

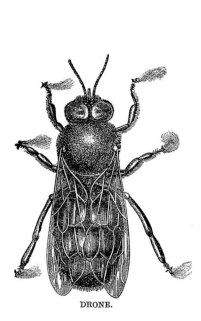

DRONE.

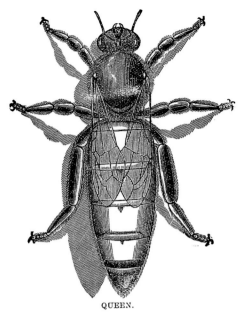

QUEEN.

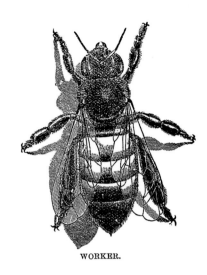

WORKER.

drone cells built by the workers. Drones have no stings and do no work, but ready themselves to chase and inseminate virgin queens during nuptial flights. In a curious sexual wrinkle, drones literally explode their genitalia in the act of copulation, falling lifeless to the ground thereafter. A queen copulates only once, storing enough sperm to last the rest of her life of up to five years—a relatively long span compared to workers, who may live only a few weeks at the height of the brood-rearing and foraging seasons. Drones are kept around until late summer or autumn, as long as there may be a need for their services. When the time for possible nuptial flights is over, workers ruthlessly eject the drones from the hive into the cruel world, where they either starve or freeze to death.

As the season advances, larvae spin cocoons and pupate, emerging as adult bees to gear up the hive for the spring nectar flows. Because whole honey bee colonies can winter over, unlike most other kinds of bees, they can be up to strength for the early dandelions, fruit trees, and other spring blossoms before other pollinators are, an important factor in their success. The main nectar flows come in spring, and this is when the hive builds up its surpluses. Summer and fall offer other nectar opportunities like purple loosestrife, goldenrod, and aster, but in smaller quantities.

In late spring, a populous hive with full frames of brood, pollen, and honey will prepare to swarm. Workers build new queen cells in preparation. Swarming is a dramatic event in which the greater

Above: Not until the seventeenth century was it realized that bees were "ruled" not by a king, but a queen, the largest member of the hive. Her function is to lay many thousands of eggs. Male drones were long thought to be female because they are not armed with stings. When drones' job of inseminating queens is done, workers unceremoniously eject them from the hive to starve or freeze. The workers, females whose ovaries have atrophied, do many tasks around the hive and gather pollen and nectar from flowers.

part of the hive tumble out of it, bearing with them the old queen, fly a short distance, and cluster on a branch or other perch. Scout bees fly off to hunt for good nest locations. When consensus is reached about the best alternative, the thousands of bees fly off to the new nest, where they will race the season to build comb, raise brood, and gather pollen and honey against the coming winter. Meanwhile, a newly hatched and inseminated queen and her remaining hive mates build up supplies in the old hive.

Swarming is colonies' way of reproducing, but it is less congruent with the needs of beekeepers, who want hive members to stay put and store up large honey reserves in a single hive rather than flying off into the wild blue yonder. The beekeeper's duties include providing suitable hives; supplying the hives with superior queens; placing them near good sources of nectar and pollen; splitting hives (removing honey and brood to other hives to discourage swarming); inspecting and treating bee diseases; feeding under-supplied hives with pollen substitute and sugar syrup; collecting, extracting, and marketing honey; and many other tasks. Practical instructions for beekeeping are obviously beyond the scope of this article, but there are many good beginning handbooks. Two are

Starting Right With Bees, published by A. I. Root, and *First Lessons in Beekeeping,* put out by Dadant and Sons.

Much has been written in recent years about "bee language," the marvelous communication system that enables a field bee to inform others of a good nectar or pollen source and direct them to the place with differently patterned dances. A "round dance" indicates a source close to the hive. The so-called "waggle dance," named by Karl von Frisch, who earned a Nobel Prize for his pioneering studies of bee communication, tells of a resource farther away. It uses gravity as a symbol of the sun: a bee telling of a source in line with the sun will align the long axis of its dance with up and down in the dark hive. It will refer to a source located at an angle to the sun's position by dancing along a corresponding angle to the perpendicular. The systems are actually much more complex than this, including both sound and scent components. Bee navigation, which uses mental maps of landmarks, the polarized light of the sun, and scent detection, is equally fascinating. Von Frisch's book, *The Dancing Bees,* is a readable account of his work. *The Honey Bee,* by James and Carol Gould, gives a very good account of more recent discoveries.

---

burning sulfur. Sometimes they were dipped in water. That some felt remorse at such cruelty is shown by Anne Hughes's *The Diary of a Farmer's Wife 1796–1797:* "It do grieve me to kill the poor things, being such a waste of good bees, to lie in a great heap at the bottom of the hole when the skep be took off it, but we do want the honey, using a great lot in the house for divers times…. The wax we do boil many times till it be a nice yaller colour and no bits of black in it, when it can be stored for use for the polishing and harness cleaning."

The New World was home to many other kinds of solitary and social bees. The different races of *Apis mellifera*, however, were all native to the Old World and originally unknown here. Some believe that in the ninth century, Irish and Norwegians brought honey bees

Amos Root recommended that apiaries include a decorative workshop and, if possible, grapevines on individual trellises to shade each hive during the hot summer months.

Above left: Invention of the honey extractor to take honey from the comb, as well as passage of the Pure Food and Drug Laws at the turn of the century, boosted popularity of extracted honey over traditional honeycomb. The laws made it more difficult to adulterate bottled honey.

Above right: Many beekeepers have discovered the difficulty of maintaining bee hives near bears. In 1889 Root photographed this pet bear sampling bottled honey and included an engraving of it in the 1895 edition of the *ABC of Bee Culture.* In certain parts of the country—New England, for example—bears still may raid hives.

with them when they established posts on the northeastern coast. Arnold and Connie Krochmal, in an article "Origins of United States Beekeeping" for the *American Bee Journal,* say that priests who lived in New Mexico in the days of Spanish rule brought bees overland from Mexico, no small feat. English colonists naturally imported bees to provide the precious honey and beeswax as well. By 1648 honey production had become a cottage industry at Jamestown, and feral colonies were well established in the wild. As early as 1666, wills listed beehives and their products as inheritable property.

Feral honey bees swarmed ahead of the colonists across North America and made the continent their own. Thomas Jefferson comments in his *Notes on the State of Virginia* that "bees have generally extended themselves into the country a little in advance of the white settlers. The Indians therefore call them white man's fly, and consider their approach as indicating the approach of the settlements of whites."

Although beekeeping methods did not change much during the Enlightenment, reliable knowledge about bee biology and behavior began to grow and built the foundation for a revolution in bee cul-

Bees naturally tend to swarm from their hives when they have filled available space. In the Midwest, this phenomenon most often occurs in spring and is something that experienced keepers try to control. Various long-poled "swarming- devices" aid in gathering these absconding clusters of bees. Fortunately, bees are generally quite docile while they are swarming.

ture. During the late seventeenth and early eighteenth centuries, French physicist René Réaumur had attempted to mate queens and drones, and it was discovered that bees produced wax from their own bodies. Later in the eighteenth century, the Swedish taxonomist Carl Linneaus gave the honey bee its scientific name, *Apis mellifera,* and a Swiss naturalist, François Huber, showed that queens mate in the air outside the hive. Jan Dzierzon, the nineteenth-century Silesian bee master, discovered parthenogenesis, the process by which queen bees, and very occasionally workers, lay unfertilized eggs. These always develop into drones.

For century upon century, though aggregate honey yields were surprisingly large, individual beekeepers harvested fairly small amounts of honey from relatively few hives using traditional methods. By the nineteenth century, when other cottage industries were giving way to large industrial operations, the feeling grew that bee culture too could be made more efficient. If beekeeping was ever to evolve into a large-scale, profitable business, however, keepers must find ways to manipulate bees more easily, reducing beekeeping's chanciness and making economies of scale possible.

But such manipulation had to work around the bees' finicky na-

A. I. Root raised queens and other bees from imported Italian stock on a two and one-half acre, honeycomb-designed plot next to his Medina factory and marketed them through an extensive mail-order network. Queens are still ordered through the mail. Emblazoned on a flag planted in the center of the complex was a motto, "By Industry We Thrive." This view was taken from the roof of the factory.

New Challenges for Beekeepers

Beekeepers, including big commercial operations, smaller sideline beekeepers, and hobby beekeepers, are facing several challenges that are sure to change beekeeping considerably in the near future. Perhaps the most important is competition from foreign bee industries, especially those in China and Argentina. Beekeeping is still relatively labor intensive, and honey can be produced more cheaply overseas. Like other farm products, domestic honey sales are protected by price supports, and a topic of deep concern for honey producers is the Clinton administration's price-support policies.

Another challenge is Africanized honey bees—the killer bees that seem to enthrall the popular media. During the 1960s, experimenters imported two African races of *Apis mellifera, A. m. adansonii* and *A. m. scutellata,* to Brazil because they were well suited to produce honey in the tropics. Several colonies escaped, and the bees have spread like wildfire through tropical South and Central America. At least five Hollywood movies have screened lurid accounts of these bees, which are nothing more than subspecies of our familiar honey bee.

Though Africanized bees are not movie monsters, they have evolved aggressiveness during millions of years of coping with their many tropical predators. More of them sting intruders with less provocation than the Italian race will do. They also swarm and abscond, or abandon their hives completely, more quickly than the Italians and have tended to out-compete them in the tropics. These traits make them hard to deal with using normal beekeeping methods.

In 1990, Africanized honey bees (known as AHBs to beekeepers) reached southern Texas, and it is clear that U.S. beekeepers will be dealing with them soon. The good news is that AHBs store less honey than Italians do, and they will probably fail to overwinter north of the southern tier of states. Though hybridization has failed to moderate their aggressive and flighty qualities in Latin America, many believe that hybridizing with the dominant numbers of Italian bees of the temperate zone, will tone down their ferocity. Finally, the United States has a highly organized and sophisticated beekeeping industry capable of altering management techniques to cope with a new strain of honey bee.

Smaller commercial and hobby beekeepers may have more trouble with AHBs and with changes in public attitudes toward bees that may result from their advent. These smaller beekeepers may also find it harder to deal with two new bee parasites that appeared for the first time in the United States in recent years.

Beekeepers learned long ago how to cope with pests like wax moths that can destroy comb in weak hives, and with bacterially caused diseases such as European and American foulbrood that attack honey bee larvae, although American foulbrood remains a serious bee disease. Nosema, an amoeba-caused intestinal disease, can also be treated effectively. However, two different kinds of mites, tiny relatives of chiggers and ticks, have appeared here in the last few years and are serious threats to American bees that have little resistance to them.

Tracheal mites were first reported early in this century on the Isle of Wight in England and have slowly spread. They live in honey bees' breathing tubes, sucking blood through the walls, and they cause bees to suffocate if their numbers are large enough. Varroa mites attack both adults and larvae. Originally parasites of *Apis cerana,* the Indian honey bee, they infected hives of *Apis mellifera* in Japan that later spread the mites to other parts of the world. Beekeepers treat tracheal mites with menthol, which has several important disadvantages. Varroa mites are treated with a product called Apistan. New ways to deal with these threats are under investigation, and many beekeepers believe that breeding resistant honey bees will eventually control the problems.

These changes are making beekeeping more complex and exacting. Decrease in forage, caused by the spread of cities and by clean farming techniques that destroy weedy areas with good nectar plants, also alters beekeeping. New beekeepers apparently take changed requirements in stride, but some older practitioners seem to be deciding that producing honey isn't worth the effort. Of three categories of beekeepers—commercial beekeepers that support themselves through their beekeeping, sideliners who derive less than half their income from bees, and hobby beekeepers who don't sell honey—the sideliners have probably been hurt the most. There are now fewer than seven thousand beekeepers in Ohio, down from about ten thousand. Nationwide, although the number of honey bee colonies, the amount of honey produced, and the price of honey have stayed steady, numbers of beekeepers decreased by more than 10 percent between 1990 and 1992. This is not so rapid a decrease as the decline of other small farmers, but it is still significant.

---

ture. James and Carol Gould, in their book *The Honey Bee,* compare bees' and humans' requirements: "From a bee's point of view, the ideal artificial cavity would have just the right volume and shape, an entrance hole of the proper size and location, and a perfect balance between ventilation and insulation. It would be dry, it would face south, and be located ten meters up. For the would-be beekeeper, the ideal cavity would be cheap and portable, located on the ground, easily opened for inspection and harvesting, and engineered so that the bees would put nothing but honey in the most accessible part of

Beekeepers need to be dexterous and confident in manipulating hive frames to avoid needlessly angering or crushing the bees. Proper handling of hives is a skill that comes with practice.

the hive. In addition, its design would allow the beekeeper to put swarms of bees directly into the hive."

Experiments aimed at improving beekeeping methods had gone on for two hundred years or more and intensified in the early years of the nineteenth century, which saw a widespread "never kill a bee" movement. Experimenters added different kinds of hive extensions, in which, it was hoped, the bees would store nothing but comb and honey, confining brood rearing to the hive's main body. But beekeepers still had little control over the hive body itself. To remove comb, they must cut it out and could not then return it. They were also unable to add brood comb to strengthen weak colonies. Even honeycomb must be laboriously and stickily cut out by hand. One improvement in hive design was the invention of various kinds of bar hives. Wooden slats were placed across an inner hive top and were spaced at the same distance apart that natural combs would be. The bees, however, still attached their combs to the hive at the sides, making them difficult to cut and lift out.

Enter Lorenzo Lorraine Langstroth, an eccentric Congregational minister who in 1851 made the final breakthrough in hive construction that revolutionized modern bee culture. As a young clergyman in Andover, Massachusetts, Langstroth became captivated by honey bees: "In the summer of 1838 the sight of a large glass globe, on the parlor table of a friend, filled with beautiful honey in the comb, led

Women also were beekeepers during the last century, and several models of beekeeping hats were available to them. A woman could order Butterick pattern no. 3696 to sew a "bee-apron" long enough to cover her whole dress.

me to visit his bees, kept in an attic chamber; and in a moment the enthusiasm [for insects] of my boyish days seemed, like a pent-up fire, to burst out into full flame. Before I went home I bought two stocks of bees in common box hives, and thus my apiarian career began."

The beekeeping task that Langstroth disliked the most was dealing with bee glue or propolis. This is a brownish, waxy, resin-like material that bees gather from tree buds and use to chink up cracks in the hive to make it weather tight. Propolis hardened into a tough glue and made it very hard to pry off hive covers. To deal with this specific problem, Langstroth inset the hive's bars, leaving a space of about three-eighths of an inch between the bars' tops and the hive cover. Langstroth had lowered the bars just one bee space; the bees respected the space and left it empty. Beekeepers now know that any space in a hive either greater or less than that needed for two worker bees to pass each other—one-fourth to three-eighths of an inch, or a "bee space"—will be filled either with propolis or, if the space is larger, with comb.

Months later, when Langstroth was pondering the old problem of how to take combs from the hive without cutting them out, his mind suddenly synthesized what he had learned about bee space: if he converted the bars into frames and hung them from rabbets, leaving a space of one-fourth to three-eighths inch between each other and between the frames and any other part of the hive, bees would respect the bee space and not fill it up. Thus, he could easily lift the frames of brood and honey from the hive and replace them at will: "the almost self-evident idea of using the same bee space as in the shallow chamber came into my mind, and in a moment the suspended movable frames, kept at suitable distances from each other and the case containing them, came into being. Seeing by intuition,

When a hive swarms, the old queen absconds with her subjects to form another colony, while a newly reared queen remains in the hive to build its population up again. Certain bees scout for a new home and return to the waiting swarm to report on their findings, which they appear to communicate by ritualized "dancing." By some means which is not fully understood, the swarm decides among its options and then takes off for its new home. Photo courtesy of H. J. Lamberth/H. Armstrong Roberts.

as it were, the end from the beginning, I could scarcely refrain from shouting out my 'Eureka!' in the open streets."

At a stroke, beekeepers had gained infinitely better control over their bees. Hive bodies with hanging frames could be stacked, with the bees tending to confine brood rearing to the lower bodies, while storing honey in the upper ones, or supers. Frames of honey could be removed easily and be replaced for refilling. Bees' health and prosperity could be checked and pollen substitutes, sugar syrup, or medication given. And to some degree, removing full frames and substituting empty ones could discourage the instinct of all honey bees to swarm when the hive becomes too crowded, thus lowering honey production in that hive. The Langstroth hive made it easier to ensure that colonies wintered with enough pollen and honey stores and, because it discouraged swarming, maintained large forces of workers to produce bigger honey surpluses for harvest. Before many decades had passed, modified Langstroth hives had become the standard in this country.

Modern beekeepers provide their hives with sheets of wax embossed with a six-sided pattern that worker bees then "draw up" by adding wax produced in their bodies by special glands. This results in more uniform comb with fewer large drone cells, desirable since drones consume rather than produce honey. It is the size and shape of the cell that determines whether the queen will lay an egg that produces a drone or a worker. Photo courtesy of L. Fritz/H. Armstrong Roberts.

Poor Langstroth himself never profited much from his invention, though he soon patented it. He had poor business sense, and vehicles for punishing patent infringements and for mass marketing were still in the future. Most importantly, he was prey to what he called his "head trouble," savage depressions that left him prostrate and unable to work much of the time. Fortunately, a brother-in-law gave him and his family a brick house and eight acres of land in Oxford, Ohio, where they moved in 1858. Langstroth lived in this house for nearly thirty years, moving to Dayton in 1887 with his daughter and son-in-law and dying there in 1895 at age eighty-five. The Langstroth House, now on the Miami University Campus, was dedicated and placed in the National Register of Historic Places in 1978.

Still, Langstroth accomplished remarkable things. Besides inventing the modern beehive, he wrote in the winter of 1852–53 a book called *Langstroth on the Hive and the Honeybee: A Bee Keeper's Manual*. This was the first practical, yet scientifically sound, book on the honey bee and its culture written in this country, and it had no rival for many years. In cooperation with Jan Dzierzon in Germany, he also imported queens from the golden Italian race of the honey bee and promoted their use in American beekeeping. These bees were easier to work with than the German black honey bees that preceded them. They had gentler dispositions, swarmed less often, and stored more honey and wax. Despite hybridization, Italians are still the standard "American" bee.

Like most beekeepers, Lorenzo Langstroth never became rich through bee culture, although he did inspire loyalty from a group of more practical men who, during the last quarter of the nineteenth century, publicized Langstroth's and others' innovations and successfully commercialized beekeeping. These included Samuel Wagner of York, Pennsylvania, who encouraged Langstroth to write his beekeeping manual, and who in 1861 founded *The American Bee Journal,* the nation's oldest bee magazine. It is published today in Hamilton, Illinois, by Dadant and Sons, a company founded by Charles Dadant, a French beekeeper who had emigrated and set up a successful Illinois apiary. He and his son Camille took over publication of the journal after Wagner's death and revised and reissued *Langstroth on the Hive and the Honeybee* when Langstroth's "head trouble" prevented him from doing so himself. Dadant and Sons periodically updates the book, which is now collaboratively written and is a standard beekeeping text.

Medina, Ohio, saw the founding of another thriving apiary and bee supply company, the A. I. Root Company. Smitten with bees as a young man in 1865, and as passionate about them as Langstroth himself, Amos Ives Root began manufacturing beekeepers' supplies in 1869. To answer the flood of questions that poured in to him about bees and beekeeping, Root inaugurated the country's second oldest bee magazine, *Gleanings in Bee Culture*, in January 1873. So enthusiastic was the response that the magazine immediately went to monthly rather than quarterly issues. "Improved bee culture was my end and aim," recalled Root in his autobiography, *An Eyewitness Account of Early American Beekeeping*. Root was unusually willing to share information about his own and others' experiments in beekeeping, and the magazine became an essential clearing house for practical information in the early years of work with the Langstroth hive and with other innovations.

Root simplified and promoted the new hive, which he called the Simplicity hive, and he also urged importation of Italian queen bees.

A Mr. Manum of Bristol, Vermont, invented a tripod swarming device shown in *ABC of Beekeeping* for ease in manipulating honey bees. Scientists spell "honey bee" as two words because it is a member of the bee family, just as the house fly is a type of fly. Dragonflies, on the other hand, are neither flies nor dragons but a separate order and thus are spelled as one word. Dictionaries tend not to recognize this principle, insisting that honey bee is a single word.

Charles Muth of Cincinnati, Ohio, was another early bee entrepreneur. Here he advertises various beekeeping supplies, including products from A. I. Root. Other pioneers included Samuel Wagner of Pennsylvania and Charles Dadant of Illinois.

Chas. F. Muth & Son,

Dealers in

Pure Honey and Beeswax.

Manufacturers of
and Dealers in

Bee=hives, Smokers,

Honey=Extractors,

and a General Assortment of

Bee=Keepers' Supplies

Root's Goods

at Root's Prices.

1 POUND PURE HONEY

2 POUNDS PURE HONEY

½ POUND PURE HONEY

PURE HONEY

Square Glass Honey=Jars,

A Specialty.

Landreth's Garden and Field Seeds.

Muth's Pure Baking Powder

Is Second to None.

Practical Hints to Bee=keepers

Will be Mailed for 10c in Stamps.

For Illustrated Catalog Apply to

Chas. F. Muth & Son,

Freeman & Central Avenues.　　　Cincinnati, O., U. S. A.

P. S.—Always in the market for Honey and Wax.

He developed a warm friendship with Langstroth and sometimes helped him financially. The company sold honey, as well as manufactured beekeeping supplies, until after World War I, when it went out of the honey business. During the 1920s, A. I. Root's son Huber began supplying beeswax candles to churches, and since then Root has specialized increasingly in high-quality church and home decorator candles. The company stopped manufacturing beekeeping supplies in 1991, although it continues to sell them. A. I. Root Company, operated in Medina by fourth and fifth generations of the Root family, still publishes *Gleanings in Bee Culture*. The magazine is a practical companion for beginning and more advanced beekeepers and a forum for new products and ideas, while *The American Bee Journal* orients more toward reporting on honey bee research. Root also publishes and sells other beekeeping books and pamphlets, the best known of which is the *ABC and XYZ of Beekeeping*.

Other inventions followed Langstroth's movable-frame hive. The most important was foundation—thin sheets of wax embossed with a honeycomb pattern to fit into the hive frames. Bees would build on the patterned foundation, or "draw it up," as beekeepers say. Thus bees would produce an even comb with few drone cells (drones exist only to inseminate queens, and they eat honey rather than make it) and would spend less time and honey energy producing comb. Another invention was the queen excluder, a grid placed between the brood chamber and the honey chamber that would admit worker bees but barred the larger queen from laying eggs in the honey supers. The honey extractor, a drum that whirled honey from the comb, changed honey processing and marketing and, along with the Pure Food and Drug Laws of the turn of the century that curbed adulterating honey with other syrups, boosted popularity of extracted honey over traditional comb honey.

Despite these inventions, and despite bee culture fads that have come and gone, basic beekeeping technology has not altered very much in more than a hundred years. The simple, flexible Langstroth hive still houses the nation's apiaries. What has changed during the last quarter century is what one might call the macro-management of bees. These changes originate not from new hives or hive equipment, but from the interstate highway system, big trucks, pallets, and fork lifts. Today, large beekeeping operations do not stay put. Their bees winter in the southern states where nectar flows and harvests of pollen, the high-protein food needed to raise brood, begin early. In spring the hives are split to discourage swarming, given new queens, fork-lifted onto tractor-trailers, and shipped north to New England for blueberries and cranberries, to California almond groves, or to the sunflowers, clover, and alfalfa of the Plains states. Hives number in the thousands: the country's biggest operation runs forty-eight thousand of them.

The beekeepers' goal is honey in amounts vaster than the pioneer apiarists of the last century could imagine. The farmers who supply the hive locations gain by crop pollination. Insecticides kill off many native pollinators—wild bees, flies, and butterflies—so the highway honey bees are crucial in getting high yields from crops that depend on insects rather than wind to pollinate them. One author estimates that a colony of bees needs about eighty pounds of pollen in the active season as well as supplies for overwintering. Using a figure of fifty flowers for each bee-load of pollen, a single hive would visit 81,454,500 flowers to gather eighty pounds of pollen for brood raising. This does not count incidental pollination done by bees seeking nectar to make honey, the principal food of adult bees.

Honey bees may be forever wild, but as one beekeeper puts it, the science of beekeeping depends largely on hoodwinking the gullible little creatures. Crafty human beings have taken this art to such heights that beekeepers purloin about 105,000 tons of honey a year in this country alone. According to the International Bee Research Association, worldwide production in 1980 was about 800,000 tons. In 1985, the value of American crop pollination was thought to be $9.3 billion. Lorenzo Langstroth would be amazed.

Invention of the Langstroth hive enabled beekeepers to remove and inspect brood comb and to perform other housekeeping duties much more easily. Frames for honey, commonly called "supers," are placed in the top of the hive, and the larger queen is barred from laying eggs in them by means of a queen excluder, a sort of sieve that allows the smaller workers access to the honeycomb but shuts her away from it. Photo courtesy of K. Scholz/H. Armstrong Roberts.

Of course, it all depends on what you want. I know a hobby bee-keeper with one hive who tells me that when he retires, he will get rid of his Langstroth hive and offer his bees traditional domed skeps. He doesn't care about harvesting much honey—after all, he can buy it at the store for about a dollar and a half a pound—and he doesn't like the frowsy tenement look of many large apiaries. Sweetness for him lies less in producing a lot of honey than in having bees around, eating a little of his own honey, and getting some beeswax to make a few candles. "Bees are wonderful to watch," he says. "My wife and I watch them flying to the flowers and back. The kids watch them. Even the cats like to follow them."

Others, like this writer, care even less about producing honey, though we do very much like to eat it. For us, to see honey bees on early crocuses, to hear them humming noisily over apple blossom or basswood flowers, and to muse over the intricate adaptations of these sophisticated insects adds an aspect to life even sweeter than the golden product of their hives.

ADDITIONAL READING

A Book of Bees by Sue Hubbell, Ballantyne Books, 1988.

The Honey Bee by James L. Gould and Carol Grant Gould, Scientific American Library, 1988.

A Book of Honey by Eva Crane, Charles Scribner's Sons, 1980.

ABC and XYZ of Bee Culture by A. I. Root et al., A. I. Root Company, 1983.

The Hive and the Honey Bee by E. L. Atkins et al., Dadant and Sons, 1975.

The Life of Langstroth by Florence Naile, Cornell University Press, 1942.

The Dancing Bees by Karl von Frisch, Harcourt, Brace and Company, 1953.

Killer Bees: The Africanized Honey Bee in the Americas by Mark L. Winston, Harvard University Press, 1992.

Following the Bloom: Across America With the Migratory Beekeepers by Douglas Whynott, Stackpole Books, 1991.

The articles in this volume, with the exception of "Waterfowl Back from the Brink," originally appeared (in different format) in The Ohio Historical Society's magazine *Timeline* in these issues:

"Man's Best Enemy: The Wolf"—February–March 1986

"Furbearers"—April–May 1988

"Amphibious Architect: The Beaver"—August–September 1992

"A Respectable Bird: The Wild Turkey"—February–March 1991

"The Trouble with Bambi"—May–June 1997

"Owl: Sorcerer, Spirit-Bird, Predator"—December 1984–January 1985

"Snakes"—December 1990–January 1991

"Fire Lizard: The Humble Salamander"—March–April 1993

"Frogs and Toads Are Friends" appeared as "Jumping Flytraps: Frogs and Toads"—
    March–April 1997

"Darters"—May–June 1994

"Bright Shiners"—July–August 1995

"Butterflies"—June–July 1991

"Spiders: Laying for Flies and Bugs" appeared as "Laying for Flies and Bugs"—
    September–October 1996

"Coyote Arrives" appeared as "Coyote Returns"—February–March 1992

"The Raccoon: Nature's Artful Dodger"—August–September 1985

"Nature's Confectioner: The Honey Bee"—July–August 1993

Creatures of Change

was designed and composed by Will Underwood
in 10½/15 ITC Galliard with captions set in 8.7/12½ Frutiger Light
on an Apple Power Macintosh 7100/80 using Adobe PageMaker 5.0
at The Kent State University Press;
printed by offset lithography on 157 gsm enamel gloss stock,
Smyth sewn and bound over 1640 gsm binder's boards in Toyo
cloth, and wrapped with dust jackets printed in four color process
on 157 gsm enamel gloss stock with polyester gloss lamination
by Everbest Printers, Ltd., of Hong Kong;
and published by

The Kent State University Press

KENT, OHIO 44242 USA